CompTIA Security+ Certification

Student Manual

Exam SY0-301

CompTIA Security+ Certification, Exam SY0-301

Chief Executive Officer, Axzo Press:	Ken Wasnock
Series Designer and COO:	Adam A. Wilcox
Vice President, Operations:	Josh Pincus
Director of Publishing Systems Development:	Dan Quackenbush
Writers:	Tim Poulsen, Andy LaPage
Developmental Editor:	Andy LaPage
Copyeditor:	Catherine Oliver
Keytester:	Cliff Coryea

Trademarks

ILT Series is a trademark of Axzo Press.

Some of the product names and company names used in this book have been used for identification purposes only and may be trademarks or registered trademarks of their respective manufacturers and sellers.

Disclaimers

We reserve the right to revise this publication and make changes from time to time in its content without notice.

The logo of the CompTIA Authorized Quality Curriculum (CAQC) program and the status of this or other training material as "Authorized" under the CompTIA Authorized Quality Curriculum program signifies that, in CompTIA's opinion, such training material covers the content of CompTIA's related certification exam.

The contents of this training material were created for the CompTIA Security+ exam (SY0-301), covering CompTIA certification objectives that were current as of April 2011.

ISBN 10: 1-4260-2832-6
ISBN 13: 978-1-4260-2832-8

Printed in the United States of America

1 2 3 4 5 GL 06 05 04 03

Contents

Introduction   **iii**
Topic A: About the manual.. iv
Topic B: Setting your expectations... vii
Topic C: Re-keying the course xiv

Mitigating threats   **1-1**
Topic A: System maintenance 1-2
Topic B: Application security 1-19
Topic C: Physical security 1-24
Topic D: Malware 1-33
Topic E: Social engineering 1-42
Unit summary: Mitigating threats 1-52

Cryptography   **2-1**
Topic A: Symmetric cryptography 2-2
Topic B: Public key cryptography 2-16
Unit summary: Cryptography... 2-33

Authentication   **3-1**
Topic A: Authentication factors and requirements 3-2
Topic B: Authentication systems.. 3-9
Topic C: Authentication system vulnerabilities................................... 3-22
Unit summary: Authentication 3-34

User- and role-based security   **4-1**
Topic A: Baseline security policies 4-2
Topic B: Resource access 4-15
Unit summary: User- and role-based security....................................... 4-23

Peripheral security   **5-1**
Topic A: File and disk encryption.. 5-2
Topic B: Peripheral and component security.. 5-12
Topic C: Mobile device security... 5-20
Unit summary: Peripheral security.. 5-29

Public key infrastructure   **6-1**
Topic A: Public key cryptography 6-2
Topic B: Implementing public key infrastructure................................. 6-10
Topic C: Web server security with PKI... 6-31
Unit summary: Public key infrastructure 6-37

Application and messaging security   **7-1**
Topic A: Application security... 7-2
Topic B: E-mail security.. 7-10
Topic C: Social networking and messaging 7-26
Unit summary: Application and messaging security............................... 7-32

Ports and protocols   8-1
Topic A: TCP/IP basics 8-2
Topic B: Protocol-based attacks 8-20
Unit summary: Ports and protocols 8-38

Network security   9-1
Topic A: Network devices 9-2
Topic B: Secure network topologies 9-20
Topic C: Secure networking 9-32
Topic D: Virtualization and cloud computing 9-41
Unit summary: Network security 9-50

Wireless security   10-1
Topic A: Wireless network security 10-2
Topic B: Mobile device security 10-25
Unit summary: Wireless security 10-29

Remote access security   11-1
Topic A: Remote access 11-2
Topic B: Virtual private networks 11-16
Unit summary: Remote access security 11-28

Vulnerability testing and monitoring   12-1
Topic A: Risk and vulnerability assessment 12-2
Topic B: Auditing and logging 12-10
Topic C: Intrusion detection and prevention systems 12-15
Topic D: Incident response 12-28
Unit summary: Vulnerability testing and monitoring 12-33

Organizational security   13-1
Topic A: Organizational policies 13-2
Topic B: Education and training 13-22
Topic C: Disposal and destruction 13-27
Unit summary: Organizational security 13-31

Business continuity   14-1
Topic A: Business continuity planning 14-2
Topic B: Disaster recovery 14-9
Topic C: Environmental controls 14-22
Unit summary: Business continuity 14-27

CompTIA Security+ acronyms   A-1
Topic A: Acronym list A-2

Course summary   S-1
Topic A: Course summary S-2
Topic B: Continued learning after class S-5

Glossary   G-1

Index   I-1

Unit 8

Ports and protocols

Unit time: 90 minutes

Complete this unit, and you'll know how to:

A Identify TCP/IP protocols and network services.

B Mitigate protocol-based attacks.

Topic A: TCP/IP basics

This topic covers the following CompTIA Security+ objectives for exam SY0-301.

#	Objective
1.3	**Distinguish and differentiate network design elements and compounds** • Subnetting
1.4	**Implement and use common protocols** • SNMP • HTTPS • DNS • SFTP • TLS • SCP • SSL • ICMP • TCP/IP • IPv4 vs. IPv6 • FTPS
1.5	**Identify commonly used default network ports** • FTP • HTTP • SFTP • HTTPS • FTPS • SCP • TFTP • SSH • TELNET • NetBIOS

The TCP/IP suite

Explanation

The most common communication protocol used today is actually a suite of protocols called TCP/IP, which stands for two of the primary protocols it uses: Transmission Control Protocol and Internet Protocol.

A four-layer reference model is used to describe the TCP/IP protocol architecture, sometimes known as the Department of Defense (DoD) model. This model can be compared to the OSI model. The four architectural layers in the TCP/IP model are:

- Application
- Transport
- Internet
- Network Interface

The Application, Transport, and Internet architectural layers contain the TCP/IP protocols that make up the TCP/IP protocol suite. The TCP/IP model is also referred to as the *TCP/IP stack*. Exhibit 8-1 shows the protocols in each of the four layers in the TCP/IP model and how they relate to the OSI model.

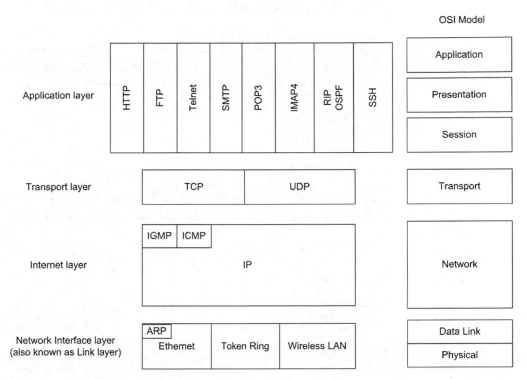

Exhibit 8-1: TCP/IP architecture

In the TCP/IP architecture, the *Application layer* provides access to network resources. It defines the rules, commands, and procedures that client software uses to talk to a service running on a server. This layer also contains a series of protocols that are useful on TCP/IP networks such as the Internet. For example, HTTP is an Application-layer protocol that defines how Web browsers and Web servers communicate.

The *Transport layer* prepares data to be transported across the network. This layer breaks large messages into smaller packets of information and tracks whether they arrived at their final destinations. It is also responsible for establishing the connection, handling error checking, and guaranteeing delivery (with TCP only).

The *Internet layer* is responsible for logical addressing and routing. IP addresses are logical addresses.

The *Network Interface layer* consists of the network card driver and the circuitry on the network card itself.

All these standards are published in what are known as *Requests for Comments* (RFCs), and are maintained at http://www.ietf.org/ by the Internet Engineering Task Force (IETF).

Do it!

A-1: Discussing the TCP/IP architecture

Questions and answers

1 On which layer of the TCP/IP model does the network card operate?

    A   Application

    B   Transport

    C   Internet

    D   Network Interface

2 Which layer of the TCP/IP model breaks large messages into smaller packets of information and tracks whether they arrived at their final destinations?

    A   Application

    B   Transport

    C   Internet

    D   Network Interface

Application-layer protocols

Explanation

The TCP/IP architecture's Application layer accepts information from applications on the computer and sends this information to the requested service provider. In addition, Application-layer protocols are available only on TCP/IP networks, and each of these protocols is associated with a client application and service. For example, FTP clients use the FTP protocol, and Telnet clients use the Telnet protocol. However, some client software can use more than one protocol. For example, Web browsers can use HTTP to communicate with Web servers and use FTP to communicate with FTP servers.

HTTP

Hypertext Transfer Protocol (HTTP) is the most common protocol used on the Internet today. This is the protocol used by Web browsers and Web servers. HTTP defines the commands that Web browsers can send and the way Web servers can respond. For example, when requesting a Web page, a Web browser sends a GET command. The server then responds by sending the requested Web page. Many commands are defined as part of the protocol.

HTTP can also be used to upload information. Submitting a survey form on a Web page is an example of moving information from a Web browser to a Web server. You can extend the capabilities of a Web server by using a variety of mechanisms that allow it to pass data from forms to applications or scripts for processing. These are some of the common mechanisms for passing data from a Web server to an application:

- Common Gateway Interface (CGI)
- Internet Server Application Programmer Interface (ISAPI)
- Netscape Server Application Programmer Interface (NSAPI)

The World Wide Web consortium (W3C) is the standards body responsible for defining the commands that are part of HTTP. To read more about the standards definition process, visit the W3C website: www.w3c.org.

HTTPS connections

Secure Web servers use *SSL* (Secure Sockets Layer) or *TLS* (Transport Layer Security) to enable an encrypted communication channel between themselves and users' Web browsers. SSL is a public-key/private-key encryption protocol used to transmit data securely over the Internet, using TCP/IP. The URLs of websites that require SSL begin with `https://` instead of `http://`. When you connect through SSL, the connection itself is secure, and so is any data transferred across it.

Secure HTTP (S-HTTP) is another protocol used to secure Internet transmissions. Whereas SSL secures a connection between two computers, S-HTTP secures the individual data packets themselves.

FTP

File Transfer Protocol (FTP) is a simple file-sharing protocol. It includes commands for uploading and downloading files, as well as for requesting directory listings from remote servers. This protocol has been around the Internet for a long time and was originally implemented in UNIX during the 1980s. The first industry-distributed document describing FTP was created in 1985; it was an RFC (Request for Comments).

Web servers (using HTTP) and e-mail software (using SMTP, or Simple Mail Transfer Protocol) must encode data so it appears as text when it travels over the Internet. FTP, however, offers an alternative. FTP can transfer binary files over the Internet without the encoding and decoding overhead, making it a popular protocol for moving files over the Internet.

Although there are still FTP servers running on the Internet, there are fewer than in previous years. FTP is slowly becoming obsolete because of its inherent lack of security and because HTTP can upload and download files, although not as efficiently.

FTP is implemented in standalone FTP clients as well as in Web browsers. It is safe to say that most FTP users today are using Web browsers, although there are a number of commercially available and free FTP clients, including SmartFTP, FTP Commander, and FileZilla. *FTP Secure* (or FTP-SSL), known as FTPS, uses TLS and SSL to encrypt data transfers.

TFTP

Another protocol similar to FTP is *Trivial File Transfer Protocol* (Trivial FTP or TFTP). TFTP has fewer commands than FTP and can be used only to send and receive files. It can be used for *multicasting*, in which a file is sent to more than one client at the same time, using the UDP Transport-layer protocol.

SFTP

Secure Shell FTP (SFTP) is used for secure, encrypted file transfers, using the *Secure Shell* (SSH) protocol. SSH enables users to securely access a remote computer by encrypting all passwords and data and using a digital certificate for authentication.

Telnet

Telnet is a terminal emulation protocol that is primarily used to remotely connect to networking devices. All of the administrative tasks for these systems can be done through a character-based interface. This feature is important because Telnet does not support a graphical user interface (GUI); it supports only text. The Telnet protocol specifies how Telnet servers and Telnet clients communicate.

The way Telnet works is similar to the concept of a mainframe and dumb terminal. The Telnet server controls the entire user environment, processes the keyboard input, and sends display commands back to the client. A Telnet client is responsible only for displaying information on the screen and passing input to the server. Many Telnet clients can be connected to a single server at one time. Each client that is connected receives its own operating environment; however, these clients are not aware that other users are logged into the system.

Because Telnet sends data, including passwords, in plaintext, SSH was developed as a replacement in order to provide a more secure communication channel.

DNS

The *Domain Name System* (DNS) is used to resolve host names to IP addresses. When you visit a website, you normally specify a *fully qualified domain name* (FQDN), such as www.yahoo.com, in a Web browser. DNS servers match host names to IP addresses. These specialized servers maintain databases of IP addresses and their corresponding domain names. For example, you could use DNS to determine that the name www.yahoo.com corresponds to the IP address 69.147.76.151.

Additional protocols

Some of the other protocols in the IP suite are covered in the following table.

Protocol	Description
SCP	*Secure Copy Protocol* uses SSH for data encryption and authentication when copying data between computers.
SNMP	*Simple Network Management Protocol* uses UDP to collect management statistics and error information about the network communication between TCP/IP hosts. It enables remote device control and management of parameters.
POP3	*Post Office Protocol version 3* is the most common protocol used for retrieving e-mail messages. It has commands for downloading and deleting messages from the mail server. POP3 does not support sending messages. By default, most e-mail client software using POP3 copies all messages onto the local hard drive and then erases them from the server. However, you can change the configuration so that messages can be left on the server. POP3 supports only a single inbox and does not support multiple folders for storage on the server.
SMTP	*Simple Mail Transfer Protocol* is used to send and receive e-mail messages between e-mail servers. It is also used by e-mail client software, such as Outlook, to send messages to the server. SMTP is never used by a client computer to retrieve e-mail from a server. Other protocols control the retrieval of e-mail messages.
IMAP4	*Internet Message Access Protocol version 4* is another common protocol used to retrieve e-mail messages. The capabilities of IMAP4 are beyond those of POP3. For example, IMAP can download message headers, which you can use to choose which messages you want to download. In addition, IMAP4 allows the use of multiple folders to store messages on the server side.
ARP, RARP	The maintenance protocols *Address Resolution Protocol* (ARP) and *Reverse Address Resolution Protocol* (RARP) translate between IP addresses and MAC addresses. ARP is used to request a MAC address when the IP address of a node is known. The information is stored in cache for use later on. RARP is used when the IP address is unknown and the MAC address is known. When a new node is added to the network, it uses its RARP client program to ask the RARP server to send its IP address from a table set up by the administrator on the local network gateway router.
ICMP	The *Internet Control Message Protocol* controls and manages information that is sent using TCP/IP. ICMP enables nodes to share error and status information. The ICMP information is passed on to upper-level protocols to inform the transmitting node about hosts that can be reached and to provide information that can be used to figure out and resolve the cause of the transmission problem. Rerouting of messages is also handled by ICMP to get around failed or busy routes. The ping command uses ICMP.

Transport-layer protocols

TCP/IP architecture Transport-layer protocols are responsible for getting data ready to move across the network. The most common task performed by Transport-layer protocols is breaking messages down into smaller pieces, called segments, that can move more easily across the network. The two Transport-layer protocols in the TCP/IP protocol suite are *Transmission Control Protocol* (TCP) and *User Datagram Protocol* (UDP).

TCP

The Transmission Control Protocol (TCP) provides connection-oriented, acknowledged communication. It provides guaranteed delivery, checks data integrity, and ensures the proper sequencing of packets. If an error occurs during transmission, TCP ensures that the sender resends the data. This is a Transport-layer protocol in the OSI reference model.

UDP

The User Datagram Protocol (UDP) is used for connectionless, unacknowledged communication. UDP uses IP as the protocol carrier, and then adds source and destination socket information to the transmission.

UDP is also used by applications as an alternative to TCP. TCP has a lot of overhead due to the acknowledgment packets. Applications use UDP when they don't need guaranteed delivery. For example, DNS and most online games use UDP instead of TCP.

Do it! **A-2: Examining protocols in the TCP/IP suite**

Questions and answers

1 Which protocol provides connection-oriented, acknowledged communication, and which protocol provides connectionless, unacknowledged communication?

2 Compare the three file-transfer protocols.

3 Which protocols are used for e-mail, and what are their purposes?

4 Compare ARP and RARP.

5 Why would you use SSH rather than Telnet?

Ports

Explanation

One of the defining characteristics of Transport-layer protocols is the use of port numbers. A port number is a 16-bit integer ranging from 0 to 65535. There are three types of port numbers, described in the following table.

Port type	Description
Well-known ports	Port numbers 0 to 1023 are reserved for privileged services.
Registered ports	These port numbers range from 1024 through 49151. Port 1024 is reserved for TCP and UDP and shouldn't be used. A list of registered ports can be found on the IANA website: www.iana.org/assignments/port-numbers.
Dynamic ports	A short-lived (*dynamic*) port is a Transport-protocol port for IP communications. The TCP/IP stack software automatically allocates the port from the IANA-suggested range of 49152 to 65535. Dynamic ports are typically used by TCP, UDP, or the *Stream Control Transmission Protocol* (SCTP).

Each network service running on a server listens at a port number. Each Transport-layer protocol has its own set of ports. When a packet is addressed to a particular port, the Transport-layer protocol knows which service to deliver the packet to. The combination of an IP address and port number is referred to as a *socket*.

A port number is like an apartment number for the delivery of mail. The network ID of the IP address ensures that the packet is delivered to the correct street (network). The host ID ensures that the packet is delivered to the correct building (host). The Transport-layer protocol and port number ensure that the packet is delivered to the proper apartment (service).

The following table shows well-known services and the ports they use:

Service	TCP and UDP ports
FTP	TCP 21, 20 20 is used for FTP data; 21 is used for FTP control
SSH, SFTP, SCP	TCP 22
Telnet	TCP 23
SMTP	TCP 25
DNS	TCP and UDP 53
BOOTP and DHCP	UDP 67, 68
Trivial FTP (TFTP)	UDP 69
HTTP	TCP 80
POP3	TCP 110
NetBIOS	UDP 137 (Name Service) UDP 138 (Datagram service) TCP 139 (Session service)
IMAP	TCP 143
SNMP	UDP 161 & 162
HTTPS	TCP 443
FTPS	TCP, UDP 989 (data) TCP, UDP 990 (control)

Do it!

A-3: Using port numbers

Here's how	Here's why
1 Open Internet Explorer	
2 In the address bar, type **http://www.msn.com:21**	
Press (↵ ENTER)	The Web browser can't connect because port 21 isn't used for HTTP.
3 In the address bar, type **http://www.msn.com:80**	
Press (↵ ENTER)	The Web browser connects and gives you the default Web page.
4 In the address bar, type **ftp://ftp.microsoft.com**	
Press (↵ ENTER)	The Web browser automatically connects you to port 21 when you use FTP.
5 In the address bar, type **ftp://ftp.microsoft.com:80**	
Press (↵ ENTER)	The Web browser can't connect because port 80 isn't used for FTP.
6 In the address bar, type **ftp://ftp.microsoft.com:21**	
Press (↵ ENTER)	The Web browser connects and gives you the same information as in step 4.
Close Internet Explorer	
7 Open a Command Prompt window	

8 At the command prompt, type
   netstat —an |find /i "listening"

Press ↵ ENTER

```
C:\Users\ESSADMIN01>netstat -an |find /i "listening"
  TCP    0.0.0.0:80             0.0.0.0:0              LISTENING
  TCP    0.0.0.0:135            0.0.0.0:0              LISTENING
  TCP    0.0.0.0:443            0.0.0.0:0              LISTENING
  TCP    0.0.0.0:445            0.0.0.0:0              LISTENING
  TCP    0.0.0.0:10049          0.0.0.0:0              LISTENING
  TCP    0.0.0.0:49152          0.0.0.0:0              LISTENING
  TCP    0.0.0.0:49153          0.0.0.0:0              LISTENING
  TCP    0.0.0.0:49154          0.0.0.0:0              LISTENING
  TCP    0.0.0.0:49155          0.0.0.0:0              LISTENING
  TCP    0.0.0.0:49156          0.0.0.0:0              LISTENING
  TCP    0.0.0.0:58850          0.0.0.0:0              LISTENING
  TCP    192.168.157.100:139    0.0.0.0:0              LISTENING
  TCP    192.168.157.101:139    0.0.0.0:0              LISTENING
  TCP    [::]:135               [::]:0                 LISTENING
  TCP    [::]:445               [::]:0                 LISTENING
  TCP    [::]:49152             [::]:0                 LISTENING
  TCP    [::]:49153             [::]:0                 LISTENING
  TCP    [::]:49154             [::]:0                 LISTENING
  TCP    [::]:49155             [::]:0                 LISTENING
  TCP    [::]:49156             [::]:0                 LISTENING
```

The first column shows the service, and the second column shows the port the service is listening on.

9 At the command prompt, type
   exit

Press ↵ ENTER   To close the Command Prompt window.

Internet-layer protocols

Explanation   Internet Protocol (IP) is a routable, unreliable connectionless protocol. Its sole function is the addressing and routing of packets. IP doesn't verify that data reaches its destination. It relies on other protocols, such as TCP, to ensure proper data sequencing and data integrity. This is a Network-layer protocol in the OSI reference model.

IPv4

Version 4 of the Internet Protocol (IPv4) has been the standard since September of 1981. This is the protocol that all Internet traffic was based on until recently.

IPv4 supports 32-bit IP addresses; this means that you can uniquely identify up to 2^{32} addresses. However, some of those addresses are unavailable for general use.

IP addresses are written in dotted-decimal notation. The Internet Assigned Numbers Authority (IANA) implemented classful IPv4 addresses in order to differentiate between the portion of the IP address that identifies a particular network and the portion that identifies a specific host on that network. These classes of IP addresses are shown in the following table.

Class	Addresses	Description
A	1.0.0.0 – 126.0.0.0	First octet: network ID. Last three octets: host ID. Default subnet mask: 255.0.0.0.
B	128.0.0.0 – 191.255.0.0	First two octets: network ID. Last two octets: host ID. Default subnet mask: 255.255.0.0.
C	192.0.0.0 – 223.255.255.0	First three octets: network ID. Last octet: host ID. Default subnet mask: 255.255.255.0.
D	224.0.0.0 – 239.0.0.0	Multicasting addresses.
E	240.0.0.0 – 255.0.0.0	Experimental use.

Subnet masks are used to identify the network-ID and host-ID portions of an address. Subnet masks allow additional addresses to be implemented within a given address space. The default mask for each of the classes is listed in the table.

Reserved addresses also take up some of the available addresses. About 18 million addresses are reserved for private networks. About 16 million addresses are reserved for multicast addresses. The number for "this network" is also reserved; it is 0.0.0.0. The local loopback address is another reserved address: 127.0.0.1. In addition, specific IP addresses are reserved for internal network use and are non-routable:

- 10.0.0.0 through 10.255.255.255
- 172.16.0.0 through 172.31.255.255
- 192.168.0.0 through 192.168.255.255

IPv4 headers contain 13 fields. The source and destination addresses are included in the header. These are shown in Exhibit 8-2.

Version	Header Length	Type of Service	Total Length	
Identification			Flags	Fragment Offset
Time to Live		Protocol	Header Checksum	
Source Address				
Destination Address				
Options			Padding	

Exhibit 8-2: The IPv4 header

CIDR

In the early 1990s, it became apparent that the number of available unique IP addresses would be used up soon. Several methods were developed to cope with the need for more addresses while a new IP version was being developed and implemented.

Classless Inter-Domain Routing (CIDR) was implemented in 1993 to help alleviate the problem. CIDR allows you to use *variable-length subnet masking* (VLSM) to create additional addresses beyond those allowed by the IPv4 classes. You can group blocks of addresses together into single routing-table entries known as CIDR blocks. These addresses are managed by IANA and Regional Internet Registries (RIRs).

CIDR addresses are written in the standard four-part dotted-decimal notation, followed by /N, where N is a number from 0 to 32. The number after the slash is the prefix length. The prefix is the number of bits (starting at the left of the address) that make up the shared initial bits (the network portion of the address). The default for a class B address would be /16, and for a class C address, it would be /24.

NAT

Network address translation (NAT) is another strategy that was implemented to help alleviate the problem of insufficient IP addresses. NAT modifies network address information in the packets it transmits from an internal network onto the Internet. NAT allows a single address from a router to rewrite originating IP addresses from the internal network so that they all appear to come from the router's IP address. As a result, you no longer need an Internet-valid IP address for each computer on the internal network. Instead, you can configure the hosts on your internal network to use private IP addresses and then assign only a single Internet-valid IP address to the router interface that connects your network to the Internet.

In addition to providing more IP addresses, NAT helps to prevent attacks initiated by sources outside the network from reaching local hosts. This feature is part of the protection provided by NAT-enabled firewalls.

IPv6

Internet Protocol version 6 (IPv6) development began in the mid-1990s. IPv6 uses 128-bit addresses, providing many more possible addresses than IPv4 provided. IPv6 provides 2^{128} addresses.

You write IPv6 addresses as eight 16-bit fields. They are written as eight groups of four numbers in hexadecimal notation, separated by colons. You can replace a group of all zeros by two colons. Only one set of colons (::) can be used per address. Leading zeros in a field can be dropped. However, except for the :: notation, all fields require at least one number. For example, fe80:0000:0884:0e09:d546:aa5b can be written as fe80::884:e09:d546:aa5b.

You indicate the network portion of the address by a slash and the number of bits in the address that are assigned to the network portion. If the address ends with /48, the first 48 bits of the address are the network portion. An example of a link-local IPv6 address is fe80::884:e09:d546:aa5b. The link-local IPv6 address is automatically configured in Windows Vista, Windows 7, and Windows Server 2008.

The loopback address is a local host address and can be written as ::/128. The address fe80::/10 is equivalent to the IPv4 address 169.254.0.0.

IPv6 header fields

IPv6 reduced the number of header fields from 13 in IPv4 to 7. The header fields are shown in Exhibit 8-3.

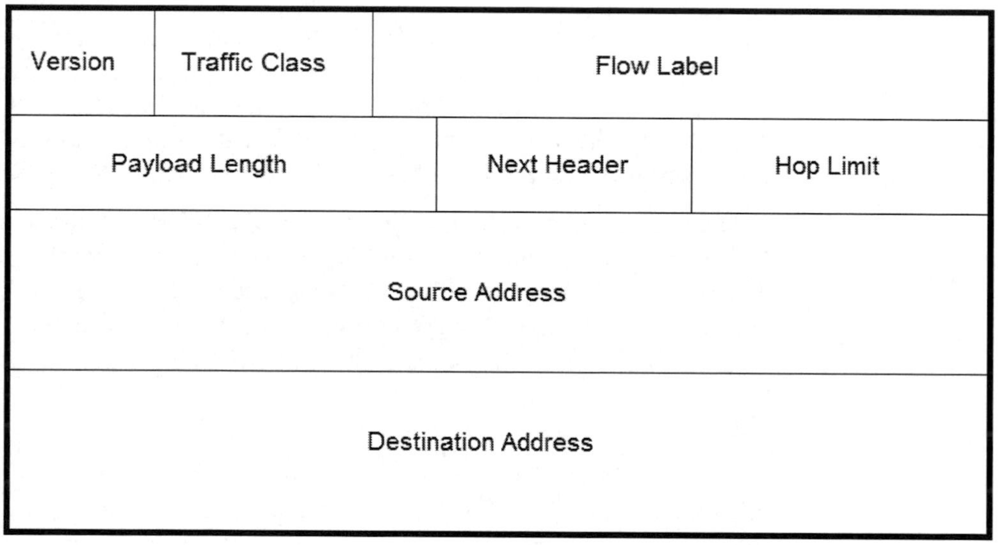

Version	Traffic Class	Flow Label	
Payload Length		Next Header	Hop Limit
Source Address			
Destination Address			

Exhibit 8-3: The IPv6 header

The following table describes the IPv6 header fields.

Field	Description
Version	Identifies the IP version.
Traffic Class	Replaces the IPv4 Type of Service field. The packet is tagged with the Differentiated Services (DS) class used for Quality of Service (QoS) traffic-management functions.
Flow Label	A new 20-bit field. Tags the packet as part of a specific flow. This allows multilayer switches and the router to handle packets based on flow rather than on a packet-by-packet basis, so packet-switching performance is faster.
Payload Length	Replaces the IPv4 Total length field.
Next Header	Identifies the information type following the basic IPv6 header, such as TCP or UDP or an extension header. This field is similar to the Protocol field in IPv4.
Hop Limit	Specifies the maximum number of hops the IP packet can go over. This field is similar to the IPv4 TTL field. No checksum is used in IPv6, so if an IPv6 router decreases the field value and it reaches 0, the message is returned to the source and the packet is discarded.
Source Address	A 128-bit field; identifies the packet source's IP address.
Destination Address	A 128-bit field; identifies the packet destination's IP address.

The data follows these fields. If any extension headers are used, they also follow the fields, but before the data.

Extension headers are processed in the following order and include:

Header	Description
Hop-by-Hop Options	Processed by all routers in the packet path.
Destination Options	Processed at the final destination and any destinations specified by the header. Can also follow an Encapsulating Security Payload, where the Destination Options header is processed only at the final destination. The Next Header value for this header is 60.
Routing	Used for source routing and mobile IPv6. The source identifies at least one intermediate node to be crossed before the packet reaches the destination. The Next Header value for this header is 43.
Fragment	Used when the source requires that a packet be fragmented. The header is used in each packet of the fragmentation. The Next Header value for this header is 44.
Authentication (AH) and Encapsulating Security Payload (ESP)	Used by IPSec to ensure packet authentication, integrity, and confidentiality. The Next Header value for the AH is 51. The Next Header value for ESP is 50.
Upper Layer	Transports headers inside a packet such as TCP or UDP. The Next Header value for TCP is 6; for UDP, it is 17.

IPv6 address scopes

Address *scopes* define regions, also known as *spans*. Addresses are defined as unique identifiers of an interface. The scopes are link-local, site network, and global network. A device usually has a link-local address and either a site-local or global address.

Using ICMPv6 router discovery messages, a host can automatically connect to a routed IPv6 network. The host sends a link-local multicast router solicitation request to obtain configuration parameters. You can use DHCPv6 instead of auto-configuration, or you can configure a host's IPv6 address information manually. Routers are usually configured manually.

A network address can be assigned to a scope zone. A link-local zone is made up of all the network interfaces connected to a link. Addresses are unique within a zone. A zone index suffix on the address identifies the zone. The suffix follows a % character. An example is fe80::884:e09:d546:aa5b%10.

IPv6 address types

IPv6 has three types of addresses: unicast, anycast, and multicast. A *unicast* address is identified for a single interface. Packets sent to a unicast address are delivered to the interface identified by the address. *Anycast* addresses identify a group of interfaces, typically on separate nodes. Packets sent to an anycast address are delivered to the nearest interface, as identified by the routing protocol distance measurement. *Multicast* addresses also identify a group of interfaces on separate nodes. However, the packet is delivered to all interfaces identified by the multicast address (instead of to a single interface).

IPv6 doesn't use broadcast addresses; that functionality is included in multicast and anycast addresses. The all-hosts group is a multicast address used in place of a broadcast address.

Do it!   **A-4:   Comparing IPv4 and IPv6 packets**

Here's how	Here's why
1 On your Windows 7 computer, click **Start**	
In the Start Search box, type **cmd** and press (↵ ENTER)	To open a command prompt window.
2 At the command prompt, enter **ipconfig**	To display the IP configuration.
3 Record the IPv4 address and subnet mask	IPv6 is disabled. IPv4: _____
4 Identify the network and host portions of each address	
5 Close the command prompt window	
6 Open the Control Panel; then open **Network and Internet** and the **Network and Sharing Center**	
Under Tasks, click **Change adapter settings**	
7 Right-click **Local Area Connection** and choose **Properties**	IPv6 was disabled during setup.
Enter administrator credentials	If prompted.
8 Display properties for **Internet Protocol Version 4 (TCP/IPv4)**	
Click **Advanced**	There are tabs for IP Settings, DNS, and WINS. Your address might be manually or automatically configured, depending on how it was set up for the course.
Click **Cancel** twice	
9 Close all open windows	

Topic B: Protocol-based attacks

This topic covers the following CompTIA Security+ objectives for exam SY0-301.

#	Objective
3.1	**Analyze and differentiate among types of attacks**
	• Man-in-the-middle • Xmas attack
	• DDoS • Pharming
	• DoS • DNS poisoning and ARP poisoning
	• Relay • Transitive access
	• Smurf attack • Client-side attacks
	• Spoofing
3.5	**Analyze and differentiate among types of application attacks**
	• Session hijacking
3.7	**Implement assessment tools and techniques to discover security threats and vulnerabilities**
	• Tools
	– Sniffer – Port scanner
	– Vulnerability scanner

Attack types

Explanation

Attacks aimed at a server or servers in a network are called *server-side attacks*. These attacks can disrupt e-mail servers or routers and prevent Web and e-mail access for an extended period of time. Attacks aimed at individual client computers are called *client-side attacks;* these are usually aimed at Web browsers and instant-messaging applications. Because most organizations concentrate resources to protect against server-side attacks, and client systems aren't typically hardened like server systems are, client-side attacks often have a better chance of succeeding.

Denial-of-service attacks

Denial-of-service (DoS) attacks consume or disable resources so that services to users are interrupted. Rather than destroying or stealing data, a DoS attack is designed to disrupt daily standard operation. This disruption can damage an organization's reputation and cause a loss of revenue.

DoS attacks are conducted in a variety of ways by using a variety of methods. Many of the attack tools are easy to use, making the attacks easy to implement. Some of the attack modes cause the user's application or operating system to crash. Other attack modes clog Web server connections with illegitimate traffic or consume disk space, buffers, or queues, making server response time slow or causing the server to be unable to respond to valid user requests. Another attack mode involves attempting to log onto the server multiple times until the account is locked due to too many incorrect logon attempts. An attacker might also cause a DNS server to crash by sending so many DNS lookup requests that the server runs out of memory and crashes, causing Web pages within the domain to be inaccessible.

SYN flood attacks

Establishing a TCP connection requires three steps. The process is illustrated in Exhibit 8-4.

1 The client sends a packet to the server with the SYN flag set (this is called a *SYN packet*).

2 The server responds with a SYN packet that also has the ACK (acknowledge) bit set. The server maintains a record of the initial request and its response, and awaits the client's response, which comes next.

3 The client responds with a third packet, which has just the ACK bit set. At this point, a connection has been established between the systems and data transfer can begin.

| Client: Send SYN (SEQ=X) | Server: Receives SYN (SEQ=X) |

| Server: Send SYN (SEQ=Y, ACK=x+1) | Client : Receive SYN (SEQ=Y, ACK=X+1) |

| Client: Send ACK (ACK=Y+1) | Server: Receive ACK (ACK=Y+1) |

Exhibit 8-4: The TCP three-way handshake

The basic nature of TCP enables a type of attack called a *SYN flood*, or simply a flood. It is a DoS attack in which an attacker sends large volumes of SYN packets without ever sending the follow-up ACK packets. These partial connections squeeze out legitimate connections, effectively taking the server out of service.

Because SYN packets are required for normal communications, you cannot simply block them entirely. Various techniques exist to limit a server's vulnerability to SYN floods. With the `iptables` command, for example, you can set a threshold that, when reached, will cause further SYN packets to be blocked.

For example, to block SYN flood attacks, you might enter:

```
iptables -A INPUT -p tcp --syn --dport 25 -j ACCEPT
iptables -A INPUT -p tcp --syn --dport 80 -j ACCEPT
iptables -A INPUT -p tcp --syn -m limit --limit 1/s ▶
    --limit-burst 4 -j ACCEPT
iptables -A INPUT -p tcp --syn -j DROP
```

The first two rules permit connections to ports 25 and 80. You'd need additional rules to permit traffic over other ports. The last two rules limit such connections (one per second, with a burst of up to four connections) and drop excessive connections.

Some routers implement a feature called *TCP intercept*. In this mode, the router accepts and responds to SYN packets on behalf of the server. If the client finishes the connection, that connection is passed through to the server. Otherwise, it is dropped. The firewall uses relatively aggressive timeouts to prevent itself from falling victim to a SYN flood attack. In Cisco's IOS software, you'd use commands like the following to enable the TCP intercept and to block SYN flood attacks:

```
access-list INBOUND line 10 extended permit tcp any
ip tcp intercept list 10
ip tcp intercept mode intercept
ip tcp intercept max-incomplete high number 1100
ip tcp intercept max-incomplete low number 900
```

The first three rules permit inbound TCP connections, turn on TCP intercept for the access list noted in the first rule, and then set the TCP intercept to Intercept mode (rather than Watch mode). The second-to-last line specifies the number of partial connections at which the router will consider itself to be under attack. At that point, it will begin dropping packets. The last line specifies the point at which the router backs off on dropping packets, under the assumption that the attack has stopped or slowed.

The Windows firewall does not provide the means to protect against SYN flood attacks. With older versions of Windows, you could harden the operating system by adjusting a couple of Registry entries. Such protections are built into the TCP/IP stack in Windows Vista, Windows 7, and Windows Server 2008. According to Microsoft, you cannot (and shouldn't need to) adjust these operating systems' handling of SYN packets.

If you're running Windows Server 2003 or older, or Windows desktop operating systems older than Windows Vista, you can enable SYN flood protection by adjusting the keys listed in the following table. You'll find these values in the HKEY_LOCAL_MACHINE\SYSTEM\CurrentControlSet\Services\Tcpip\Parameters key.

Key	Description
SynAttackProtect	When set to a value greater than 0, enables SYN flood protection. The recommended value is 2.
TcpMaxConnectResponseRetransmissions	Specifies how many times TCP will retransmit an unanswered SYN-ACK packet. The default value of 5 is probably sufficient for most situations.
TcpMaxHalfOpen	Specifies how many connections the server will maintain in a half-open state before TCP/IP initiates SYN-flood attack protection. This value should be larger than that set for TcpMaxHalfOpenRetried.
TcpMaxHalfOpenRetried	Specifies how many connections remain in the half-open state even after a connection request has been retransmitted.
TcpMaxPortsExhausted	Specifies how many connection requests the system can refuse before TCP/IP initiates SYN-flood attack protection.

Information on Windows Server 2008 TCP/IP Registry keys is available at http://tinyurl.com/6hvvsob ("Registry settings that can be modified to improve operating system performance," an MSDN article) and http://tinyurl.com/69r766n ("TCP/IP registry values for Microsoft Windows Vista and Windows Server 2008," a Microsoft white paper). Recommendations for older Windows versions can be found at various guides, such as http://tinyurl.com/65yv3w6 ("Hardening the TCP/IP stack to SYN attacks," a Symantec article).

Smurf attacks

A *smurf attack* overwhelms a host by flooding it with ICMP packets. It uses a third-party network to do so. The hacker sends a ping to the broadcast address of the intermediary network. The IP address for the packet source appears to be from the victim system. Every host on the subnet replies to the broadcasted ping request on the victim's address. Without knowing it, the hosts on the third-party network inundate the victim with ping packets. The hacker achieves two results: the smurf attack overwhelms the system that receives the echo packet flood; and the attack saturates the victim's Internet connection with fraudulent traffic, thereby preventing valid traffic from getting through.

To prevent smurf attacks, you can configure routers to drop ICMP packets that originate outside the network and that have an internal broadcast or multicast destination address. You can also configure hosts to ignore echo requests targeted at their subnet broadcast address.

Ping-of-death attacks

Operating systems have been updated so that ping-of-death attacks are no longer much of a threat, but at one time, they were successfully used to crash systems. An IP packet has a maximum size of 65,535 bytes. The attacker would send a 65,536-byte fragmented ping packet; when the packet was reassembled, it caused a buffer overflow, which could crash the system.

Christmas (Xmas) attacks

A *Christmas packet attack* is a DoS attack that overwhelms a router with packets on which every option for the selected protocol is set. Such packets require more processing than normal packets do, and therefore can cause routers and hosts to spend too much time processing these requests.

Christmas packets are also used to determine protocol settings by examining responses to the packets sent to the target network or host. How hosts respond to unusual packets, such as Christmas packets, can provide information about a host's operating system.

Do it!

B-1: Preventing common protocol-based attacks

Here's how	Here's why
1 On your Windows Server 2008 computer, while logged on as Administrator, click **Start**	You will configure your server to prevent SYN flood attacks.
In the Start Search box, enter **regedit**	To open the Registry Editor.
2 Expand **HKEY_LOCAL_MACHINE**, **SYSTEM**, **CurrentControlSet**, **Services**, **Tcpip**	
3 In the console tree, select **Parameters**	
Right-click **Parameters**	To prepare to add a new DWORD value.
Choose **New**, **DWORD (32-bit) Value**	
4 Type **SynAttackProtect** and press (↵ ENTER)	
5 Right-click **SynAttackProtect**	
Choose **Modify...**	
In the Value data field, enter **1**	To enable the parameter.
Click **OK**	
6 In the console tree, select **Parameters**	
Right-click **Parameters**	To prepare to add a new DWORD value.
Choose **New**, **DWORD (32-bit) Value**	
7 Type **TcpMaxConnectResponseRetransmissions** and press (↵ ENTER)	
Right-click **TcpMaxConnectResponseRetransmissions**	
Choose **Modify...**	
In the Value data field, enter **2**	SynAttackProtect with a value of 1 is enabled if this value is set to at least 2. The valid range of retransmission attempts is between 0 and 255.
Click **OK**	

8 Close the Registry Editor

Restart your computer   To put the changes into effect. In the Shutdown Event Tracker, select "Operating System: Reconfiguration."

Log back in as Administrator

9 How does a SYN attack inhibit services?

10 How can you defend your systems from Smurf attacks?

Distributed denial-of-service attacks

Explanation

A network attack in which the attacker manipulates several hosts to perform a DoS attack is known as a *distributed denial-of-service* (DDoS) attack. This attack usually causes the target to be inaccessible for a time. It also results in revenue and reliability losses for the victim.

DDoS attacks use automated tools, which make the attacks easy to execute. They are often used to attack government and business Internet sites.

A DDoS assault requires that the hacker first finds a computer to use as the handler. The compromised system is usually one with lots of disk space and a fast Internet connection. The hacker uses this computer to upload his chosen attack toolkit. The hacker needs to remain undetected, so for the handler, he often chooses a host with many user accounts or one with a careless administrator.

The next step after the handler has been set up is to use automated scripts to scan large areas of IP address space to locate targets to use as *zombies* or agents. The scripts often exploit known weaknesses in Windows operating systems. The zombie software is loaded onto these systems transparently to the system user. The hacker typically creates hundreds or thousands of zombies to launch the DDoS attack. A collection of zombies is sometimes called a *botnet*. Home PCs that aren't adequately protected and that use DSL or cable connections which are always on are often targeted as zombies.

The attack is usually launched through Internet Relay Chat (IRC) connections. The compromised host is automatically logged on to an IRC channel. The host waits passively for the order to attack from the handler system. At the time of the attack, a command is delivered from the handler system to the zombies connected to the IRC channel. The zombies are instructed remotely to flood the victim's network. All of this happens without the owner of the machine ever knowing that it was compromised.

There are several steps you can take to prevent your system from being compromised by DDoS attacks. Clients and servers should install all security patches issued by software vendors. Personal firewalls should be configured on PCs, along with antivirus software that regularly scans hard disks. E-mail servers should also have antivirus software installed. Firewalls and routers should be configured in the following ways:

- If packets are entering the network with a broadcast address for the destination, they should be filtered.
- Directed broadcasts on internal routers should be turned off.
- For any source address that is not permitted on the Internet, the packet should be blocked.
- Any port or protocol not used for Internet connections on your network should be blocked.
- Packets with a source address that originates inside your network should be blocked from entering the network.
- Packets with counterfeit source addresses should be blocked from leaving your network.

Do it!

B-2:   Assessing your vulnerability to DDoS attacks

Here's how	Here's why
1 On your Windows Server 2008 computer, while logged on as Administrator, open Server Manager	
Under Security Information, click **Configure IE ESC**	By default, the Internet Explorer Enhanced Security Configuration is enabled on servers. This feature blocks many sites, requiring many extra clicks to view even basic content. You're going to disable Internet Explorer Enhanced Security Configuration for Administrative users to make working with the downloads in this unit easier.
2 Under Administrators, select **Off**	
Click **OK**	
3 Close Server Manager	
4 Open Internet Explorer	You will use DDoSPing to scan for zombies on your network.
5 Go to **foundstone.com**	DDoSPing is a utility that scans for common DDoS programs. It will detect Trinoo, Stacheldraht, and Tribe Flood Network programs on the computer.
6 Install Adobe Flash Player	(If necessary.) Do not install bundled software if asked.
7 Click **Free Tools & Resources**	
Click **Scanning Tools**	
8 Under Scanning Tools, click **DDoSPing™**	Scroll down.
9 Click **Download this Tool Now**	
10 Read the Terms of Use and click **Download Now**	
11 Click **Save**	
Save the file in the Administrators\Downloads folder	
12 Click **Open Folder**	

13 Right-click **ddosping** and choose **Extract All...**

Click **Extract**

14 In the Administrator\Downloads\ddosping folder, double-click **ddosping**

15 Click **Run**

16 Observe the Target IP address range

By default, the DDoSPing utility scans the IP subnet your computer is on. Make note of this range. You'll need it in the next activity:

Start IP: _____

End IP: _____

17 Move the Transmission speed control setting to **Max**

18 Click **Start**

The scan runs quickly and should complete in a few seconds. The message "Program stopped," followed by the date and time, indicates that the scan was completed.

A scan of this type is often detected by a network administrator and might violate computer use policies if permission has not been granted to perform the scan.

19 Examine the Infected Hosts and Status boxes

Any host infected with a zombie is listed. If no hosts are listed, no zombies were found. The Status box will indicate whether any zombies were detected.

20 Close all open windows *except* the Internet Explorer window with Foundstone Free Tools

Man-in-the-middle attacks

Explanation

To conduct a man-in-the-middle attack, the attacker positions himself between the two hosts that are communicating with each other. The attacker then listens in on the session. Each of the hosts thinks that it is communicating only with the other host. However, the hosts are actually communicating with the attacker.

Man-in-the-middle attacks can be used for several types of attacks. They can be used for DoS attacks, for corrupting transmitted data, or for analyzing the traffic to gather information about the network. Other types of attacks include:

Attack	Description
Web spoofing	The attacker puts a Web server between the victim's Web browser and a legitimate server. The attacker monitors and records the victim's online activity. The attacker can also modify the content viewed by the victim.
Information theft	The attacker passively records data passing between hosts to gather sensitive information, such as usernames and passwords or even industrial secrets.
TCP session hijacking	The attacker between the two hosts takes over the role of one of the hosts and assumes full control of the TCP session.

Anyone with access to network packets that travel between hosts can conduct a man-in-the-middle attack. Some of the methods used to do so include:

Attack method	Description
ARP poisoning	This attack can be conducted by using programs such as Dsniff, Hunt, ARPoison, Ettercap, or Parasite, which allow the attacker to monitor and modify a TCP session. The attacker needs to be on the same Ethernet segment as the victim or as the host.
ICMP redirect	The attacker instructs a router to forward packets with a victim's destination to instead go through the attacker's system. ICMP redirect packets are used to bring about this attack. The attacker can monitor and modify packets before sending them to their destination. To prevent these attacks, configure your routers to ignore ICMP redirect packets.
DNS poisoning	The attacker redirects traffic by changing the victim's DNS cache so that the host-name-to-IP-address mappings are wrong.

Spoofing

When you impersonate someone else, that is called spoofing. Presenting credentials that don't belong to you in order to gain access to a system is spoofing the system. Information security staff needs to be concerned about several types of spoofing. These include:

- IP address spoofing
- ARP poisoning
- Web spoofing
- DNS spoofing

IP address spoofing

TCP/IP packets generated by the attacker and using the source address of a trusted host are used to gain access to a victim through IP address spoofing. Using this trickery, the attacker can bypass filters on routers and firewalls to gain network access.

Following are the steps used to stage an IP spoofing attack:

1 The attacker identifies the victim to be the target, and identifies a machine trusted by the victim. The attacker uses SYN flooding to disable the trusted machine's ability to communicate.

2 Using a sniffer, sampling packets, or some other method, the attacker determines the sequence numbers used by the victim in the communication. The source IP address of the trusted host is spoofed by the attacker and used to send his own packets to the victim.

3 The victim accepts and responds to the spoofed packets. Even though the packets are routed to the trusted host, they can't be processed by the trusted host because of the SYN flood attack.

4 The attacker guesses the content of the victim's response and creates a response, using the spoofed source address, and guesses at what the appropriate sequence number should be.

One way to prevent IP spoofing is to disable source routing on internal routers. You can also filter out packets that come from outside the network and that have a local network source address.

Do it!

B-3: Scanning ports

Here's how	Here's why
1 In Internet Explorer, go back to the Free Tools page	On the Foundstone.com website.
Under Scanning Tools, click **SuperScan™**	You will use SuperScan, which is a connection-based TCP port scanner, pinger, and host-name resolver, to scan IP addresses.
2 Click **Download this Tool Now**	
3 Read the Terms of Use and click **Download Now**	

4 Click **Save**

   Save the file in the
   Administrators\Downloads folder

5 Click **Open Folder**

6 Right-click **superscan4** and
   choose **Extract All...**

   Click **Extract**

7 Double-click **SuperScan4**   If you get a prompt stating that you need local
                                                    administrator privileges to run this, use Run as
                                                    Administrator.

   Click **Run**

8 Enter the Start IP address for your   You recorded this range in the previous activity.
   network

   Click in the End IP box   The end IP address is automatically entered for
                                                    the subnet, based on the IP address you entered.

9 Click the arrow button next to the   To add the starting and ending IP addresses to
   IP address range   the scanned range.

10 Click the blue Start arrow   It is located in the bottom-left corner of the
                                                    SuperScan 4.0 window.

                                                    A scan of this type is often detected by a
                                                    network administrator and might violate
                                                    computer use policies if permission has not been
                                                    granted to perform the scan.

11 Review the results   The IP address of the host performing the scan
                                                    isn't included in the list because no ports are
                                                    open on the host performing the scan. By
                                                    default, hosts without open ports are not listed.

                                                    The ports that are open on the system are of
                                                    great use to attackers.

12 Close all open windows *except* the
   Internet Explorer window with
   Foundstone Free Tools

ARP poisoning

Explanation

ARP (Address Resolution Protocol) sends out ARP request packets to obtain a computer's MAC address when its IP address is known. This information is stored in a table in the computer's cache. ARP poisoning corrupts the table so that a hacker can redirect traffic to another computer's MAC address in order to carry out a network attack. The attacker needs to be on the same local network as the computers being targeted.

The attacker sends forged ARP replies so that the compromised computer sends network traffic to the attacker's computer. The user with the compromised computer doesn't realize that anything is amiss. The attacker meanwhile is receiving all of your network traffic, which might include clear text passwords or even your secured Internet session.

The attacker can use ARP poisoning to launch DoS attacks or man-in-the-middle-attacks, and use *MAC flooding* to overload a switch and force it to drop into hub mode. In hub mode, a switch is so busy handling traffic that port security features are not enforced and network traffic is broadcast to all computers on the network.

Because the attacker needs local access to perform ARP poisoning, the best precaution is to physically secure your network from attackers. ARP poisoning takes advantage of the lack of security in the ARP protocol needed for TCP/IP, so there isn't a whole lot you can do to fix that particular part of the problem. However, you can take some steps to address the problem. On a small network, you can use static IP addresses and static ARP tables. On large networks using switches, you can enable the port security feature that allows only one MAC address for each physical port on the switch; this feature prevents attackers from mapping another MAC address to the attack computer. A tool such as ARPwatch or XArp can alert you to any unusual ARP communications on the network.

Do it!

B-4:   Checking the ARP cache

Here's how	Here's why
1 In Internet Explorer, go to **www.chrismc.de/development/xarp**	
	You will use XArp to check for ARP attacks.
Download XArp 2.2 or later	
2 Click **Open Folder**	
3 Double-click **XArp**	
Click **Run**	
4 Click **Next**	
Click **I Agree**	
Click **Next**	
Click **Install**	
Click **Finish**	To start the program.
5 Examine the results	If no ARP attacks are detected, all of the entries in the ARP table are listed with green checkmarks.
6 Choose **File**, **Exit**	
Close all open windows	

Web spoofing

Explanation

Another term for phishing is *Web spoofing*. Users are tricked into visiting a website that looks and acts like an official, legitimate website. However, the attacker has created this page to dupe the victim into providing information such as user names, passwords, credit card numbers, and other personal information. These pages can use man-in-the-middle attacks or DoS attacks to get the user to the attacker's site instead of the real site.

For man-in-the-middle Web spoofing, the attacker changes the URL in a Web page to direct the user to the attacker's website instead of to the legitimate site. The site request passes through the attacker's computer on the way to the real site, and the page sent from the server also passes through the attacker's computer on the way to the victim's browser.

A DoS attack displays what appears to be the legitimate website requested by the user, but the website was actually created by the attacker to mimic the requested site. The page content redirects traffic to the attacker's computer.

To protect themselves from such attacks, users can be on the lookout for sites with misspellings, poor grammar, or other tip-offs that the sites aren't the real ones. Users can disable the use of JavaScript, Java applets, and ActiveX in their browsers, and can enable a phishing filter in the browser if one is available. Users should examine the URL for the site and report it to Security or the administrator for review if something looks wrong about it.

DNS spoofing

You use DNS every time you go to a website. You don't need to know the IP address of the site; instead, DNS takes the URL that you enter and looks up the IP address, which is used to connect you to the site. In *DNS spoofing*, rather than going where you want to, you are sent to another server that the attacker has set up. There are several ways that the attacker can accomplish his goal of getting you to his server.

In *DNS poisoning*, the cache on the DNS server is hacked. The attacker creates his own domain with a DNS server. This DNS server changes the mappings from the real site's IP address to the attacker's server IP address. To create the hacked DNS server, the attacker first requests your DNS server and asks it to resolve the attacker's domain. Your DNS server doesn't know the attacker's IP address because it isn't part of your domain, so it asks another name server. The hacked DNS server replies to your DNS server and gets all of your records. This action is referred to as a *zone transfer*. This poisons your DNS server until the cache is cleared or updated. A request for a website now sends users to the attacker's site, where a Web server is running, or the attacker could bounce forward packets going to the legitimate site so that they pass through the attacker's site. This attack has come to be known as *pharming* in recent years.

Another DNS spoofing technique is *DNS ID spoofing*. In this type of attack, the attacker uses a sniffer to intercept DNS requests and find the request ID. A fake reply is sent, using the correct ID number but with the IP address of the attacker's computer. The user believes he is communicating with the server he requested, but is actually communicating with the attacker instead.

Some measures you can take to prevent DNS spoofing include ensuring that the latest versions of DNS software and security patches are installed on your server. All of the DNS servers in your organization should have auditing enabled. Security systems should not use or rely on DNS. Limit the size of the cache so that it doesn't hold on to DNS records for too long; this way, if the cache is poisoned, it won't last for long.

Using SSL or other forms of encryption will make the attack more difficult for the attacker to conduct. You can also configure the DNS server to secure the cache against pollution; this setting puts filters in place to protect the cache from spoofing.

Do it!

B-5:   Examining spoofing attacks

Questions and answers

1   What types of attacks are used for Web spoofing?

2   What are some of the ways users can protect themselves from Web spoofing?

3   What happens when a DNS server's cache is poisoned?

4   What happens in DNS ID spoofing?

5   What steps can you take to protect your DNS server from spoofing attacks?

Replay attacks

Explanation

When an attacker reuses valid transmission data to gain access to the network, this action is known as a *replay attack*. The most common type of replay is to use a packet sniffer to intercept and retransmit data. This mechanism is used in masquerade attacks and IP packet substitution attacks. Another type of replay involves reusing authentication tokens from an unencrypted Web session by sniffing out the user's cookies. Attackers might also try faking out biometric security devices with a copy of a fingerprint or other biometric feature.

To prevent replay attacks, you should make sure that your software is up-to-date and has all of the security patches applied. Web sessions should use SSL to encrypt data. Use a secure authentication system that has anti-replay features which make every packet unique.

TCP/IP hijacking

In *TCP/IP hijacking*, the attacker takes over an established session between two nodes that are already communicating. The attacker impersonates one of the nodes, usually a client communicating with a server, and disconnects the legitimate client. This is usually launched as a man-in-the-middle attack and uses ARP cache poisoning. The client thinks it is still communicating with the server but is connected to the attacker's system instead.

Unencrypted protocols, such as DNS, FTP, and Telnet, are vulnerable to TCP/IP session hijacking. The session is sniffed by the attacker's system to learn the sequence numbers used to synchronize the session between the nodes. For each packet that is sent, the sequence number is increased; this guarantees that packets are processed in the proper order at the receiving node's end of the connection. The attacker predicts the sequence numbers and prevents the legitimate client from sending packets that would cause the sequence number to be increased.

The attacker disconnects the session from the client system and takes its place with a spoof of the client address. The attacker poisons the ARP cache on the server or uses ICMP redirects, enabling the attacker to reroute the information from the server to the attacker's computer.

Attackers often use the free Linux Hunt tool to monitor traffic on the Ethernet segment. Hunt sniffs the packets after putting the attacker's network card in promiscuous mode. Hunt has an option called "arp/simple attack," which sends three ARP packets that bind the victim's IP address to the attacker's MAC address. Any packets originally intended for the victim's IP address are now being sent to the attacker's computer instead.

To protect your network from such attacks, you should implement encrypted transport protocols. IPSec, SSH, and SSL are examples of encrypted transport protocols. They generate session keys dynamically, providing a secure transmission channel. You can also use digital signatures so that even if an attacker did obtain the session keys, it would be that much harder for the attacker to hijack the session.

Transitive attacks

Transitive attacks occur when a user is granted administrative privileges in a Windows domain that has a transitive trust relationship with another Windows domain. In such a scenario, a user in Domain A, which has a trust relationship with Domain B, which in turn has a trust relationship with Domain C, can access resources in Domain C through the transitive trust relationship. To prevent transitive trust attacks, you must limit user access to a single domain, and limit transitive trust relationships to situations in which they are absolutely necessary. For more information about Windows transitive trusts, see this Web page: http://technet.microsoft.com/en-us/library/ cc754612.aspx.

Do it!

B-6: Examining replay and hijacking attacks

Questions and answers

1 Attackers reuse valid transmission data to gain access to the network in a(n) _____ attack.

2 When a replay involves intercepting data captured through a packet sniffer, what types of attacks can be launched?

3 A Web replay reuses what type of data from the client's session?

4 To hijack a TCP/IP session, what does the attacker need to obtain?

5 List examples of unencrypted TCP/IP protocols that are often used by attackers when sniffing out packets to hijack a TCP/IP session.

6 What Linux tool is often used to conduct TCP/IP hijacks?

7 What are some ways to protect your systems from TCP/IP hijacking?

Unit summary: Ports and protocols

Topic A   In this topic, you reviewed **TCP/IP protocols** and network services. First you examined the protocols in the IP suite, including TCP, IP, UDP, ARP, and RARP. Then you examined IPv4 and IPv6 and compared their features.

Topic B   In this topic, you examined **protocol-based attacks**. You started out by examining denial-of-service (DoS) attacks, such as SYN flood, smurf, and ping-of-death attacks. Next, you looked at distributed DoS (DDoS) attacks. Then you examined man-in-the-middle attacks and spoofing attacks. You also looked at ARP poisoning. Next, you examined Web spoofing and DNS spoofing attacks. Finally, you examined replay attacks and TCP/IP hijacking.

Review questions

1   The protocols that make up the IP suite are documented in _____ documents.

2   _____ provides connection-oriented, acknowledged communication.

3   _____ is a routable, unreliable, connectionless protocol.

4   Compare ARP and RARP.

5   What are some of the ways in which more IPv4 addresses were made available?

6   What are the three IPv6 scopes?

7   Compare the format of IPv4 and IPv6 addresses.

8   Rather than destroying or stealing data, a(n) _____ attack is designed to disrupt daily standard operation.

9   _____ attacks flood a server with half-open TCP connections, which prevent users from being able to access the server.

10 A smurf attack overwhelms a host by flooding it with _____ packets.

11 The target systems in a DDoS attack use _____, which are later woken up to launch the attack.

12 Man-in-the-middle attacks can be used for what types of attacks?

13 List four types of spoofing attacks that administrators need to be aware of.

14 How is TCP/IP hijacking usually conducted?

Independent practice activity

Your manager has asked you to assemble a toolkit to create various protocol-based attacks in a lab setting. You also need to assemble a toolkit to identify the attacks and ways to prevent the attacks from recurring.

1 Identify the tools you need to launch protocol-based attacks in the lab.

2 Identify the tools you need to identify the attacks and prevent them from recurring.

Unit 9
Network security

Unit time: 180 minutes

Complete this unit, and you'll know how to:

A Describe common networking devices, including switches, bridges, routers, and firewalls; and identify the vulnerabilities of common networking devices.

B Describe the security considerations associated with network design, including virtual private networks and network interconnection techniques.

C Apply and implement the principles of secure network administration.

D Explain the purpose and benefits of virtualization and cloud computing technologies, particularly as these relate to system security.

Topic A: Network devices

This topic covers the following CompTIA Security+ objectives for exam SY0-301.

#	Objective
1.1	**Explain the security function and purpose of network devices and technologies**
	• Firewalls
	• Routers
	• Switches
	• Load balancers
	• Proxies
	• Web security gateways
	• VPN concentrators
	• Spam filters, all-in-one security appliances
	• Web application firewall vs. network firewall
	• URL filtering, content inspection, malware inspection
1.2	**Apply and implement secure network administration principles**
	• Loop protection
1.3	**Distinguish and differentiate network design elements and compounds**
	• Subnetting
	• NAT
1.5	**Identify commonly used default network ports**
	• FTP
	• HTTP
	• HTTPS
2.7	**Execute disaster recovery plans and procedures**
	• Redundancy and fault tolerance
	– Load balancing
3.6	**Analyze and differentiate among types of mitigation and deterrent techniques**
	• Hardening
	– Disabling unnecessary services
	– Protecting management interfaces and applications
	– Disabling unnecessary accounts

The OSI stack

Explanation

To better describe the various functions in most networks and to further the development of compatible products by vendors, the International Organization for Standardization developed the Open Systems Interconnection (OSI) reference model. The seven-layer model is illustrated in Exhibit 9-1.

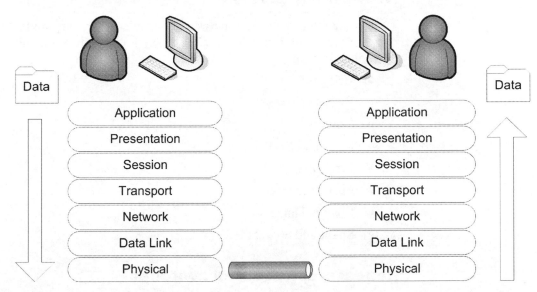

Exhibit 9-1: The OSI seven-layer model

The four-layer TCP/IP model is not based directly on the OSI model. The OSI model is generic and defines no specific protocols at any particular layer. Still, it is instructive to correlate the TCP/IP protocols with the OSI model. Additionally, both models divide network functionality into layers, assigning specific functionality to each layer and describing a communication flow between layers. With that in mind, the following description of the OSI model's layers includes the TCP/IP protocols at the layers to which they correspond:

- The Physical layer (Layer 1) deals with the electrical signals, the media access method (Ethernet, Token Ring, etc.), and the actual hardware of networking, including cables, connectors, hubs, and network cards.

- The Data Link layer (Layer 2) deals with the MAC address. This is the layer where bridges and older switches function.

- The IP protocol works at the Network layer (Layer 3), providing addressing and routing functions.

- The Transport layer (Layer 4) is responsible for host-to-host communications. In the TCP/IP suite of protocols, this is the layer at which the TCP and UDP protocols operate.

- The Session layer (Layer 5) establishes, manages, and terminates connections.

- The Presentation layer (Layer 6) translates the application's data format into the network's communication format.

- The Application layer (Layer 7) defines how protocols like FTP, HTTP, and Telnet exchange data.

A function at each layer needs to be able to communicate with the layers above and below it and to communicate with its peer level. Changes at one level should not affect the ability of the other layers to function.

For instance, if a Token Ring network is migrated to an Ethernet system, only the cabling, hardware, and drivers that represent the Physical and Data Link layers need be modified; the IP network should still function, as well as all protocols and applications above it.

Networking devices

To provide interconnections between LAN clients, servers, and networks, networks use one or more of the following devices. Each device will be examined in further detail in upcoming sections.

- Bridges
- Switches
- Routers
- NAT and PAT devices
- Firewalls
- Proxy servers
- Load balancers
- Spam and content filters

Repeaters, hubs, and switches

Many network devices—including repeaters, hubs, bridges, and switches—have both physical and logical configurations. *Repeaters* and *hubs* function at the Physical layer and extend the Ethernet segment by re-creating the transmission signals. Hubs are simply multiport repeaters, with all ports existing on the same collision domain.

Bridges function at Layer 2 (the Data Link layer). They filter and forward packets based on their MAC addresses. Bridges separate the network into two or more collision domains, also called *subnets*. Their function is based on a table of MAC addresses and host locations; this table is built from the moment the bridges are turned on.

Switches also function at Layer 2, but they divide the network into multiple domains, with the number depending on the number of ports on the switch. Although bridges and switches divide collision domains, they forward broadcasts to all hosts on the Layer 2 network.

Just as switches made moving information within an intranet more efficient, a new breed of switches is now operating at Layer 3, the Network layer. It's now possible to combine the speed of hardware switching with the optimized path choosing of Layer 3.

Switch security

Modern switches offer a variety of security features, including *access control lists* (ACLs) and *virtual local area networks* (VLANs). From a security perspective, the major benefit of a switch over a hub is the separation of collision domains, limiting the possibility of easy sniffing.

Access control lists

Modern switches often support ACLs so that you can control network access. An ACL is essentially a list of permitted addresses. Your list might permit or deny selected inbound or outbound addresses. When a switch receives a packet, it can compare the addresses within the packet to those in its ACLs and then take action accordingly.

Switch ACLs operate at either Layer 2 or Layer 3 of the OSI model, and thus make switching decisions based on MAC addresses or IP addresses. ACL-based filtering is a function that was, until recently, available only in routers.

MAC flooding

Switches can be vulnerable to MAC flooding. Switches maintain a table of MAC addresses associated with each port. This table is what enables the switch to forward traffic to the correct port, rather than sending the data out on all ports, as a hub does. In a *MAC flooding attack*, the attacker sends many packets, each with a different MAC address, in an attempt to overwhelm the storage capacity in the switch's address table.

Simple switches and older models sometimes fail-open when overwhelmed by a MAC flood. In *fail-open mode*, switches fall back to hub-like behavior, forwarding packets to every port. With the network in such a state, the hacker can use a sniffer to view packets from across the network.

Modern and advanced switches better manage port table space and won't fail open. They can also permit only a limited number of MAC addresses per port before they assume that something's wrong and stop recording new addresses in the table.

Loop protection

Network loops form when a segment is connected back onto itself via an intervening switch. In such a configuration, broadcast packets, ARP requests, and so forth can repeatedly travel through the network, consuming bandwidth and interfering with normal traffic.

A network loop can form when a user connects an Ethernet port on the wall to a switch on the desk, and then connects a wire to a second port on the wall. Also, a technician could inadvertently daisy-chain switches in a rack such that a loop is formed.

You can use some basic configuration techniques to limit problems with loops. You can disable broadcast forwarding on gateways, routers, and switches. You can make sure that ARP requests are configured to be self-canceling (this is the default setting, but it might have been overridden on your network).

Many products include loop protection safeguards. These techniques rely on configuring *bridge protocol data unit* (BPDU) handling. The exchange of these packets enables switches to self-configure to block forwarding on selected ports. You should enable BPDU handling if your equipment supports it. Juniper calls its implementation "bpdu-block-on-edge"; Cisco calls it "bdpuguard" or "loopguard."

Do it!

A-1:   Examining low-layer networking devices

Questions and answers

1 Given that TCP/IP doesn't implement the OSI model, what purpose is there in learning that reference model?

2 What factors about collision domains must you consider when designing a secure network?

3 What is the function of a switch?

4 True or false? Modern switches can reduce broadcast traffic by forwarding packets based on their IP addresses.

5 Describe a loop and the techniques you would use to prevent the problems that a loop would create.

Routers

A *router* is a network management device that sits between different network segments and routes traffic from one network to another. Routers operate at Layer 3 of the OSI model, meaning that they work with logical IP addresses as opposed to physical MAC addresses. The benefit of logical IP addresses is that you can build a hierarchical network structure that is not possible with Layer 2 physical addresses.

A router's role of digital go-between is essential because it allows different networks to communicate with one another and allows the Internet to function. With the addition of packet filtering, however, routers can take on the additional role of digital traffic cop.

Packet-based networking

TCP/IP networks divide communications into small discrete packages called *packets*. Packets are sent between computers over whatever route is available and is best suited to link the sender and receiver.

Packet-switched networks are well suited to providing shared access to a common network medium. They are cost-effective because devices can share the common medium. And they offer fault-tolerance, because any of several routes between devices can be used.

Route selection

Each packet is sent to its destination using the best available route, which might differ for each packet. So how does a router choose the best route? There are many common techniques that routers use to select routes. These techniques can be broadly divided into four categories:

- Manually configured routing tables
- Distance-vector algorithms
- Link-state algorithms
- Path-vector protocols

Manually configured routing tables

The earliest routers required administrators to enter tables of information that associated inbound and outbound connections. The administrator would configure a list of network addresses connected to the router. By examining the contents of the packet and comparing the destination address to the list of addresses contained in the lookup table, the router would be able to determine which router to send the packet along to next.

Manually configuring routers is time-consuming and error prone. Therefore, nearly all routers now support dynamic methods for selecting routes.

Distance-vector algorithms

With distance-vector algorithms, a router dynamically assigns a cost to each link between nodes in a network. The router routinely shares this data with neighboring routers, which in turn share their tables. Using this data, a router will select the lowest-cost route between networks and send the packet via that route.

Various distance-vector algorithms have been developed, such as RIP (routing information protocol) and IGRP (Interior Gateway Routing Protocol). Each algorithm uses its own method to calculate route costs. RIP, for example, simply considers the number of hops; more hops means a more expensive route. IGRP considers delay, bandwidth, and other information.

Distance-vector algorithms are fast and efficient for small networks within one autonomous domain (e.g., one company's network). However, they do not scale up well and could not be used for routing on large internetworks or the Internet.

Link-state algorithms

Routers using a link-state algorithm build a map of the network, showing which nodes are connected to which other nodes. The map includes information about link cost, availability, and so forth. When it receives a packet, a router examines its map to determine the best next hop for the packet, and then sends it to that node.

Routers build their maps by sharing the information used to build their maps. This method involves less data than sending the full map does, and less information than is shared by distance vector–based routers. Such sharing messages are flooded across the network. When link state information changes, a router sends its neighbors the new information. In turn, they determine if the data is in fact newer, and if so, they forward it to their neighbors. This process continues until the information has traversed the entire network.

As with distance-vector algorithms, link-state algorithms are most efficient within a single autonomous domain. Hierarchical versions can support larger internetworks. However, most link-state protocols cannot support Internet-scale routing.

Path-vector protocols

Path-vector protocols are designed to interconnect autonomous domains (networks). In general, they operate like distance-vector algorithms. A single "speaker node" in each domain shares its routing data with a speaker node in other domains.

The information shared is different. Instead of sharing node-level connectivity information, speaker nodes share large-scale path information. Such information is sufficient to get a packet from domain to domain; after that, the intra-domain routing protocol (a distance-vector or link-state algorithm) is used to route the packet to its ultimate destination. The Border Gateway Protocol (BGP) is an implementation of a path-vector algorithm.

Do it!   **A-2:   Examining routers**

Questions and answers

1   A node has 10 packets' worth of data to send to a remote host. There are multiple potential routes between the nodes. Will all of those packets take the same route across the network?

2   True or false? IP packets are routed by Layer 2 of the OSI model.

3   Classify the four routing algorithms by whether they are designed to support intra-domain or inter-domain communications: manual configuration, distance-vector, link-state, and path-vector.

NAT and PAT

Network address translation (NAT) devices correlate internal and external addresses. A small company might have just a single IP address on the Internet, yet have dozens or hundreds of private (internal) IP addresses. All Internet communications appear to come from that single public IP address. The NAT router makes sure that inbound and outbound packets arrive at the correct destination. Unless an internal system has initiated a communication session, external devices cannot find or communicate with internal devices due to the translated network addressing scheme.

There are a couple of good reasons to use NAT:

- **Availability of addresses** — The American Registry for Internet Numbers (ARIN) regulates and assigns IP addresses that can be used directly on the Internet. Companies must apply and pay for the use of address ranges, and typically must justify the addresses they request. Rather than going through the trouble for every new block of network devices they add, companies use a private range of addresses within their networks.

- **Security** — By using private addresses within the company, network administrators make it more difficult for hackers and automated malware on the Internet to discover and compromise internal systems.

In the home environment, the typical cable or DSL modem provides NAT functionality to map internal addresses to one or more IP addresses assigned by the homeowner's Internet service provider. In a corporate environment, routers, firewalls, or other devices provide large-scale address translation services.

In many cases, NAT devices use non-routable, private addresses for your internal network. These address ranges include the 10.0.0.0, 172.16.0.0, and 192.168.0.0 subnetworks. Addresses in those ranges are not valid on the Internet (and should not be routed by Internet devices). They are defined specifically for internal networks.

Port address translation

Particularly in smaller networks, many internal devices can share a single external IP address through a device that provides *port address translation* (PAT). Such a device, typically a router or firewall, performs NAT services, mapping multiple private internal IP addresses to a single public external IP address. The PAT device uses port numbers to differentiate between internal servers sharing this single address.

A *port* is the address of an application at a particular IP address. For example, a packet arriving at a server at 192.168.1.100 could be meant for the Web server application running on that computer, the mail server, or some sort of VoIP (voice over IP) processing software. The port number identifies which application should receive and process the packet. Commonly used port numbers are listed in the following table.

Port number	Protocol and purpose
21	FTP (File Transfer Protocol) for file transfer services.
25	SMTP (Simple Mail Transport Protocol) for sending e-mail.
80	HTTP (HyperText Transport Protocol) for Web server traffic.
443	SSL (Secure Sockets Layer) for secure connections over HTTP.

In a PAT environment, an internal server with an arbitrary IP address could provide publicly available Web services, while a different server would provide FTP services. To users on the Internet, both servers would appear to be located at the same IP address but with non-standard port numbers. For example, the Web server might be at port 8080, and the FTP server, at port 2121. The PAT device would receive requests from the Internet at the single IP address on these arbitrary port numbers. It would then translate to the appropriate internal addresses and ports.

Many sources describe the sharing of a single public IP address as the primary advantage of PAT. That is true; however, PAT also adds a measure of security. Many attacks, particularly automated attacks, are tuned to the standard port assignments. By using alternate ports, your systems are effectively hidden from such attackers.

Do it!

A-3:   Examining NAT and PAT devices

Questions and answers

1 What is the primary purpose of NAT? What else does it provide?

2 Why might you use PAT?

3 How can NAT and PAT provide complementary services to enhance security?

Firewalls and proxy servers

Explanation

A *firewall* is a device that controls traffic between networks, typically between a public network and a private internal network. Firewalls examine the contents of network traffic and permit or block transmission based on rules.

At their core, all firewalls protect networks by using some combination of the following techniques:

- Network address translation (NAT)
- Basic packet filtering
- Stateful packet inspection (SPI)
- Access control lists (ACLs)

Basic firewalls use only one technique, usually NAT, but firewalls that are more comprehensive use all of the techniques combined. Of course, as features are added, complexity and cost increase. Depending on the features you need, you can get firewalls that operate at various levels of the TCP/IP protocol stack. The various types of firewalls include:

- Network-layer firewalls
- Application-layer firewalls
- Proxy servers
- Content filters
- Load balancers
- Unified threat management devices

Network-layer firewalls

Network-layer firewalls, also called *packet filters*, operate at Layer 3 (IP addresses are used at Layer 3). *Stateless* packet filters examine IP addresses and ports to determine whether a packet should be passed on. *Stateful* packet filters monitor outbound and inbound traffic by watching addresses, ports, and connection data. Stateful packet filters can determine whether a packet is part of an existing communication stream or a new stream.

Application-layer firewalls

Application-layer firewalls "understand" the data contained in packets and thus can enforce more complex rules. For example, an Application-layer firewall might determine that an inbound packet is carrying an HTTP (Web) request and is going to a permitted address and port. Such a packet would be transmitted. Packets carrying other protocols or going to other addresses might be blocked.

Application firewalls are typically specific to a single application or a very small set of applications. A Web application firewall, for example, monitors Web traffic and would try to block cross-site scripting or SQL injection attacks. Other examples of Web application firewalls include database and e-mail firewalls.

In addition to monitoring inbound traffic, an application firewall can monitor, log, and sanitize outgoing traffic. For example, rules can be implemented that strip out some types of private information from the data transmitted by clients to Internet-based hosts.

Proxy servers

A *proxy server* is a server that acts as an intermediary between computers on a network and the Internet. When a proxy server is used, a client's request is not actually sent to the remote host. Instead, it goes to the proxy server, which then sends the request to the remote node on behalf of the client. Before sending the packet, the proxy server replaces the original sender's address and other identifying information with its own. When the response arrives, the proxy server looks up the original sending node's information, updates the incoming packet, and forwards it to the client.

By these actions, a proxy server masks internal IP addresses, like a NAT device does. It also blocks unwanted inbound traffic—there will be no corresponding outbound connection data in its tables, so the packets will be dropped. Many proxy servers also provide caching functions. The contents of popular Web pages, for example, could be saved on the proxy server and served from there, rather than having many client workstations sending packets out across a wide area network link.

Squid Server (www.squid-cache.org) is a popular open-source caching proxy server. It is available for most common operating systems. Squid Server offers proxy and content caching for HTTP, HTTPS, FTP, and other protocols. It also offers hierarchical load-balancing functions to enable your network to handle very high network loads.

Content filters

Content filters permit or deny traffic based on the contents of the messages, rather than based on addresses or other meta-information. On a personal level, content filters such as NetNanny and CYBERsitter permit (or block) access to websites deemed appropriate (or inappropriate) by the authors of the software. Enterprise-grade content filters enable Internet service providers and corporations to scan Web and e-mail traffic for suitability and compliance with corporate standards.

URL filters evaluate websites based on their Web addresses. Content filters can handle new websites and dynamically changing sites more easily. E-mail filters can scan incoming and outgoing messages for malware, in addition to scanning message contents.

Spam filters are also a form of content filter. Spam filters can run on the client as components of e-mail applications, or you can use network-based network appliances.

Load balancers

Load balancers, as their name implies, are devices that distribute networking or computing workloads across multiple resources. A load balancing router, for example, can dynamically adjust network routes to balance the utilization across networks.

Load balancing devices also provide additional functions:

- **SSL offloading** — Reduces the SSL processing overhead burden on Web servers by offloading SSL computations to a specialized device.
- **Denial-of-service protection** — Offloads TCP functions from protected servers and distributes network connections across devices to limit the effect of or to block DoS and DDoS attacks.
- **Health monitoring** — Monitors the state of applications on managed systems, removing crashed systems from the pool.
- **HTTP caching, compressing, and security** — Caches static HTML content, compresses HTTP data, and provides security functions, such as cookie encryption and error page hiding.

Unified threat management (UTM)

Unified threat management (UTM) represents the merger of separate network security devices into a single all-in-one appliance. UTM systems typically comprise a firewall, spam filter, malware scanner, load balancer, VPN concentrator, NAT/PAT router, and more.

Simple UTMs provide filtering and inspection based on message content and meta-information (addresses, ports, and so forth). User-identity UTMs can identify individual users, log information on a per-user basis, and even enable you to specify per-user network and content policies.

UTMs offer the convenience of a single, central console for management. Using a single appliance simplifies setup and maintenance. Vendors of UTM systems include Cisco Systems, Endian, and Vyatta.

Do it!

A-4:   Examining firewalls and proxy servers

Questions and answers

1 Describe the primary difference between a proxy server and an Application-layer firewall.

2 True or false? Firewalls operate at Layer 2 of the protocol stack.

3 Does your company use a firewall? If so, what features does it offer that encouraged your company to select it instead of another firewall solution?

4 Does your company use a proxy server? If so, do you use it for caching Web requests, filtering content, or masking internal IP addresses?

5 Describe the pros and cons of using content filtering software.

Security issues

Explanation Your network devices present a tempting target for hackers. Should they gain virtual or physical access to your devices, hackers could disrupt your network or even gain access to the data flowing over it. Devices present the following general vulnerability points:

- Built-in management interfaces
- Firmware and operating system weaknesses
- Susceptibility to physical attack

Built-in management interfaces

Devices such as switches, routers, and firewalls include management interfaces so that you can monitor or configure the devices without physically visiting them. You might use a Web browser, Telnet application, or SNMP console to connect to and manage these devices. Such interfaces are a crucial feature for many of these devices. However, they are also vulnerable to attacks. Attackers attempt to log in, using default account credentials, in order to gain escalated permissions and take control of the devices.

Security problems with switches

Switch hijacking occurs when an unauthorized person obtains administrator privileges for a switch and changes its configuration. Once a switch has been compromised, the hacker can do a variety of things, such as changing the administrator password on the switch, turning off ports to critical systems, reconfiguring VLANs to allow one or more systems to talk to systems they shouldn't, or configuring the switch to bypass the firewall altogether. There are two common ways to obtain unauthorized access to a switch: trying default passwords, which might not have been changed; and sniffing the network to get the administrator password via SNMP or Telnet.

Almost all switches come with multiple accounts with default passwords (or sometimes no password at all). Although most administrators know enough to change the administrator password for the Telnet and serial console accounts, sometimes people don't know that they should change the SNMP (Simple Network Management Protocol) strings that provide remote access to the switch. If the default SNMP strings are not changed or disabled, hackers might be able to obtain a great deal of information about the network or even gain total control of the switch. The Internet is full of sites that list the various switch types and their administrator accounts, SMTP connection strings, and passwords.

If the default passwords do not work, the switch can still be compromised if a hacker is using a protocol analyzer to sniff the network while an administrator is logging onto the switch. Contrary to popular belief, it's very possible to sniff the network when an administrator is logged onto some switches. This means that even if you change the administrator passwords and the SNMP strings, you might still be vulnerable to switch hijacking.

The easiest way to sniff a switched network is to use a software tool called "dsniff," which tricks the switch into sending packets to the sniffer that were supposed to go to other systems. Dsniff not only captures packets on switched networks, but also has the functionality to automatically decode passwords from insecure protocols, such as Telnet, HTTP, and SNMP, which are commonly used to manage switches.

Firmware and operating system weaknesses

Firmware and operating system weaknesses are built-in vulnerabilities. Usually, these result from mistakes or oversights by equipment designers rather than being purposeful "back doors." The problems come to light after the device is released and many users have a chance to fully use and stress its capabilities. Most vendors quickly release firmware or software updates to fix such problems.

In this context, "operating system" refers to the software running on the network device. Higher-functioning devices, such as routers, are in essence specialized computers. These devices run their own operating system software. In some cases, this operating system is a custom, proprietary system, such as Cisco's IOS (Internetwork Operating System). In other cases, networking functions are built upon a Linux kernel, or perhaps even a complete Linux distribution. The Endian UTM system, for example, runs on a hardened Linux operating system.

Susceptibility to physical attack

Devices are susceptible to attack whenever someone gains physical access. The range of possible attacks is nearly limitless. Someone could simply steal your router, server, or switch. For example, someone might steal a server or external storage device in order to bypass data security controls later.

In the case of networking appliances, hackers are more likely to attempt to reconfigure the devices to block traffic or permit unwanted communications. Another form of physical susceptibility involves access to your communications medium. Such problems can lead to eavesdropping or even network hijacking.

Network hijacking

If a hacker has physical access to your network, he or she can mount attacks that could disrupt or reroute your communications. Consider what would happen if a hacker were able to put his own router onto your network. The server could be configured to send packets to the wrong destinations or cause packets to simply be lost along the way.

This scenario might sound far-fetched, but it has happened on the Internet. The BGP (Border Gateway Protocol) is susceptible to an attack known as *prefix hijacking*. In this scheme, a rogue router with a modified routing table is placed on the network. The table is configured to report that the router can service various network routes. When packets are sent via that router, they are either dropped or sent to the wrong locations. In one event in 2004, one such rogue device provided incorrect routing information for over 100,000 IP ranges.

With bus topology networks, stations are attached to the backbone via *vampire taps*, also called *piercing taps*. These devices clamp around the network cable, pierce its insulation, and make contact with the conductors within. Vampire taps are rarely used in modern networks. If you use an older-style bus network, or if you use broadband copper backbones to span long distances, your network could be susceptible to physical attack by someone attaching a vampire tap to your network cables.

Fiber taps are devices that work in a somewhat similar fashion. In normal operations, the light flowing down a fiber is completely reflected within the fiber, with no light escaping through the walls of the fiber strand. However, at sharp bends in the strand, some light can escape. Fiber taps can take advantage of this by capturing that light and giving an attacker access to your network transmissions. Such taps are often easy to detect due to the attenuation they introduce into the line.

Another such problem would be *Wi-Fi hijacking*. In this scheme, a hacker configures his or her computer to present itself as a wireless router. So, you're at the coffee shop and think you're connecting to the shop's router, when in fact you're connecting to the hacker's rogue hotspot. He then has the option to intercept your communications or even access your computer's files.

Do it!

A-5:   Identifying inherent weaknesses in network devices

Questions and answers

1   What is switch hijacking?

2   What are some malicious acts someone could perform if he or she had physical access to your network's communication medium?

3   What are the default administrator usernames and passwords for Linksys and DLink brand routers? (Hint: Use your favorite search engine if you don't already know the answer.)

Overcoming device weaknesses

Explanation

Network and security administrators need to be aware of the vulnerabilities of their hardware and software systems. If you work in such a role, you will need to take specific actions to limit your risk of attacks. These actions include:

- Changing default passwords
- Disabling features, protocols, and options you do not need
- Applying firmware and software updates regularly
- Monitoring physical and virtual access to your network and devices

Changing default passwords

Always set strong passwords on network devices. Passwords should be seemingly random strings of letters, numbers, and punctuation characters. Use long passwords of more than eight characters if they are supported by your device.

A device might offer multiple accounts, such as one for Telnet access and another for browser-based access. Make sure that you change default passwords and user IDs for all access methods.

Many switches and routers use Telnet or HTTP—both being open text protocols—for management. Wi-Fi routers sometimes permit management access over both wired and wireless interfaces.

You need to limit the chances that your management passwords will be discovered. You should manage devices via a serial port connection or by using a Secure Shell (SSH) or another encrypted communications channel, if one is available. For wireless devices, when possible, perform management functions over wired connections only.

Disabling features, protocols, and options you do not need

When installing or reconfiguring a device, turn off options and protocols that you do not need and won't use. For example, unless you absolutely need to enable a LAN client to reconfigure your Internet router, you should turn off UPnP (Universal Plug and Play). There are known vulnerabilities in UPnP.

For wireless devices, disable access to management functions via wireless connections. For wired devices, turn off protocols (such as SNMP or Telnet) that you won't be using for management.

Applying firmware and software updates regularly

You must stay alert for notices of new updates and then take action quickly to prevent problems. If your software vendor provides regular notices of updates, via e-mail or RSS, make sure to subscribe and read the notices regularly. Then, as they become available, you should quickly test and then install firmware and OS updates.

Monitoring physical and virtual access to your network and devices

Cameras and key-card entry systems provide a way to monitor physical access to network devices. However, simple awareness might be the key to catching someone trying to access your network media. For example, you might want to ask someone what he's doing if you find him at the top of a stepladder with suspended-ceiling tiles removed.

Network monitoring software will enable you to monitor access to servers. You will need to rely on device logs to monitor access to non-server devices. Collect such logs regularly on a central console for archiving and examination.

Do it!

A-6:   Examining ways to overcome device threats

Questions and answers
1 List the four tasks you should perform to overcome device threats:
2 What is the advantage of disabling features or services you don't need?
3 Should you immediately apply firmware and other device software updates?

Topic B: Secure network topologies

This topic covers the following CompTIA Security+ objectives for exam SY0-301.

#	Objective
1.1	**Explain the security function and purpose of network devices and technologies** • VPN concentrators
1.2	**Apply and implement secure network administration principles** • Rule-based management • Firewall rules • VLAN management • Secure router configuration • Prevent network bridging by separation
1.3	**Distinguish and differentiate network design elements and compounds** • DMZ • VLAN • Telephony • NAC
1.4	**Implement and use common protocols** • IPSec

3.6	**Analyze and differentiate among types of mitigation and deterrent techniques**
	• Port security
	   – MAC limiting and filtering
	   – Disabling unused ports

Network design for security

Explanation

Designing a secure network involves accounting for both internal and external threats. This topic focuses on mitigating external threats. We'll start by looking at virtual private networks and then look at the way you connect your network to the Internet.

Security zones

Any network that is connected (directly or indirectly) to your organization, but is not controlled by your organization, represents a risk. To alleviate these risks, security professionals create *security zones*, which divide the network into areas with various levels of security (trusted, semi-trusted, and untrusted). You create the security zones by putting all your publicly accessed servers in one zone, putting restricted-access servers in another zone, and then using firewalls to separate both zones from external networks like the Internet.

The three main zones into which networks are commonly divided are the intranet, the perimeter network, and the extranet.

The intranet zone

An *intranet* is the organization's private network; it is fully controlled by the company and is trusted. The intranet typically contains confidential or proprietary information relevant to the company and consequently restricts access to internal employees only. The private internal LANs are protected from other security zones by one or more firewalls, which restrict incoming traffic from both the public and DMZ zones.

As an additional safeguard to prevent intrusion, intranets use private address spaces. These IP addresses are reserved for private use by any internal network and are not routable on the Internet. The following address ranges are reserved:

- Class A: 10.0.0.0–10.255.255.255
- Class B: 172.16.0.0–172.31.255.255
- Class C: 192.168.0.0–192.168.255.255

You would use addresses in these ranges with a NAT device. Such devices translate private, internal, non-routable addresses into public, routable addresses.

Additional security measures include:

- Installing antivirus software
- Removing unnecessary services from mission-critical servers
- Auditing the critical systems' configurations and resources
- Subnetting to divide the intranet into distinct segments, thereby isolating unrelated traffic

The perimeter network

You have various options for connecting your network to a public, insecure network such as the Internet. The topology you choose will have a profound impact on the security of your network and its hosts.

Small networks, such as those in users' homes or small businesses, will often be directly connected to the Internet over a connection provided by an ISP. Such connections should always be secured through the use of a firewall. A typical configuration involves a cable or DSL connection and a hardware-based firewall built into a router, which might include wired or wireless internal network connections.

In such topologies, connections are permitted from inside the network to points on the Internet. However, unsolicited connections from the Internet to nodes on the internal network are blocked. Of course, you could permit some connections to the internal network by opening selected ports, but that is rarely needed.

A different topology is often used in larger networks or when access to internal systems is regularly needed. These systems often employ a perimeter network, kept separate from the intranet. A perimeter network is also known as a *demilitarized zone* (DMZ).

DMZ configurations

A DMZ is an area between the private network (intranet) and a public network (extranet) such as the Internet. A DMZ isn't a direct part of either network but is instead an additional network between the two networks.

Computers in the DMZ are accessible to nodes on both the Internet and the intranet. Typically, computers within the DMZ have limited access to nodes on the intranet. However, direct connections between the Internet and nodes on the internal network are blocked.

For example, you might put your company's mail server in a DMZ. Users on both the internal network and the Internet will need access to the mail server. The mail server might need to communicate with internal storage servers to save files and other data. But Internet users shouldn't have access to your internal network.

You can set up a DMZ in several ways:

- Screened hosts
- Bastion hosts
- Three-homed firewalls
- Back-to-back firewalls
- Dead zones

Screened hosts

With a screened host, a router is used to filter all traffic to the private intranet while allowing full access to the computer in the DMZ. The router is solely responsible for protecting the private network (see Exhibit 9-2). The IP address of the DMZ host is entered in the router configuration. This IP address is allowed full Internet access, but other computers on the network are protected behind the firewall provided by the router. The disadvantage of this setup is that sometimes a router firewall can fail and allow traffic through to the intranet.

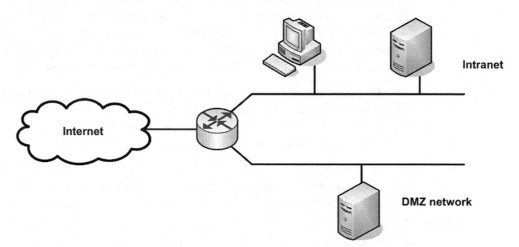

Exhibit 9-2: A screened-host DMZ

In addition to using a router to protect a network, an administrator can use subnets and subnet masks to protect the private network from a screened host. If the screened host is on one subnet and all other computers on the private intranet are on another subnet, the intranet on another subnet is less likely to be compromised if the screened host is penetrated.

Bastion hosts

Another DMZ configuration is the bastion host. The word "bastion" means a protruding part of a fortified wall or rampart. *Bastion hosts* are computers that stand outside the protected network and defend it by using two network cards, one for the DMZ and one for the intranet, as shown in Exhibit 9-3. Network communication isn't allowed between the two network cards in the bastion host server, or if it is allowed, the bastion host must be the proxy server to the network. With this configuration, only one host, the bastion host, can be directly accessed from the public network. Bastion hosts are also known as *dual-homed hosts* or *dual-homed firewalls*.

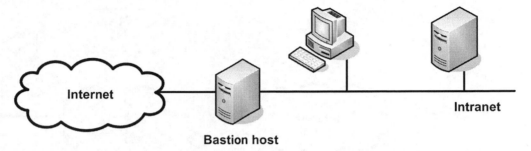

Exhibit 9-3: A bastion host

Three-homed firewalls

If your DMZ contains several computers, such as a Web server, a DNS server, and an FTP server, you can use a *three-homed firewall* (see Exhibit 9-4). In such a configuration, the entry point to the DMZ requires three network cards. One network card is connected to the Internet, the second card is connected to the DMZ network (or perimeter network), and the third card is connected to the intranet. Firewall software, such as Microsoft Internet Security and Acceleration Server, is required to control traffic on the server or group of servers that have these three network cards installed. Traffic is never allowed to flow directly from the Internet to the private intranet without filtering through the DMZ.

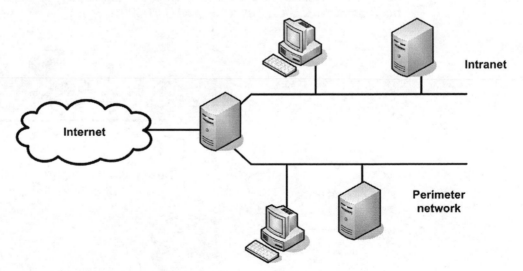

Exhibit 9-4: A three-homed firewall

Back-to-back firewalls

The *back-to-back firewall* configuration offers some of the best protection for networks. In this design, the DMZ network is located between two firewalls, as shown in Exhibit 9-5. The two firewalls—between the Internet and the DMZ and between the DMZ and the intranet—each have two network cards. In addition, the server within the DMZ has two network cards. Although this design offers exceptional protection, it's also expensive and complicated to implement. Therefore, only those companies that require the highest level of security use it.

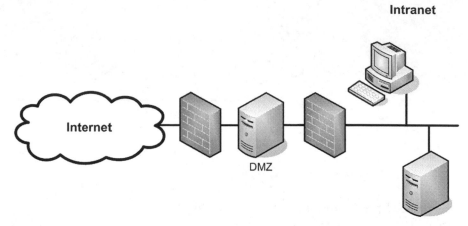

Exhibit 9-5: A back-to-back firewall

Dead zones

A *dead zone*, illustrated in Exhibit 9-6, is a network that is placed between two routers and that uses a network protocol other than TCP/IP. If the DMZ is using some other protocol, such as IPX/SPX, the network between the two routers is a dead zone. This is the most secure of all DMZ configurations, but it comes with a price. Network protocol switching must happen at each router for communication to take place among the networks. This configuration is especially resistant to ping-of-death attacks and SYN flooding because these attacks depend on TCP/IP.

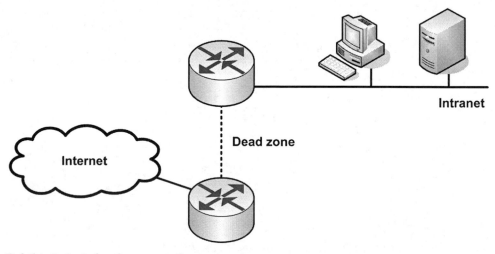

Exhibit 9-6: A dead zone configuration

Traffic filtering

You might set up filtering rules that control the flow of packets between the three zones: intranet, perimeter network, and extranet. You would configure such rules in your firewalls and routers. You could use rule-based management to drop unwanted packets or to trip intrusion detection alarms—console notifications, e-mail messages, log entries, and so forth.

You can configure filtering rules based on IP addresses, MAC addresses, or port numbers. MAC-based filtering is a common technique for wireless network security. In general, you would define a set of MAC addresses permitted to connect to your network. Such filtering rules could also be used in a wired network.

Filtering outgoing traffic

You might filter outgoing traffic that originates from a DMZ computer. Doing so would prevent an attack in which a hacker configures a DMZ computer to initiate communications with his or her host. It would also keep your DMZ computers from being used as traffic-generating agents in distributed denial-of-service (DDOS) attacks.

However, you might have legitimate reasons for your DMZ computers to initiate communications with remote hosts. For example, the mail server in your DMZ might periodically contact a remote mail host to download mail messages. Your local DNS server will likely initiate contacts with higher-level DNS servers in order to keep tables up to date. Make sure you know all of the legitimate data flows in use before configuring a firewall rule that might drop critical data packets.

Filtering incoming traffic

You might filter incoming traffic. For instance, at the interface between your DMZ and intranet, you would want to block all traffic with a source network address other than that of your DMZ. Such traffic is likely to be spoofed traffic associated with an attack.

You will also likely configure the firewall between your DMZ and the extranet to filter some types of incoming traffic. For example, you might permit only inbound connections to your mail servers, while dropping all other uninitiated inbound traffic.

Do it!

B-1: Comparing firewall-based secure topologies

Questions and answers

1 How do NAT and PAT differ from a DMZ?

2 A computer that resides in a DMZ and hosts Web, mail, DNS, and/or FTP services is called a(n) _____ _____.

3 Which of the following are features of a DMZ?

    A   It is a network segment between two routers.

    B   Its servers are publicly accessible.

    C   Its servers have lower security requirements than other internal servers.

    D   It commonly contains bastion, public Web, FTP, DNS, and RADIUS servers.

    E   All of the above.

Network bridging

Explanation

Bridging joins two networks into a single network. Bridging can be accomplished by design, using devices called *bridges*. Bridging can also occur unintentionally due to poorly configured network devices and workstations.

For example, a wireless router interconnects a wired network (such as your LAN) with a wireless network. For the best security, the wired and wireless networks should be separate, isolated networks with a firewall or other security device providing the required interconnection. However, many devices are configured by default to simply extend the wired network into the wireless spectrum.

A user's workstation could include multiple network adapters. Typically, this is the case for laptops with both wired and wireless network adapters. System features, such as Windows' Internet Connection Sharing, can create a bridge between the networks. You should disable such bridging to isolate networks.

The following table lists the ways you can disable bridging in a few of the popular end-user operating systems. Consult your system documentation for other operating systems.

Operating system	To disable bridging...
Windows XP	In the Control Panel, Network, right-click an active network connection and de-select Bridge Connections.
Windows 7	In the Network and Sharing Center, click Change Adapter Settings. Right-click a network connection and de-select Bridge Connections.
Mac OS X	In System Preferences, under Internet & Wireless, click Sharing. If necessary, click the lock icon and enter the system password. Select Internet Sharing, clear any connection sharing options, and set Internet Sharing to Off.

Do it!

B-2:   Disabling connection bridging

Here's how	Here's why
1 On your Windows 7 computer, open the Network and Sharing Center	
2 Click **Change Adapter Settings**	In the left pane.
3 Right-click each of your connections	Bridge Connections should be unchecked for each of your connections, unless your instructor tells you otherwise.
Press (ESC)	If necessary, to close the context menu.
4 Close the Network and Sharing Center	

Virtual local area networks

Explanation

A *virtual LAN* (VLAN) is a virtual network segment enabled by a Layer 2–compatible switch. Nodes on the same physical segment can be made to interoperate as if they were on separate segments, or various physical network segments can be made to appear as if they were on the same segment. By formal definition, a VLAN is a distinct broadcast domain within a larger network.

The IEEE 802.1Q standard formalizes a method called *VLAN tagging* by which you can create VLANs. Proprietary protocols that provide similar functionality include the VLAN Trunking Protocol, Dynamic Trunking Protocol, and Inter-Switch Link, all created by Cisco Systems.

Bridging between virtual segments can be restricted or permitted as needed. In this way, nodes can co-exist on the same wire, yet be logically separated and protected from each other.

VLANs increase security by clustering users in smaller groups, thereby making the job of the hacker harder. Rather than just gaining access to the network, a hacker must now gain access to a specific virtual LAN as well.

VLAN configurations are often used with VoIP (Voice over IP) telephony systems. Distinct VLANs are created for voice and data traffic. In this way, traffic on each VLAN is isolated and protected from traffic on the other VLAN. For example, if someone launches a denial-of-service attack against one of your servers, your VoIP phones will continue to operate.

Do it!

B-3: Examining VLANs

Questions and answers

1 Name at least two benefits of VLANs compared to physical LANs.

2 Describe how VLANs improve or reduce security.

3 If you are planning to add VoIP to your data network, what else do you need to consider?

Network Access Control

Explanation

Computers on your network should adhere to your corporate security policy. For example, let's say your policy dictates that all computers on your network run an up-to-date antivirus program. How do you know that the antivirus definitions are actually current? Is the computer running a firewall? Is the operating system up-to-date?

Consider what might happen if a laptop that has been disconnected from your network has become infected with a virus and is then reconnected to the network. All of your systems might be vulnerable to attacks from this laptop.

Network Access Control (NAC) is the means to ensure that computers comply with your security policies. NAC is a process or architecture through which computers are verified to be in compliance, and are brought into compliance if they fall short, before they are permitted access to the network.

Microsoft's implementation of NAC is called *Network Access Protection* (NAP). It is a feature introduced in Windows Server 2008. Cisco offers the Network Admission Control architecture, and the Trusted Computing Group's Trusted Network Connect (TNC) system is another implementation of NAC.

Vendors such as Microsoft, Juniper, IBM, Computer Associates, and Cisco offer NAC components. These tools work together to support an overall NAC architecture. For example, IBM's Tivoli network management system might be the central reporting and management console for other NAC components, such as an antivirus scanner from Computer Associates.

Do it!

B-4:   Identifying the benefits of NAC

Questions and answers
1   Why might you want to implement NAC on your network?
2   Is NAC a product you buy?

Virtual private networks

Explanation

A *virtual private network* (VPN) is a private communications network transmitted across a public, typically insecure, network connection. With a VPN, a company can extend a virtual LAN segment to employees working from home by transmitting data securely across the Internet. A VPN, illustrated in Exhibit 9-7, is a means of providing secure communications across the extranet zone. (A *Point of Presence* is an access point from one place to the rest of the Internet.)

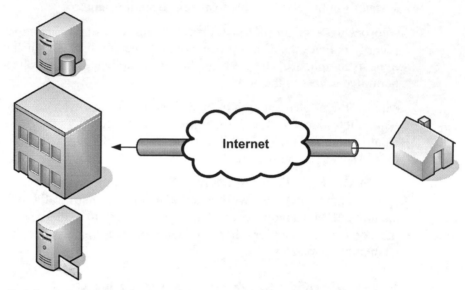

Exhibit 9-7: A typical VPN using Point of Presence (POP)

With a VPN, TCP/IP communications are encrypted and then packaged within another TCP/IP packet stream. The VPN hardware or software can encrypt just the underlying data in a packet or the entire packet itself before wrapping it in another IP packet for delivery. If a packet on the public network is intercepted along the way, the encrypted contents cannot be read by a hacker. Such encryption of data or packets is typically implemented by using a protocol suite called *Internet Protocol Security* (IPSec).

A *VPN concentrator* is the hardware device that serves as the connection point between clients on the WAN and the corporate LAN. The VPN concentrator enables many relatively low-speed devices to connect to the high-speed LAN. VPN concentrator functionality is often provided by a device that also serves other purposes. For example, a unified threat management (UTM) system typically provides VPN concentrator features. Integrated devices like this ease management because you have only one device to manage. They can also improve your security by simplifying or automating administration tasks.

IPSec encryption

IPSec was initially developed for Internet Protocol version 6 (IPv6), but many current IPv4 devices support it as well. IPSec enables two types of encryption. With *transport encryption*, the underlying data in a packet is encrypted and placed within a new packet on the public network. With *tunnel encryption*, the entire packet, including its header, is encrypted and then placed in the public network's packet.

The following steps illustrate the process:

1   A remote user opens a VPN connection between his computer and his office network. The office network and the user's computer (or their respective VPN gateways) execute a handshake and establish a secure connection by exchanging private keys.

2   The user then requests a particular file.

3   Assuming that the user has sufficient rights, the network begins to send the file to the user by first breaking the file into packets.

- If the VPN is using transport encryption, then the packet's data is encrypted and the packets are sent on their way.

- If the system is using tunneling encryption, then each packet is encrypted and placed inside another IP envelope, with a new address arranged for by the VPN gateways.

4   The packets are sent along the Internet until they are received at the user's VPN device, where the encryption is removed and the file is rebuilt. If the VPN is using tunneling encryption, the peer VPN gateway forwards the decrypted packets to the appropriate host on its LAN.

With IPSec in place, a VPN can virtually eliminate packet sniffing and identity spoofing. Only the sending and receiving computers hold the keys to encrypt and decrypt the packets being sent across the public network. Anyone sniffing the packets would have no idea of their content and might not even be able to determine the source and destination of the request.

Do it!

B-5:   Identifying the security enabled by VPNs

Questions and answers

1   What could you use a VPN for?

2   Which encryption method encrypts the entire packet, including its header, before packaging it into the public network's packet stream?

A   CHAP

B   IPSec

C   Tunneling

D   Transport

3   Do you have to use IPSec to enable a VPN?

4   Is a VPN concentrator a stand-alone device or an integrated appliance?

Topic C: Secure networking

This topic covers the following CompTIA Security+ objectives for exam SY0-301.

#	Objective
1.2	**Apply and implement secure network administration principles**
	• Rule-based management
	• Firewall rules
	• VLAN management
	• Secure router configuration
	• Access control lists
	• Port security
	• Flood guards
	• Implicit deny
3.6	**Analyze and differentiate among types of mitigation and deterrent techniques**
	• Port security
	– Disabling unused ports

Firewall administration

Explanation

Host-based firewalls filter traffic arriving at and leaving a specific computer. Network firewalls filter traffic for an entire network or subnetwork. Windows Firewall is an example of a host-based firewall. Many vendors, including Cisco, IBM, Endian, and Vyatta, make network firewalls.

Another way to distinguish firewalls is by the techniques by which they are created. A software-based firewall is implemented as an application that runs on a general-purpose computer configured with multiple network adapters. A dedicated firewall uses embedded software and custom hardware to perform its duties.

Rules-based firewalls

A rules-based firewall uses predefined rules that permit or deny communications to a specific combination of address and port number. Such rules are relatively easy to configure and understand. Most rules-based firewalls are configured to deny by default so that you don't have to configure every conceivable rule to establish a basic level of security.

Cisco calls firewall rules "access control lists" (ACLs). You can enter these rules through the Cisco IOS console or through Cisco's other administration tools. A sample rule—in this case, to permit network access from a given host—would look like this:

```
access-list INBOUND line 10 extended permit tcp 192.168.1.123
```

Linux-based systems can use the built-in `iptables` command to set up firewall rules. Although some Linux distributions offer GUI-mode configuration tools, most reference sources describe commands you can issue to block or permit traffic. An `iptables` rule, which you would enter at the command line or in a configuration file, would look like this:

```
iptables -A INPUT -p tcp --syn -m limit --limit 1/s ▶
        --limit-burst 4 -j ACCEPT
```

Some vendors attempt to differentiate their products by labeling them as policy-based or zone-based firewalls. The implication is that these products offer additional features for blocking or permitting traffic or that the firewalls can automatically adapt to changing network configurations.

Network-layer vs. Application-layer firewalls

A Network-layer firewall, also called a *packet filter*, operates at the bottom layers of the OSI stack. Rules block or permit traffic based on IP addresses, port numbers, or MAC addresses. This is the type of device most people envision when considering firewalls.

Application-layer firewalls work at the OSI Application layer and block or permit traffic based on the application communicating. At a simple level, you might block all Telnet traffic but permit HTTP (Web) traffic. You could also use such a system to block SQL injection attacks from reaching your database server while permitting valid data queries. Or you could block requests from one type of Web browser (that has known vulnerabilities) but permit other browsers to communicate.

Rule planning

You should plan your firewall rules prior to implementation. This will help ensure that required protections are enabled while required communications are still permitted. In general, you should plan with *implicit deny* in mind. In other words, plan to lock down your configuration and then relax rules where required so that unconfigured options are blocked by default.

When you're planning firewall rules, consider the following factors:

- What traffic must always be allowed? What traffic must always be blocked?
- Which systems must accept unsolicited inbound connections? For example, public-facing Web servers must accept all inbound connections.
- Can all of your devices take advantage of secure technologies, such as IPSec, Kerberos v5 authentication, and so forth?
- Do you need to permit remote access, VPN access, or mobile access to internal systems? If so, would a different network configuration provide better security?
- Do the default firewall rules meet your needs? If not, can you use them as a starting point, or should you start from scratch?

Do it!

C-1: Configuring firewall rules

Here's how	Here's why
1 On your domain server, open Server Manager	You will configure firewall rules.
Expand **Configuration**, **Windows Firewall with Advanced Security**	We're using the Windows host-based firewall, but the principles apply to dedicated and network firewalls as well.
2 Select **Inbound Rules**	
3 Scroll to find **File and Printer Sharing (Echo Request – ICMPv4-In)**	This rule controls whether your server will respond to ping requests (over IPv4). Depending on your version of Windows Server, the rule might be disabled already. If so, you will have to skip ahead to Step 6. There might also be two versions of the rule: one for public networks and one for private networks.
4 On your client workstation, open a command prompt and ping your server	(You can use `ipconfig` at the server to determine its IP address if you don't know it already.) You should be able to ping your server.
5 On the server, double-click **File and Printer Sharing (Echo Request – ICMPv4-In)**	If two rules are listed, choose the Domain, Public rule.
Under Action, select **Block the connections** and click **OK**	This alters the rule to block IPv4 Ping traffic.
6 On your client workstation, attempt to ping your server	This time, the ping should fail.
7 To fully block ping requests (and some associated attacks), what else would you need to do?	
8 Close Server Manager	

Port security

Explanation

Stopping services is one way to close a port. The port might actually remain open and available on the system, but nothing will use it for inbound or outbound communications. However, such a configuration would not prevent a rogue application, such as a virus, from communicating over that port.

Let's say your corporate policy prohibits users from running a Web server on their workstations. You could use group policy objects or other tools to remove known Web servers, such as Internet Information Services or Apache. But what if the user's computer were infected with a virus that installed its own Web server? The virus would likely escape the notice of your software deployment tools.

By blocking ports at the firewall instead, you effectively stop all communications from known and unknown applications. For the scenario described here, you would use a GPO or provisioning tool to push a firewall configuration out to every desktop. In many cases, you could also establish port blocking at the network firewall to simply prevent communications beyond your LAN.

Do it!

C-2: Blocking ports with a firewall

Here's how	Here's why
1 On your client computer, open the Control Panel	You will block a port on your client workstation.
Click **System and Security**	
Click **Windows Firewall**	
In the left pane, click **Advanced Settings**	To open Windows Firewall with Advanced Security.
2 In the left pane, select **Inbound Rules**	
In the Actions pane, click **New Rule...**	The Actions pane is the rightmost pane.
3 Select **Port** and click **Next**	We'll block a port, rather than a program.
4 Confirm that TCP is selected; then, in the "Specific local ports" box, enter **80, 443**	To block the two common HTTP (Web) ports.
Click **Next**	
5 Select **Block the connection** and click **Next**	
6 Observe the profile options and click **Next**	You could limit this rule to certain conditions, such as when the computer is connected to only a public network.
7 In the name box, enter **WWW ports**	
Click **Finish**	To save and enable your rule.
8 Observe the list of rules	Your custom rule is shown first, with a circle-slash "no" symbol indicating that you're blocking ports.
9 How would you conveniently set this sort of rule on multiple computers?	
10 Close all open windows	

VLAN security

Explanation

Traffic on one VLAN is supposed to be unavailable to nodes on other VLANs. *VLAN hopping* is an attack in which packets that start on one VLAN end up on another VLAN. VLAN hopping attacks can be carried out in various ways, including by switch spoofing and double encapsulation.

In *switch spoofing*, an attacker uses special software to configure his computer to mimic a switch. Switches are meant to be able to "see" packets on all VLANs so that they can direct traffic to appropriate destinations. In this case, the attacker could inspect traffic across all VLANs at will.

Double encapsulation is another VLAN hopping technique. VLANs based on 802.1Q are defined by ID tags inserted into fields within the TCP packet. Each VLAN you define is assigned a unique ID. Furthermore, there is a default, or native, VLAN defined by the switches you use. An attacker uses special software to double-tag packets so that they carry two VLAN IDs. The first tag is the native VLAN ID; the second tag is the ID of the VLAN the attacker wants to reach. Native VLAN IDs are not supposed to be used and are stripped off by switches. So when the packets arrive at the first switch in line, the switch dutifully strips off the outer, native VLAN ID and then sends the packets onward toward their destination. At this point, they are tagged with the target VLAN's ID and thus pass through the remaining switches to reach the destination.

Switch flooding is another means of attack, though not generally a successful one. An attacker sends a flood of multicast packets (such as broadcast packets) to a switch in an attempt to overflow buffers, corrupt memory, or cause similar failures. The hope is that the switch will default open, sending subsequent packets to all VLANs rather than segregating data. Switches generally withstand such attacks, but software bugs could make this attack possible.

Network monitoring software, such as Wireshark, typically includes the ability to view traffic across VLANs. Such access is enabled by putting the network adapter into promiscuous mode, in which it reads all packets on the network, rather than just those destined for the local computer. Such software would give an attacker information about the VLANs in use and thereby enable subsequent real attacks via one of the other techniques listed here.

Countermeasures

Network monitoring and anti-malware software are two ways to stop switch spoofing attacks. Intrusion detection systems (IDSs) can also detect packets crossing VLANs and raise warnings.

Some vendors claim that their proprietary networking protocols are immune to double-encapsulation attacks. Adopting standards-based technologies generally rewards you with costs savings and vendor flexibility. If security is your utmost concern, however, you might consider implementing proprietary systems, such as Cisco's ILS, instead of 802.1Q for your VLAN.

You can configure many switches to automatically drop double-encapsulated packets. There's no legitimate purpose for such packets. If this setting is available in your switch, you should enable it.

Keep switch management software and firmware up-to-date. Bugs that might enable switch flooding attacks would likely be quickly identified and fixed. Choosing products from established and reputable vendors is another way to survive such attacks.

Do it!

C-3: Considering VLAN security

Questions and answers

1 List the types of VLAN attacks.

2 In your opinion, which is the most serious or likely threat?

3 Summarize the basic VLAN security principles you should implement.

Secure router configuration

Explanation

Secure router configuration is a broad topic that covers everything from setting strong passwords on management accounts and patching the router OS to configuring routing rules to stop ongoing network attacks. In this section, we'll examine some ways to handle network attacks.

In general, you should attempt to detect and block traffic as close to the source as possible. This generally means that you should detect and block traffic on the router that connects your LAN to the Internet. But in a large internal network, it could also mean detecting and blocking traffic at the LAN on which a flood of traffic is originating. The principle is to stop unwanted traffic as early as you can, before it impairs performance and communications on your network.

Basic configuration principles

Microsoft published an article describing six router configuration principles that should stop most denial-of-service attacks. These six principles are as follows:

1   Block inbound traffic in which the source address matches that of your internal network.

2   Block outbound traffic in which the source address isn't from your internal network. (Someone, or someone's infected computer, is spoofing addresses, and such traffic shouldn't be sent out to the Internet for others to deal with.)

3   Block inbound and outbound traffic with private IP addresses or Windows automatic private IP addresses for either the source or destination address.

4   Block all source-routed packets. Source routing is not used on the Internet and probably indicates some sort of attack.

5   Block all broadcast packets, including directed broadcasts.

6   Block all packet fragments unless you're using IPSec, which legitimately uses packet fragments during the authentication sequence.

Real-Time Black Hole (RTBH) filtering

When an attack is detected, such as a DoS (denial-of-service) attack, you can route packets to a null, or non-existent, network. Routing packets to a null port is called *Real-Time Black Hole (RTBH) filtering*. Make sure that such a rule doesn't propagate to other routers, though, or you could have trouble disabling the rule quickly after the attack stops.

RTBH filtering can be implemented in a source-based or destination-based method. In a source-based method, you send all packets with a specific sender's address to the digital trashcan. You would do this if many hosts were being attacked from a single address or a small number of attacking addresses.

In destination-based filtering, all traffic being directed to a specific host is sent to the black hole. You would use this sort of filtering if many distributed hosts were attempting to attack a single host or a small number of target hosts.

Do it!

C-4: Considering router security

Questions and answers

1 Which of the six principles published by Microsoft are, in your opinion, the most important to implement?

2 Which is more likely to be effective: source-based or destination-based RTBH filtering?

Topic D: Virtualization and cloud computing

This topic covers the following CompTIA Security+ objectives for exam SY0-301.

#	Objective
1.3	**Distinguish and differentiate network design elements and compounds**
	• Virtualization
	• Cloud computing
	– Platform as a Service
	– Software as a Service
	– Infrastructure as a Service
2.1	**Explain risk-related concepts**
	• Risks associated with cloud computing and virtualization
4.2	**Carry out appropriate procedures to establish host security**
	• Virtualization
4.3	**Explain the importance of data security**
	• Cloud computing

Virtual computers

Explanation

Virtualization is a technology through which one or more simulated computers run within a physical computer. The physical computer is called the *host*. The simulated computers are typically called *virtual machines* (VMs), though other terms are sometimes used.

Virtualization offers a range of benefits and is a suitable solution largely because many user and system functions typically consume far less than the full power of a modern computer. For example, if a user's activities on her PC use just 30% of the computer's capabilities, 70% is being wasted. Through virtualization, potentially three VMs could be run on a single system at this level of utilization, giving similar performance levels.

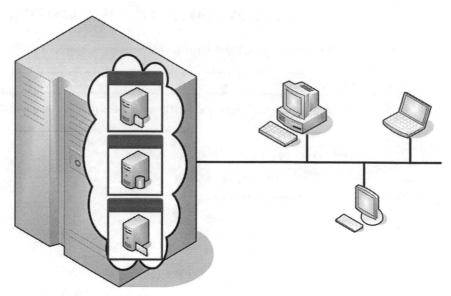

Exhibit 9-8: Multiple VMs on a single physical host

Virtualization is generally offered in three levels:

- Virtual applications
- Virtual desktops
- Virtual servers

Virtual applications

Organizations must often purchase one copy of an application for every employee. Typically, however, only a small percentage of employees use the application regularly, and even fewer use it simultaneously.

With virtual applications, users share a pool of software licenses. Typically, the users connect to a central host that is operating various VMs configured to run the application. Because the company purchases only enough licenses to service average demand (or maybe peak demand), rather than one license per employee, the company saves money.

Beyond cost savings, virtual applications provide centralized control over applications. Software managers control which applications employees can use. Managers can even configure computer security to deny employees the permissions to install local copies of software. Because virtual applications are loaded from a locked "image," users cannot make changes or apply updates, and viruses cannot infect the executables.

Finally, in most cases, virtual applications can be configured to limit where users can save and print their data. For example, the software manager can force users to save files on a shared network volume and prohibit the saving of files on local drives, including removable drives like USB drives. This setup prevents users from secretly removing data from the premises.

XenApp (formerly known as Presentation Server) from Citrix Systems, Inc., is an example of a virtual application product.

Virtual desktops

Virtual desktops go beyond virtual applications to provide multiple applications, a logon environment, and local user preferences. Essentially, a virtual desktop is a virtualized PC running within a VM on a host computer. Users connect to their own virtual desktops by using a "thin" terminal or specialized Windows software.

The virtual desktop environment can be configured and treated just like a real Windows computer. It exists solely within software. Many virtual desktop systems enable users to log on from anywhere on the network. Some systems even permit managers to move virtual desktops dynamically between physical host computers to balance loads and recover from failed hosts.

As with virtual applications, virtual desktops provide additional security by giving IT managers greater control over user environments. Managers can configure save and print locations, determine which settings can be changed by the users, and so forth.

Examples of virtual desktop technologies include XenDesktop from Citrix Systems, Inc., and VMWare Virtual Desktop Infrastructure from VMWare, Inc.

Virtual servers

Virtual servers extend virtualization to the data center. Instead of virtualizing end-user systems, you virtualize servers. For example, you can run multiple print servers as virtual machines in a single host.

The primary benefits of virtual servers include better utilization of computer hardware, simplified provisioning (setting up new servers), and simplified backup and disaster recovery. Typically, virtual servers would store their data on a central storage device, such as a SAN (storage area network) or disk array.

A typical host would be a rack-mounted "blade" computer without optical drives. Additionally, hosts could be configured with no local disk storage, instead using the services of a networked storage device. Eliminating drives removes options for hackers and thieves to boot to alternate operating systems or steal your storage media.

If your organization uses VLANs, each virtual server could be logically located within the network segments serving individual departments. Yet the host would be in the central computer room and not out "on the floor." This system reduces opportunities for theft and hacking.

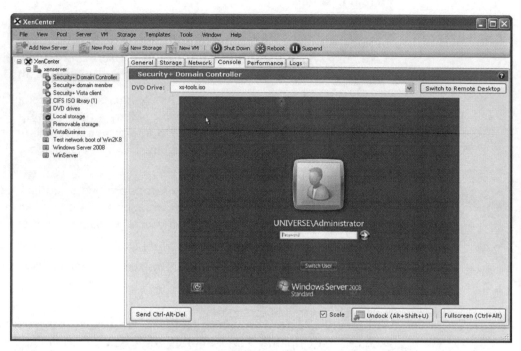

Exhibit 9-9: The Citrix XenCenter management application, showing the console of a virtual Windows Server 2008 domain controller

Examples of virtual server technologies include Hyper-V Server from Microsoft Corp., XenServer from Citrix Systems, Inc., and VMWare Server from VMWare, Inc.

Security concerns with virtualization

While virtualization offers efficiencies and some opportunities for improved security, it also comes with risks that you must manage. A few of the risk areas you'll want to consider are:

- Compliance with corporate security standards
- Rogue VMs
- Orphaned VMs
- Compliance with other standards

Compliance with corporate security standards

Virtual computers are not immune to malware. Even more insidious is the growing crop of virtual-aware malware. Such threats "know" when they're being run within a VM. They might stay dormant to avoid detection, under the assumption that you're testing an application to see if it's a Trojan horse before you install it on a non-virtualized system. As unlikely as it sounds, there are also means by which malware can escape the virtualization system to infect the physical host.

Virtual machines must therefore be hardened to meet your corporate security standards, just as physical computers are. Using anti-malware software within VMs is recommended. Stopping unnecessary services, configuring the host-based firewall, and all the other hardening recommendations apply to virtual systems.

Rogue VMs

Some virtualization systems can be installed within an existing operating system without requiring extensive operating system permissions. This capability enables users to create their own virtual machines.

Users might install such rogue VMs in order to camouflage their use of prohibited or untested applications. It's also likely that rogue VMs won't be hardened and secured to the same level as the systems your IT staff deploys.

Rogue VMs will likely be missed by security or legal audits. It's possible that important data they contain won't be backed up properly. If an employee sets up a rogue VM and then leaves the company, you might not be able to access the data and applications contained within it.

Orphaned VMs

Related to rogue VMs is the problem of the deadwood that accumulates over time. For example, you might set up a VM to test a new service, and then forget to decommission it later. Even if they are initially properly hardened, forgotten VMs will fall behind on updates and patches, becoming a prime target for attack.

Compliance with other standards

Just because a system is virtual, it doesn't mean that you're relieved of legal or contractual obligations. If you'd be required to separate customer data on physical servers, you should do so on virtual servers. Separating customer data into two VMs running on the same physical host might not meet these requirements.

The Payment Card Industry Data Security Standard (PCI DSS) and the Health Insurance Portability and Accountability Act (HIPAA) apply to VMs as well as to physical hosts.

Do it!

D-1: Exploring the benefits and risks of virtualization

Questions and answers

1 How can simulating multiple computers on a single physical computer provide better utilization of hardware?

2 Describe the ways in which virtualization can enhance security.

3 Many of the security benefits associated with virtualization can be accomplished with standard Windows and network security. Speculate on the real reason that organizations are increasingly using virtualization technologies.

4 Speculate on the ways you can manage and account for the risks associated with virtualization.

Cloud computing

Explanation   Cloud computing is a model for providing or purchasing computing services. In broad terms, cloud computing is a service (that you purchase or set up on your own) by which you can dynamically expand or contract computation or storage capabilities on an as-needed basis.

According to the U.S. National Institute of Standards and Technology (NIST), cloud computing is defined this way:

> "Cloud computing is a model for enabling convenient, on-demand network access to a shared pool of configurable computing resources (e.g., networks, servers, storage, applications, and services) that can be rapidly provisioned and released with minimal management effort or service provider interaction."

Key features of cloud computing include:

- Dynamic, or elastic, provisioning (addition or removal of resources), which can give the illusion of infinite supply
- Cost benefits, namely a low entry price and accounting differences. Because cloud computing is typically implemented as an outsourced service, it shifts IT expenditures from a capital expense to an operational expense.
- A standardized API (application programming interface) for using or developing applications that run "within the cloud."
- Simplified installation and maintenance because you don't have to install applications on users' computers. End-user cloud-based applications are typically accessed via a Web browser.
- Multi-tenancy, meaning that your data and the computing resources you consume are intermingled with others' resources in the provider's pool of resources.
- Improved reliability and redundancy because of the device independence and elastic provisioning.

Cloud deployment models

Cloud computing can be deployed following a public, private, or mixed model.

- A *public cloud* is one operated by a third-party service, such as Rackspace or Amazon.
- A *private cloud* is one that you set up on your own to enable private, and probably more secure, cloud computing services. The OpenStack project (www.openstack.org) is the key example of a technology you could use to implement your own cloud computing infrastructure.
- A *mixed cloud* exhibits characteristics of both public and private clouds. Google's "Gov Cloud" is an example. This cloud can be used by government branches within the U.S., but it is not available to consumers or businesses.

Cloud computing categories

Cloud computing can be categorized according to the services provided or purchased. The following are popular labels assigned to cloud computing services:

- **Software as a Service (SaaS)** — Cloud applications enable you or a service provider to make applications available over the Internet. This capability eliminates the need to install software on user computers, and it can be helpful for mobile or transient workforces. Perhaps the most well-known SaaS example is the Google Apps suite of office applications. Other notable SaaS examples are the Zoho suite of applications and Microsoft's Office Web Apps.

- **Platform as a Service (PaaS)** — A platform cloud enables you to rent a fully configured system that is set up for a specific purpose. An example is Rackspace's CloudSites offering, in which you rent a virtual Web server and associated systems (such as a database or e-mail server). Amazon's Relational Database Service (RDS) enables you to rent fully configured MySQL database servers, with Oracle services announced for availability in mid-2011.

- **Infrastructure as a Service (IaaS)** — Rather than purchasing equipment and running your own data center, you rent those resources as an outsourced service. In an IaaS arrangement, you are typically billed based on the resources you consume, much like a utility company bills you for the amount of electricity you use. Examples of IaaS include Rackspace's CloudServers offering, in which you rent a virtual server running an operating system of your choice. You then install the applications you need onto that virtual server. Other examples include Amazon's Elastic Compute Cloud (EC2) service and Amazon's Simple Storage Service (S3).

Security concerns with cloud computing

The obvious and largest security concern with cloud computing is that your data and computing resources might reside outside your corporate network, in the hands of others. Such an arrangement means that you must trust your provider and have the tools available to manage security options and audit your provider's compliance.

You need to carefully evaluate services and systems to make sure that your data is kept private from other customers that your provider might serve. Your provider should explain the methods they use to implement physical and user security in their data center so that you can be assured that a rogue administrator won't compromise your security.

You'll also want to investigate the backup and redundancy features provided. You want to be sure that your data is protected from loss and that information can be recovered if systems fail. Looking further out, you should investigate the provider's business continuity plans to account for both technological and operational failings.

Your business might need to comply with legal or industry regulations. For example, e-commerce websites must comply with the Payment Card Industry Data Security Standard (PCI DSS). Systems that collect or store medical information must comply with the Health Insurance Portability and Accountability Act (HIPAA). You must make sure that your cloud service supplier provides the features you need to maintain compliance with such standards.

Finally, you probably have intellectual-property agreements in place with suppliers, employees, or customers. You must make sure that existing agreements don't preclude the use of a cloud service. You also need to evaluate cloud service offerings to make sure that using a cloud computing model won't interfere with your contractual agreements to respect property ownership. A legal review of contracts and service offerings is recommended.

Do it!

D-2:   Exploring the benefits and risks of cloud computing

Questions and answers

1 Name at least three benefits of implementing a cloud computing architecture.

2 Which of the cloud computing categories—SaaS, PaaS, or IaaS—would you likely implement first?

3 Would your company be more likely to purchase cloud services or to implement a private cloud?

4 Which of the security risks is the biggest concern to your company?

Unit summary: Network security

Topic A In this topic, you learned about **networking devices**, including switches, routers, firewalls, and proxy servers. You learned how NAT and PAT devices translate between internal and external addresses to enhance security. You also examined the **vulnerabilities** in these devices, chiefly those vulnerabilities presented by built-in management accounts, firmware, and operating software.

Topic B In this topic, you learned that **firewalls** and **proxy servers** are critical devices for implementing network security. You examined **intranets**, **perimeter networks** (also called demilitarized zones or **DMZs**), and **extranets**, along with various network topology options for adding network security.

Topic C In this topic, you learned why following standard, tested network **administration principles** can improve the security of your network. You examine rules-based firewall configuration, port security, VLAN security, and secure router configuration.

Topic D In this topic, you learned that **virtualization** is a technology through which one or more simulated computers run within a physical computer. You learned that virtualization **saves money** through better hardware utilization and **improves security** through improved data storage management, more flexible network topology options, and better control over user environments. You also examined **cloud computing**, which is a model for enabling convenient, on-demand network access to a shared pool of configurable computing resources,

Review questions

1 True or false? A VPN relies on dedicated communication lines between clients and servers.

2 Define NAT.

3 True or false? A VPN and a VLAN are essentially identical security solutions.

4 Why might you filter outgoing traffic between your DMZ and the Internet?

5 Define "bastion host."

6 The three main zones into which you can divide a network are the _____, _____, and _____.

7 Name at least two actions you should take to limit the risk of attacks on your network devices (switches, routers, and so forth).

8 You're configuring your network switch to improve its security. You have changed the default password for the unit's Web interface. What else should you configure to be sure that all management interfaces have been locked down?

9 Most rules-based firewalls are configured to _____ by default so that you don't have to configure every conceivable rule to establish a basic level of security.

10 Is the following a description of a Network-layer firewall or an Application-layer firewall? You've implemented a network-connected device that examines packet data to detect and prevent SQL injection attacks.

11 True or false? Blocking ports prevents unwanted communications more effectively than does uninstalling applications.

12 Which of the following are ways that an attacker might attempt a VLAN hopping attack? [Choose all that apply.]

A Double-encapsulation

B Switch spoofing

C 802.1Q tag stripping

D Switch flooding

13 The technique of routing packets to a null port is often called _____ _____ _____ _____ _____.

14 How does server virtualization add security to your network?

15 What are the three types of virtualization?

16 Which of the following is an example of the Software as a Service category of cloud computing?

   A Your provider offers fully configured virtual systems set up for a specific purpose.

   B Your provider offers Internet-based applications for your mobile workforce.

   C Your provider rents virtual servers running an operating system of your choice.

   D Your provider installs a virtualization server in your data center to host applications and data for your user base.

17 What is elastic provisioning?

18 True or false? With a cloud solution, your provider is responsible for compliance with such regulations as the Payment Card Industry Data Security Standard (PCI DSS) and the Health Insurance Portability and Accountability Act (HIPAA).

Independent practice activity

This unit does not have an independent practice activity.

Unit 10

Wireless security

Unit time: 180 minutes

Complete this unit, and you'll know how to:

A Configure your wireless router to address common wireless networking vulnerabilities.

B Configure your cell phone and other mobile devices to address common vulnerabilities.

Topic A: Wireless network security

This topic covers the following CompTIA Security+ objectives for exam SY0-301.

#	Objective
1.2	**Apply and implement secure network administration principles** • 802.1X
1.6	**Implement wireless networks in a secure manner** • WPA • MAC filter • WPA2 • SSID broadcast • WEP • TKIP • EAP • CCMP • PEAP • Antenna placement • LEAP • Power level controls
3.4	**Analyze and differentiate among types of wireless attacks** • Rogue access points • War chalking • Interference • IV attack • Evil twin • Packet sniffing • War driving
3.6	**Analyze and differentiate among types of mitigation and deterrent techniques** • Port security – MAC limiting and filtering – 802.1X

Wireless networking standards

Explanation

Wireless networking provides a means to connect network nodes without installing network cabling. While many technologies exist for wireless networking, those in the 802.11 family of standards are the most widely implemented and least expensive.

The 802.11 standard

The IEEE 802.11 standard specifies a wireless computer networking technology that operates in the 2.4–2.5GHz radio frequency (RF) band. The IEEE 802.11 standards are defined at the Data Link layer of the Open Systems Interconnection (OSI) model.

The current and future 802.11 standards are described in the following table.

Standard	Description
802.11a	Ratified in 1999, 802.11a uses Orthogonal Frequency Division Multiplexing (OFDM) signaling to transmit data. OFDM offers significant performance benefits compared with the more traditional spread-spectrum systems. OFDM is a modulation technique for transmitting large amounts of digital data over radio waves. Capacity per channel is 54 Mbps with real throughput at about 31 Mbps. It operates at a frequency of 5 GHz, which supports eight overlapping channels.
802.11b	Ratified in 1999, 802.11b is one of the most commonly used 802.1x technologies. Uses Direct Sequence Spread Spectrum (DSSS). Capacity per channel is 11 Mbps with real throughput at about 6 Mbps. It operates at a frequency of 2.4 GHz, which supports three non-overlapping channels.
802.11d	Ratified in 2001, 802.11d aims to produce versions of 802.11b that are compatible with other frequencies so it can be used in countries where the 2.4 GHz band isn't available.
802.11e	802.11e adds Quality of Service (QoS) capabilities to 802.11 networks. It uses a Time Division Multiple Access (TDMA) data signaling scheme and adds extra error correction.
802.11g	Ratified in 2003, 802.11g is a combination of 802.11a and 802.11b. It can use either Direct Sequence Spread Spectrum (DSSS) or Orthogonal Frequency Division Multiplexing (OFDM) to transmit data. Capacity per channel is 54 Mbps with real throughput at about 12 Mbps. It operates at a frequency of 2.4 GHz and is a popular 802.11 technology.
802.11h	Ratified in 2003, 802.11h attempts to improve on 802.11a by adding better control over radio channel selection and transmission power.
802.11i	Ratified in 2004, 802.11i deals with security and is based on the Advanced Encryption Standard (AES). The 802.11i standard has a feature called Robust Security Network (RSN), which defines two security methodologies. The first is for legacy-based hardware using RC4, and the second one is for new hardware based on AES.
802.11j	Ratified in 2004, 802.11j allows 802.11a and HiperLAN2 networks to coexist on the same airwaves. The 802.11j standard changed the 5GHz signaling capabilities to support Japanese regulatory requirements.
802.11n	802.11n is a 100+ Mbps standard. Many access points are available that are compatible with 802.11n and 802.11a and b.

WiMAX (IEEE 802.16 Air Interface Standard)

WiMAX, which stands for Worldwide Interoperability of Microwave Access, provides wireless DSL and T1-level service. It's an emerging point-to-multipoint broadband wireless access standard that services wide area and metropolitan area networks, allowing wireless users with 802.16e devices to roam between wireless hotspots.

WiMAX operates in the frequency ranges of 10–66 GHz for licensed communications, and 2–11 GHz for unlicensed communications, providing a bandwidth in excess of 70 Mbps, which is shared among the network's users. It has a theoretical maximum of 31 miles with no obstructions. However, the average range for most WiMAX networks is 4–5 miles, and up to 10 miles in line-of-sight applications. (WiMAX doesn't rely on a line of sight for connection.) As a comparison, WiMAX wireless coverage is measured in square miles, while 802.11x technologies are measured in square yards. WiMAX can be deployed in areas where physical limitations, such as a lack of DSL or T1 cabling, prevent broadband access.

Device compatibility

Although devices that support the 802.11a standard are generally incompatible with those that support 802.11b, some devices are equipped to support either 802.11a or 802.11b. The newest approved standard, 802.11n, allows 802.11b, 802.11g, and 802.11n devices to operate together on the same network. Many modern APs support multiple standards. For example, one AP might offer concurrent support for 802.11a, b, g, and n clients in addition to 100 Mbps wired network clients.

Do it! ## A-1: Comparing wireless network protocols

Questions and answers
1 In wireless communications, what replaces the wire?
2 List the major wireless protocols.
3 Are 802.11b products compatible with 802.11a products?
4 Which wireless standard is currently used in airports and coffee shops?
5 Which 802.11 standard offers the fastest transmission rates?
6 What are some factors you should consider when determining which wireless technology to use?

Wireless LAN connection components

Explanation

To establish a wireless LAN, you need wireless network cards in the computers and a wireless router or wireless access point (WAP) device on the network. (The 802.11 standard defines an *access point* as a device that functions as a transparent bridge between the wireless clients and the wired network.) The router or access point broadcasts radio signals, and the wireless network cards pick up the broadcasts.

Wireless NICs

LAN network adapters of all current types (PCI, PC Card, and USB, shown in Exhibit 10-1) come in wireless versions. Wireless capability is built into most newer laptops as standard equipment and can easily be added to laptops via wireless PC Cards or USB NICs. Desktops can also be easily outfitted with wireless capabilities by adding PCI Cards or USB wireless NICs. If wireless access is available, these cards can communicate with a wireless access point—examples are shown in Exhibit 10-2— allowing you to access the network without using cables. This is especially useful in places like libraries, where wandering around with a laptop while maintaining network access can be very convenient.

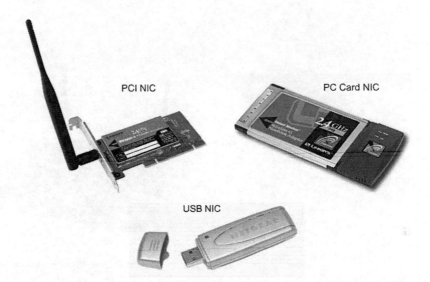

Exhibit 10-1: Wireless NICs

Wireless access points

A wireless access point connects a WLAN to a wired Ethernet network. The access point (AP) contains the following: at least one interface for connecting to the wired network (this interface is typically called the "WAN port"); transmitting equipment for connecting with the wireless clients; and IEEE 802.1D bridging software to act as a bridge between wireless and wired Data Link layers. For home users, this connection is often to a broadband router or transceiver.

Access points often integrate other networking functions. Many APs include Ethernet networking ports for connecting wired devices and thus function as switches. Many APs also include routing capabilities, and such devices most often also include firewall functions. The popular Linksys Wireless-G family of wireless routers is one such example of multifunction APs. Two brands of wireless access points are shown in Exhibit 10-2.

Cisco Aironet Access Point

Linksys Wireless-G 2.4 GHz router/wireless access point

Exhibit 10-2: Wireless access points

Manufacturers of wireless LAN equipment will often promote access ranges of 550 meters. As shown in the following table, as you move farther away from an access point, the data transfer speed drops. Remember that interference from your building's structure and environmental noise can also affect data throughput.

IEEE speed	Data speed	Distance from AP
High	4.3 Mbps	40 to 125 meters
Medium	2.6 Mbps	55 to 200 meters
Standard	1.4 Mbps	90 to 400 meters
Standard low	0.8 Mbps	115 to 550 meters

If the signal from your WAP or wireless router isn't strong enough with the built-in antennas, you can add a more powerful antenna and sometimes add a signal booster.

The WAP or wireless router should be placed in a central location within 60 to 90 meters of the people who'll be using it. As shown in the previous table, the closer the users are to the device, the stronger the signal and the better the network speed.

When determining the number and placement of WAPs, you need to account for obstructions in the floor plan. For example, in a large room with no walls, you could centrally place one WAP to service up to 200 devices.

There are two methods for determining the correct WAP placement: an informal site survey and a formal site survey.

- In an *informal site survey*, you temporarily set up the WAPs at the locations you're considering for permanent placement. Then you use a wireless client to test the signal strength of connections within the range that WAP will service, preferably testing from actual client desk locations. If the connection signals are strong where you need them to be, you go back and permanently mount and install the WAPs. If not, you move the WAPs and retest.

- In a *formal site survey*, you use field-strength measuring equipment. You install a test antenna in each estimated WAP location and then use the field-strength measuring equipment to determine the exact strength of a test signal at various points within the WAP's range. You move the test antenna to obtain the best possible signal for the wireless coverage area. Once you've determined the exact locations for the WAPs, you can permanently mount and install them.

Security threats to wireless networks

Wireless devices present a whole new set of threats that network administrators might be unaware of. The most obvious risks concerning wireless networks are theft and rogue devices. Most cell phones, text pagers, PDAs, and wireless NICs are small enough that they can easily be lost or stolen. Because they are easy to conceal and contain valuable information about a company, they have become favorite targets of intruders. Wireless LANs can be subject to session hijacking and man-in-the-middle attacks. Additional risks remain because anyone can purchase an access point and set it up.

Wireless access points, when set up right out of the box, have no security configured. They broadcast their presence—in essence saying, "Hey, my name is xxx, here I am!" The free availability of 802.11 network audit tools, such as AirSnort and NetStumbler, and even some PDAs, means that breaking into wireless networks configured with weak security is quite easy. These tools can be used to check wireless security by identifying unauthorized clients or access points and verifying encryption usage.

There are other tools, however, in the form of management software. To eliminate 802.11 shortcomings and to help improve the image of wireless technology on the market, the Institute of Electronic and Electric Engineers (IEEE) and the Wi-Fi Alliance proposed standards for significantly improved user authentication and media access control mechanisms.

Additional risks associated with wireless networks include the following:

- The 802.1X transmissions generate detectable radio-frequency traffic in all directions. Persons wanting to intercept the data transmitted over the network might use many solutions to increase the distance over which detection is possible, including the use of metal tubes such as Pringles cans or large tomato-juice cans.

- Without the use of an encryption standard of some type, data is passed in clear text form. Even though technologies such as Wired Equivalent Privacy (WEP) encrypt the data, they still lack good security. A determined listener can easily obtain enough traffic data to calculate the encryption key in use.

- The authentication mechanism is one-way, so it's easy for an intruder to wait until authentication is completed and then generate a signal to the client to trick it into thinking it has been disconnected from the access point. Meanwhile, the intruder, pretending to be the original client, begins to send data traffic to the server.

- The client connection request is a one-way open broadcast. This gives an intruder the opportunity to act as an access point to the client, and act as a client to the real network access point. An intruder can watch all data transactions between the client and access point, and then sniff, read, modify, insert, or delete packets at will.

- Wireless networks are vulnerable to war driving and war chalking (covered later in this topic), which involve using other people's open wireless access points.

WLAN security components

There are four components to security on a wireless network:

- Access control
- Encryption
- Authentication
- Isolation

For each security method you implement on the AP, you must also configure your clients to match.

Access control

You can use various techniques to control which clients can use your AP. The simplest, and least effective, method is to simply turn off SSID (service set identifier) broadcasts. Doing this hides the presence of your AP. You then configure your clients to connect to the appropriate AP by manually entering its SSID. However, the SSID is also included in routine client-to-AP traffic. Thus, it's easy for appropriately configured devices to detect SSIDs that aren't explicitly broadcast.

A stronger method of access control is to enable a MAC filter on your AP. The MAC address is the hardware-level address of a client's network adapter. On most APs, you can enter a list of permitted MACs, or blocked MACs, to limit connections.

As with the SSID, valid MAC addresses are transmitted across the wireless network. Thus, a malicious user could detect a valid MAC address and then configure his computer to impersonate that MAC address and gain access to your AP.

Encryption

You can encrypt communications between your AP and clients. Various techniques exist, with some being more secure than others. To make a connection, clients must use the same encryption scheme and possess the appropriate encryption key. After the connection is made, a static or dynamically changing key provides ongoing encryption.

In theory, encryption blocks unapproved connections to your AP. Additionally, as long as the encryption scheme is sufficiently strong, your data streams are kept private from eavesdroppers. As you will see, however, not all wireless encryption systems are sufficiently robust to actually provide these protections.

Authentication

Through RADIUS (Remote Authentication Dial-In User Service) or other systems, you can enable client authentication over your wireless network. Using a system essentially like the username and password you use when you log on, an AP can authenticate the identity of wireless networking clients.

Authentication provides much stronger access control protection than does SSID hiding or MAC and IP address filtering. You should still use encryption with authentication. Without it, eavesdroppers could access the data that legitimate clients transmit when those clients have connected to the AP. Authentication typically requires the use of additional software or hardware devices, such as a RADIUS server.

Isolation

Isolation is a means of segregating network traffic. There are two types: wireless client isolation and network isolation.

With *wireless client isolation*, also called *AP isolation*, wireless clients are put onto individual VLANs (virtual LANs) so that they cannot access each other. This method is commonly used in public wireless networks to prevent one user from accessing another user's computer. Imagine the risk you face in a library or coffee shop, where another user might attempt to access your shared folders or even mount brute-force attacks on your PC over the Wi-Fi (802.11 wireless) hotspot network.

You might also want to provide *network isolation*. For example, you might want to permit wireless clients to access the Internet and your corporate mail server, which is on your wired network. However, you might also want to prevent wireless clients from accessing other wired nodes, such as your file servers. Some APs offer network isolation through custom routing configurations. You can also enable such isolation through your general network design and firewall configuration.

Transmission encryption

You should enable transmission encryption on your wireless routers unless you have a very good reason not to. Transmission encryption limits the clients that can connect to your AP and protects data from eavesdropping during transmission.

Products certified as Wi-Fi compatible by the Wi-Fi Alliance must support at least the WPA Personal level of encryption. As of this writing, products don't have to support the 802.11i standard, but this requirement will soon take effect.

The following table describes transmission encryption methods.

Encryption method	Description
WEP	Wired Equivalent Privacy was built into the 802.11 standards for wireless connectivity that govern how data can be encrypted while in transit on the wireless network.
	WEP uses a 64-bit or 128-bit symmetric encryption cipher. For WEP to work, a key is configured on both the WAP and the client. This key is used to encrypt the data transmitted between the WAP and the client. There are no standards for how the WEP key is to be placed on the clients and the WAP. Most implementations require you to type in the key manually on each client and the WAP.
	Although WEP provides an easy way to prevent casual hackers from viewing the traffic transmitted on your wireless LAN, it is the least secure encryption technique. WEP has known design flaws that make it relatively easy to crack. However, it is the only viable option for 802.11b and other older wireless clients.
WPA Personal and WPA2 Personal	Wi-Fi Protected Access (WPA) was developed to overcome the weaknesses in WEP. It uses the RC4 symmetric cipher with a 128-bit key.
	WPA Personal uses a *pre-shared key* (PSK), which simply means that you must enter the same passphrase on both the AP and the clients. The actual encryption key is built from this passphrase and various other data, such as the sending node's MAC address. With the Temporal Key Integrity Protocol (TKIP) option, the full encryption key changes for each packet.
	WPA authorizes and identifies users based on a secret key that changes automatically at regular intervals. WPA uses TKIP to change the temporal key every 10,000 packets. This ensures much greater security than does the standard WEP.
WPA2	WPA2 builds on WPA by adding more features from the 802.11i standard. Notably, WPA2 uses the Advanced Encryption Standard (AES) cipher for stronger encryption (equivalent to IEEE 802.11i).
	WPA2 uses the version of AES called AES-Counter Mode with Cipher Block Chaining Message Authentication Protocol, or AES-Counter Mode CBC-MAC Protocol, better known CCMP. This protocol uses AES in "counter mode" to provide even stronger security by making it more difficult for potential eavesdroppers to spot data patterns, and the message authentication provides a high level of message integrity.
WPA Enterprise, WPA2 Enterprise	These methods authenticate enterprise wireless clients by using a RADIUS or TACACS server and the user's username and password or digital certificate, rather than using a pre-shared key.
	WPA- and WPA2 Enterprise work in conjunction with an 802.1X authentication server (RADIUS or TACACS). Communications between the client and AP are encrypted using the individual's key.
RADIUS	Remote Access Dial-in User Service (RADIUS) uses a specialized server for authentication and uses WEP for data encryption, as illustrated in Exhibit 10-3. The authentication server can include keys as part of the accept message that's sent back to the WAP. In addition, clients can usually request a key change. This feature ensures that keys are changed regularly to limit the ability of hackers to view information on the wireless network.

Encryption method	Description
802.11i	This standard defines security mechanisms for wireless networks (equivalent to WPA2). CCMP is the preferred encryption protocol.
EAP, LEAP, and PEAP	EAP (Extensible Authentication Protocol) provides an authentication framework for a wireless client and a wireless access point and authenticating server, such as a RADIUS server, to negotiate a connection. The framework defines different ways to authenticate a connection. These ways, called *EAP methods*, include:

- EAP-TLS, which uses TLS as the mechanism by which the client and AP authenticate each other;

- EAP-Tunneled TLS (EAP-TTLS), which uses a secure tunnel to authenticate the client; and

- EAP-Flexible Authentication via Secure Tunneling (EAP-FAST), which uses a TLS tunnel to exchange user credentials.

LEAP (Lightweight EAP) is Cisco's proprietary version of EAP, which is not natively supported in Windows. Its major flaw is the lack of strong protection for user credentials. Cisco now recommends the use of EAP-FAST, PEAP, or EAP-TLS.

PEAP (Protected EAP) was developed jointly by Cisco, Microsoft, and RSA Security. It encapsulates EAP in a TLS tunnel for stronger protection.

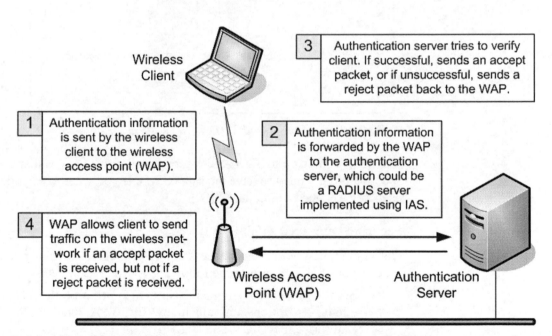

Exhibit 10-3: The 802.1X standard protocol authentication process

Configuring a wireless access point

After you've connected your wireless access point to your wired network, you need to configure it and your clients. When setting up your AP, you assign a *service set identifier* (SSID), which is essentially a name for your wireless network. The default name is usually the name of the router or WAP manufacturer. You should change this name as part of the device configuration to make your WLAN more secure. Changing the name isn't really a method of securing the network, however, because the SSID is sent in plain text over the network and can be found by anyone with the ability to read network packets. It's possible, and sometimes likely, that multiple wireless networks will be accessible from a given location. In such cases, clients use the SSID to distinguish between WLANs and connect to a particular network.

An access point typically broadcasts the SSID. In this way, clients can discover the presence of a nearby access point. Such broadcasts identify the security mechanisms in place to enable clients to auto-configure their connections. Exhibit 10-4 shows an example of the wireless channel and SSID for a wireless router.

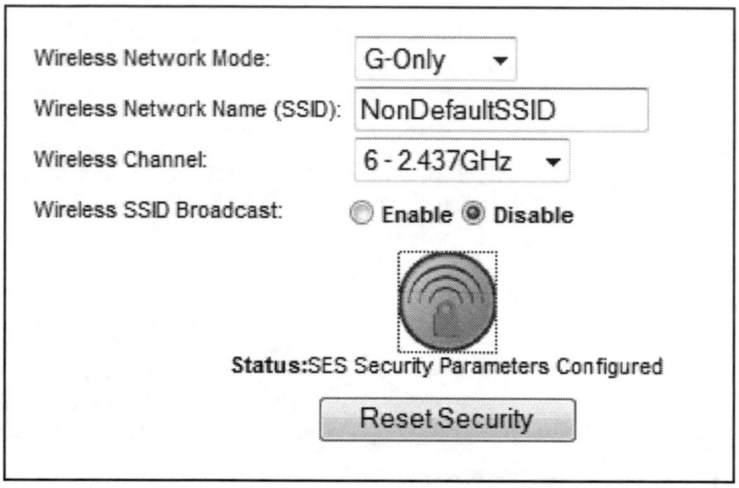

Exhibit 10-4: Channel and SSID settings for a wireless router

The SSID can be up to 32 characters long. All of the devices that need to connect to a specific WLAN need to have the same SSID. If you want to establish separate WLANs, each WLAN needs a unique SSID.

Securing your access point

Out of the box, your wireless access point isn't secure. To make your access point more secure, you should complete the following configuration tasks:

- **Set the most secure transmission encryption method compatible with your clients** — Options might include WEP, WPA Personal, WPA2, WPA Enterprise, RADIUS, and 802.11i.

- **Update the access point's firmware version** — Visit the manufacturer's website and search for firmware updates for your access point. You can also find third-party vendor sites and download open-source replacement firmware. Download both the software and the installation (sometimes referred to as "flash") instructions. Be careful to select the appropriate firmware for your particular AP model. Installing an incorrect firmware version can "brick" your access point, making it nonfunctional. If a problem occurs during installation of the new firmware, it can also brick the access point.

  You can prevent problems by doing the following:

  - Make sure that the power to the access point and to uploading computer remains on during the installation process. Use a universal power supply, if you have one.

  - Upgrade only through a wired connection, not through a wireless one.

  - Manually configure an IP address, instead of using DHCP, on the computer that will upload the firmware update to the access point.

  - Disable any firewall software, such as Windows Firewall.

  - Follow the installation instructions exactly.

- **Change default administrator accounts and passwords for the access point** — Many devices don't have a default password set on the Administrator account. Programs like AirSnort identify the manufacturer based on the MAC address, so if you change only the SSID, an informed hacker can still easily gain access. Also, changing the name of the widely available administrator accounts presents an added barrier to anyone trying to connect to the access point.

- **Change the default SSIDs** — When you change the SSID, don't use anything that reflects your company's main names, divisions, products, or address. Doing so would make your organization an easy target. If an SSID name is enticing enough, it might attract hackers.

- **Disable SSID broadcasts** — SSID broadcasting is enabled by default. When you disable this feature, an SSID must be configured in the client to match the SSID of the access point.

- **Separate the wireless network from the wired network** — Consider using an additional level of authentication, such as RADIUS, before you permit an association with your access points. RADIUS is an authentication, authorization, and accounting protocol for network access. The wireless clients can be separated so the connections not only use RADIUS authentication but are also logged.

- **Put the wireless network in an Internet-access-only zone or a demilitarized zone (DMZ)** — Place your wireless access points in a DMZ, and have your wireless users tunnel into your network through a VPN (virtual private network). Setting up a VLAN for your DMZ requires extra effort on your part, but this solution adds a layer of encryption and authentication that makes your wireless network secure enough for sensitive data.

- **Disable DHCP within the WLAN to keep tighter control over users** — Assign static IP addresses to your wireless clients. Doing this creates more administrative overhead to manage, but makes it harder to access your network.

- **Enable MAC address filtering on access points to limit unauthorized wireless NICs** — Many access points allow you to control access based on the MAC address of the NIC attempting to associate with it. If the MAC address of the wireless client's NIC isn't in the access point's table, access is denied. Although there are ways to spoof a MAC address, doing so takes an additional level of sophistication.

- **Enable 802.1X** — This is the recommended method of authentication and encryption for enhanced security on computers running versions of Windows later than Windows XP. The use of 802.1X offers an effective solution for authenticating and controlling user traffic to a protected network, as well as dynamically varying encryption keys. The 802.1X standard ties EAP to both the wired and wireless LAN media and supports multiple authentication methods, such as token cards, Kerberos, one-time passwords, certificates, and public key authentication. You configure 802.1X encryption from the IEEE 802.1X tab in the policy setting's Properties dialog box.

A network administrator should periodically survey the site, by using a tool such as NetStumbler or AirSnort, to see if any rogue access points are installed on the network. In addition, the administrator can take a notebook equipped with a wireless sniffer and an external antenna outside the office building to see what information inside the building can be accessed by someone parked in the parking lot or across the street.

Do it!

A-2: Configuring a wireless access point (instructor demo)

Here's how	Here's why
1 Open Internet Explorer and enter the IP address of your WAP	You are prompted for administrator credentials on the WAP.
2 Enter the appropriate username and password for your WAP, and click **OK**	
3 Click the **Wireless Settings** tab	
Edit the SSID box to read **123ABC567**	Remember, one of the guidelines for creating a more secure SSID is that it not reflect your company's primary names, divisions, products, or address.
For SSID broadcast, select **Disabled**	
For Security, select **WEP** and record the WEP key	WEP key: _____
Check **Apply**	The device restarts itself.
4 Click the **Tools** tab	
In the New password and Confirm password boxes, enter **!pass4321**	
Check **Apply**	
5 Click the **Advanced** tab	
Select **MAC filters**	
Choose **Only allow computers with MAC address listed below to access the network**	
In the Name box, enter your computer's name	
In the MAC address box, enter your computer's MAC address	
Check **Apply**	
6 Close Internet Explorer	

Configuring wireless clients

Explanation

The operating system that a client is running determines how you configure its connection to a wireless network. Windows 7, Windows Vista, and Windows XP use the Wireless Zero Configuration and Wireless Auto Configuration technologies to make the connection process easier for end-users. You must configure Windows 2000 Professional clients manually.

Windows 7, Windows Vista, and Windows XP wireless clients

Wireless Auto Configuration dynamically selects the wireless network to which a connection attempt is made, based on configured preferences or default settings. Computers running Windows 7, Windows Vista, and Windows XP support *Wireless Zero Configuration*, which enables computers to automatically connect to available wireless networks. By default, Windows 7, Windows Vista, and Windows XP client computers can choose from available wireless networks and connect automatically without user action. Wireless Zero Configuration automatically configures such items as TCP/IP settings and DNS server addresses.

The default settings used by Wireless Zero Configuration include:

- "Infrastructure before ad hoc mode, and computer authentication before user authentication."

  Infrastructure mode uses an access point to connect the wireless network to the wired network. It typically requires authentication in which the computer identifies itself to the authenticating server before the user credentials are sent. *Ad hoc mode* allows all wireless devices within range to discover and communicate with one another without a central access point.

- "WEP authentication attempts to perform an IEEE 802.11 shared key authentication if the network adapter has been preconfigured with a WEP shared key; otherwise, the network adapter reverts to the open system authentication."

Although the IEEE 802.1X security enhancements are available in Windows 7, Windows Vista, and Windows XP, the network adapters and access points must also be compatible with this standard for deployment.

You can change the default settings to allow guest access, which isn't enabled by default. You shouldn't turn on guest access on a laptop using Wireless Zero Configuration. An unauthorized user could establish an *ad hoc* connection to the laptop and gain access to confidential information on it.

RADIUS servers

When you implement an authenticating server, such as RADIUS, the wireless client must submit its credentials to the authenticating server before wireless network access is established. When the client computer is in range of the wireless AP, it tries to connect to the WLAN that is active on the wireless AP.

If the wireless AP is configured to allow only secured or 802.1X-authenticated connections, it issues a challenge to the client. The wireless AP then sets up a restricted channel that allows the client to communicate with only the RADIUS server.

The RADIUS server accepts a connection from only two sources: a trusted wireless AP; or a WAP that has been configured as a RADIUS client on the Microsoft Internet Authentication Service (IAS) server and that provides the shared secret key for that RADIUS client.

The RADIUS server validates the client credentials against the directory. If the client is successfully authenticated, the RADIUS server decides whether to authorize the client to use the WLAN. If the client is granted access, the RADIUS server transmits the client's master key to the wireless AP. The client and the wireless AP now share common key information they can use to encrypt and decrypt the WLAN traffic passing between them. How you configure clients to participate in this process depends on the operating system.

Do it!

A-3: Configuring a wireless client (instructor demo)

Here's how	Here's why
1 If the computer with the wireless NIC is also connected to the network through a wired NIC, unplug the cable from the NIC	
2 On the computer with a wireless NIC, click	You'll configure the client to connect by using the settings on the wireless access point.
Click **Open Network and Sharing Center**	
Under Tasks, click **Manage wireless networks**	
3 Click **Add**	
Click **Manually create a network profile**	Because you disabled the broadcast of the SSID, you must manually configure the connection.
4 In the Network name box, enter **123ABC567**	
In the Security type list, select **WEP**	
5 In the Security Key/Passphrase box, enter the WEP key you recorded in the previous activity	
6 Check **Connect even if the network is not broadcasting**	
Click **Next**	
7 Click **Connect to...**	
Select **123ABC567**	This item must match the SSID of the WAP you want to connect to.
Click **Connect**	
8 In the SSID name box, enter **123ABC567**	If necessary.
9 In the "Security key or passphrase" box, enter the WEP key you recorded in the previous activity	
10 Click **Connect**	

11	Close all open windows	
12	Open the Network and Sharing Center	Under Connections, the new wireless connection is listed, and the connection's signal strength is shown.
13	Close all open windows	
14	Open Internet Explorer and verify that you have Internet connectivity	By default, the WAP is handing out DHCP addresses to its clients, so this wireless connection has valid IP addressing information assigned to it automatically.
15	Close Internet Explorer	
16	Disconnect the wireless connection	In the Network and Sharing Center, next to Signal strength, click Disconnect.

Wireless network vulnerabilities

Through careful technology selection and configuration, you can prevent unwanted access to your access point and block client-to-client access over your wireless network. You should also consider vulnerabilities in your APs. As with other networking devices, access points include these common vulnerabilities:

- Physical access
- Firmware vulnerabilities
- Default administrator accounts

Just as you should prevent physical access to your switches, routers, and servers, you should prevent physical access to your AP. Use lockable enclosures for your APs, or mount them in physically secure locations, such as a locked room. Unlike wired devices, you must take care to consider how these physical safeguards will affect the wireless signal propagation.

You should check often for firmware upgrades. After careful testing, implement upgrades as they become available. You might also consider third-party router firmware, such as the open-source DD-WRT firmware.

As with wired devices, make sure you change the passwords on all administration interfaces on your APs. Typically, APs provide Web-based administration interfaces. Make sure you change the password on such interfaces because the default passwords for most APs are widely published on the Internet.

Additionally, make sure you change the passwords for Telnet, SSH (secure shell), and SNMP interfaces. APs often support such interfaces, but their documentation and built-in administration tools provide little information on their availability. Third-party AP firmware typically offers easier access for managing these interfaces.

Additional risks associated with wireless networks include the following:

- The authentication mechanism is one-way, so it is easy for an intruder to wait until authentication is completed and then generate a signal to the client that tricks the client into thinking it has been disconnected from the access point. Meanwhile, the intruder begins to send data traffic to the server, while pretending to be the original client.
- The client connection request is a one-way open broadcast. This gives an intruder the opportunity to act as an access point to the client, and act as a client to the real network access point. This allows an intruder to watch all data transactions between the client and access point, then modify, insert, or delete packets at will.

Data emanation

Nearly all computing devices emit electromagnetic radiation. Processors and chips, as well as electronic signals flowing through wires, create electronic signals. Unintentionally, such emanations can transmit data. With the right equipment, someone could capture and decode these emanations and reconstruct the data they represent.

Decoding data emanations is not likely. The signals are weak and don't travel far, requiring the eavesdropper to be very close to the "leaky" equipment. Additionally, it is computationally difficult to reconstruct data from the electromagnetic noise. Eavesdropping in this way is perhaps the stuff of spy movies rather than a real-world security concern. However, if you must run an extremely secure network, you should consider the risks associated with data emanation.

Do it!   **A-4:   Identifying wireless networking vulnerabilities**

Questions and answers

1 Why should you enable encryption on your wireless network?

2 Why might you *not* want to use AP isolation?

3 Speculate on the equipment that would be needed to eavesdrop on network communications via data emanation.

Wi-Fi scanners

Explanation

As was mentioned earlier, wireless access points have no security configured when set up right out of the box, so by default, they broadcast their presence. Unsecured access points in an otherwise secure network are sometimes called "rogue access points" and represent a large vulnerability.

You can purchase Wi-Fi scanners, which detect the presence of wireless signals within range. These devices often provide lights or other indicators that describe what security is in place on the network. You can also use software such as Airsnort or NetStumbler on a laptop to scan for WLANs.

The stated purpose of such tools is to help "road warriors" find wireless networks for legitimate networking purposes. In many cities, free wireless networks are available for public use. However, these tools are often used by people looking to use wireless networks without permission.

War driving is the practice of scanning for open wireless access points in a region. (War driving often involves driving around with a laptop system configured to listen for open wireless access points.) Several websites provide detailed information about unsecured networks. These sites provide locations, sometimes on city maps, for the convenience of others looking for open access links to the Internet. War driving is an attractive method not only to capture data from networks, but also to connect to someone else's network, use that person's bandwidth, and pay nothing for it.

War chalking is the process of marking buildings, curbs, and other landmarks to indicate the presence of an available access point and its connection details by utilizing a set of symbols and shorthand. Some common war-chalking symbols are shown in Exhibit 10-5.

After discovering a wireless network, attackers can launch an *interference attack*, which steals bandwidth and can result in a denial-of-service (DoS) attack by limiting the bandwidth available on your wireless network. Anyone with a network scanner, or even a laptop or mobile device, can access your network and use your bandwidth if the network isn't properly secure. You can prevent an interference attack by securing your APs to prevent unauthorized access.

Another kind of eavesdropping attack is called *IV attack* or *CBC IV attack*. It exploits a feature of TLS 1.0 in which the initialization vector (IV) used for cipher block chaining encryption can be compromised to break the encryption. This vulnerability was removed from TLS 1.1 and later.

Even worse is an *evil-twin attack*, in which an attacker sets up a bogus access point to eavesdrop on wireless communication at a public hotspot or a home or business network. Although the AP uses an SSID that appears legitimate, it is in fact an AP set up by a third party. Users then give away usernames and passwords, thinking they're logging onto a valid AP.

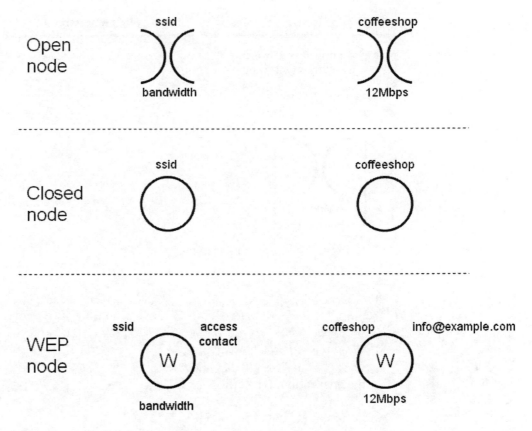

Exhibit 10-5: War-chalking symbols

Do it!

A-5: Scanning for insecure access points

Here's how	Here's why
1 You arrive at work to see the following symbol painted on the sidewalk. What does it mean? 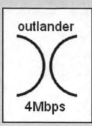	
2 Using a Wi-Fi scanner, scan the area for wireless networks	
3 What security measures are in place?	Depending on the unit you use, you might not be able to tell what type of security is in use.
4 What type of attack involves a weakness in TLS 1.0 that allows the encryption to be broken?	
5 Differentiate between an evil-twin attack and an interference attack.	

Topic B: Mobile device security

This topic covers the following CompTIA Security+ objectives for exam SY0-301.

#	Objective
3.4	**Analyze and differentiate among types of wireless attacks**
	• Bluejacking
	• Bluesnarfing
4.2	**Carry out appropriate procedures to establish host security**
	• Mobile devices
	– Screen lock
	– Strong password
	– Device encryption
	– Remote wipe/sanitation
	– Voice encryption
	– GPS tracking

Mobile security considerations

Explanation

You must consider the security implications of mobile devices, such as phones, handheld computers, PDAs, and even portable music players. The devices themselves are vulnerable to some forms of attacks. If you enable network connectivity for them, then these portable devices provide attackers with another way to compromise your systems.

Device-to-device issues

Device-to-device issues are those in which one mobile device accesses another mobile device. The following table describes some of the more common risks associated with device-to-device communications.

Vulnerability	Description	Security risk
Bluejacking	Users send unsolicited messages over Bluetooth wireless links to other devices. Typically, these messages are harmless advertising, spam-like messages.	Generally, there is no risk beyond user confusion as to why some message appears on his or her phone.
Bluesnarfing	Bluesnarfing is any form of unauthorized access of a device over a Bluetooth connection. In theory, hackers can obtain address books, files, call records, and more over a Bluetooth link. Additionally, hackers could install a virus on an unsuspecting user's device via Bluetooth, perhaps even turning the device into a zombie so that it propagates the virus to other devices.	In general, the risk is low because devices must be paired in order for bluesnarfing to work. Known flaws in the Bluetooth protocol have been patched to prevent unauthorized pairing.
Bluebugging	A hacker takes control of a victim's phone to make calls and perform other functions as if the hacker had physical possession of the device. A hacker can also bluebug to eavesdrop on a call.	The risk is modest in that the hacker could incur usage or other charges without the victim's knowledge or consent. A bluebugging attack has been demonstrated, though software for making such attacks is not widely available.

Most Bluetooth-related attacks can be prevented through prudent device configuration. You should disable Bluetooth on your phone unless you need to connect to Bluetooth devices (such as a hands-free headset). Furthermore, you should disable auto-discovery and auto-pairing unless you need those services.

With auto-discovery enabled, Bluetooth devices can learn of the presence of each other. Devices broadcast their availability. Bluetooth has a range of about 10 meters (approximately 32 feet), though some laptops and PCs can have even further reach. Your phone is vulnerable to bluejacking with auto-discovery enabled, though it is unlikely to be vulnerable to bluesnarfing or bluebugging.

If you have auto-pairing enabled, nearby Bluetooth devices can automatically connect to your phone. Devices must generally be paired to be vulnerable to bluesnarfing or bluebugging. This configuration is not normally required to use a hands-free headset. So unless you absolutely need it, disable auto-pairing.

Infrastructure issues

Infrastructure issues are those caused when a mobile device connects to your network. The following table describes some of the most common vulnerabilities you might face.

Vulnerability	Description	Security risk
Minimal security features supported	Many mobile devices, particularly older models, lack basic security features. For example, those devices that support wireless networking might not support transmission encryption or might support only the older WEP protocol.	To support such devices, you might be forced to provide unsecured access points, which then open up your entire network to attack.
Airsnarfing	A hacker configures his or her computer to masquerade as an access point. Victims connect to the airsnarf AP instead of to a real AP. Typically, the victims are granted network connectivity to complete the illusion that they are connected to a legitimate AP.	When victims connect, their usernames and passwords can be captured. Furthermore, the hacker could access local resources (hard drives, etc.) on a victim's computer. Thus, the potential for damage is high.
Slurping	An attacker uses a removable storage device to steal data. For example, a user connects his USB drive to a PC and downloads sensitive information.	Both the risk and the consequences of slurping can be high. It is relatively easy to configure security permissions that prevent users from connecting USB drives. However, so many users require this functionality that such measures are often not enabled.
Pod slurping	This is slurping using a wireless mobile device, such as an iPod.	The risks are the same same as for slurping.

Protecting against attacks

There are several methods you can use to protect mobile devices.

Method	Description
Screen lock	A screen lock, similar to a password-protected screen saver on a computer, provides one level of security from most casual intruders. A strong password, rather than something easily guessed, can help prevent access to mobile devices from all but sophisticated intruders. Strong passwords include upper- and lowercase characters and symbols and are typically at least 8 characters long.
Device encryption	Encrypted devices make it difficult, if not impossible, to access the data without a password. It's important not only to encrypt the onboard flash memory but also to encrypt any removable memory cards.
Remote wipe; sanitation	The ability to wipe your device's memory if the device is lost or stolen can protect the data from falling into the wrong hands. Not all devices offer this feature, but it can be useful when your device has been stolen.
GPS tracking	Devices' GPS features can be used to locate and retrieve lost devices. Some of the same services that let you track your phone let you wipe its memory remotely, but if you think your device is secure (for example, left at home), you can retrieve the device without having to wipe its memory and lose your data.
Voice encryption	This feature can encrypt voice transmissions to protect them from eavesdropping. Some methods include using AES 128-bit encryption to secure voice transmissions, and using an SD or microSD card to provide the encryption mechanism.

Do it!

B-1: Identifying threats related to cell phones and PDAs

Questions and answers

1 How can you reduce the risk of someone's bluejacking your cell phone?

2 How can you reduce the risks of bluesnarfing and bluebugging attacks?

3 How can you mitigate the risk when you must support older mobile devices that don't support WPA transmission encryption?

Unit summary: Wireless security

Topic A   In this topic, you learned that wireless networks are vulnerable to many forms of attack. You learned that **transmission encryption**, such as WEP, WPA, and WPA2, prevents unauthorized access and eavesdropping. You also learned that you need to secure or disable **default management accounts**, turn off SSID broadcasts, and enable AP isolation to close security holes.

Topic B   In this topic, you learned that **mobile devices** can fall victim to attacks, such as bluejacking, bluesnarfing, and bluebugging. You also learned that mobile devices present an entry point to the rest of your network though their inherent vulnerabilities. You examined ways to secure **Bluetooth**-capable devices and measures you can take to prevent **snarfing** and **slurping** attacks.

Review questions

1 True or false? Bluejacking represents a significant security risk and one that could result in data theft or destruction.

2 According to the 802.11 standard, an access point is _____.

3 What are the four components of wireless security?

4 A typical wireless router offers management interfaces over multiple protocols. Name them.

5 You see the following symbol spray-painted on the sidewalk outside your business. Is it a cause for concern?

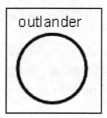

outlander

6 What does enabling AP isolation in your wireless router accomplish?

7 Name the basic configuration changes you should make in your wireless router to enable a base level of security.

8 WPA with AES is equivalent to what type of transmission encryption?

9 How do you log out of the Web-based management interface of most router firmware systems?

10 You have enabled auto-discovery on your phone. What attacks is it susceptible to?

Independent practice activity

In this activity, you will install a wireless router and use a Windows client to connect to it.

1 Obtain a wireless router and its documentation from your instructor (or download the documentation, if necessary). Connect the power supply.

2 Connect to the router, following the manufacturer's instructions. Use the default administrator username and password.

3 Using the documentation as a guide, configure the following settings to secure your router.

- Change the default administrator username and password to **SECADMIN** and **!pass1234**, respectively.
- Disable SSID broadcasts. Change the name of the SSID to **SECSSID##**, where ## is the number of your lab station.
- Configure WPA/TKIP with a pre-shared key. Note the key for future use.
- Disable DHCP.

4 Connect your router to a wired network from which it can obtain IP addressing information, including a default gateway and a DNS server address.

5 On your Windows client, configure an IP address that's on the same subnet as the router. Configure the router's IP address as the default gateway.

6 Open the Network and Sharing Center, and choose to manage wireless networks. Add a new network, and enter the SSID you created earlier. Configure the WPA pre-shared key and TKIP encryption.

7 Connect to the wireless router. Verify that you can access the Internet.

8 Disconnect from the wireless network. Close any open windows.

Unit 11

Remote access security

Unit time: 150 minutes

Complete this unit, and you'll know how to:

A Compare the RADIUS, TACACS+, and 802.1X authentication systems, and implement a RADIUS server.

B Describe VPN technologies and tunneling protocols.

Topic A: Remote access

This topic covers the following CompTIA Security+ objectives for exam SY0-301.

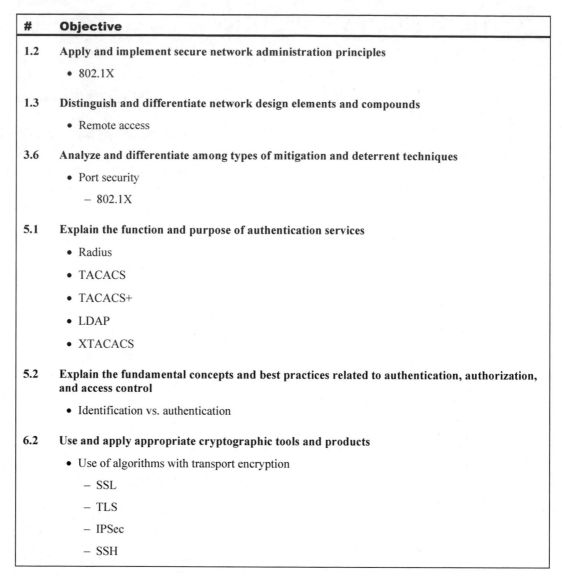

#	Objective
1.2	**Apply and implement secure network administration principles** • 802.1X
1.3	**Distinguish and differentiate network design elements and compounds** • Remote access
3.6	**Analyze and differentiate among types of mitigation and deterrent techniques** • Port security − 802.1X
5.1	**Explain the function and purpose of authentication services** • Radius • TACACS • TACACS+ • LDAP • XTACACS
5.2	**Explain the fundamental concepts and best practices related to authentication, authorization, and access control** • Identification vs. authentication

6.2	**Use and apply appropriate cryptographic tools and products**
	• Use of algorithms with transport encryption
	  − SSL
	  − TLS
	  − IPSec
	  − SSH

Remote network access

Explanation

Telecommuters and traveling employees often need access to your network beyond what a simple Internet connection can provide. For example, these users might need access to internal file storage locations, application servers, or printers. Your security needs might preclude the use of an Internet connection, or perhaps you want to use Active Directory–integrated security, which is not available via the Internet. In these situations, remote access solutions such as RADIUS and TACACS+ might enable you to provide the needed connectivity solutions. In this topic, you will examine these systems, starting with a basic look at the principles of authentication, authorization, and accounting.

AAA

Access security can be thought of as a three-phase process:

1 Authentication
2 Authorization
3 Accounting

Authentication is the stage in which a user's identity is verified. This could be done through a username and password, a smart card, or a fingerprint scan. At the end of this stage, you know that the user is either who he or she claims to be or an imposter.

Assuming that the user has been successfully authenticated, the next stage is *authorization*. In this stage, the user is granted the permissions necessary to use specific network resources.

Finally, *accounting* is the stage that involves tracking the user's actions. This tracking can include determining how long the user is connected, what systems he accesses, how much data she transfers, and so forth. While such information is great if you plan to bill users based on usage, it's also helpful in determining whether you have sufficient bandwidth and optimal connectivity.

The remote access systems described in the upcoming sections typically provide solutions for all three AAA phases. Older systems often provided only authentication and authorization.

RADIUS

Remote Authentication Dial-in User Service (RADIUS) provides centralized AAA remote access services. RADIUS is a client/server system. Although it was originally developed for dial-in user authentication, RADIUS is often applied to wireless and virtual private network connections.

RADIUS clients

The role of the RADIUS client is provided by the *network access server* (NAS), sometimes called the *remote access server* (RAS). It accepts user connections and passes authentication requests to the RADIUS server. After connections are authenticated, the RADIUS client acts as a middleman between the user's system and the RADIUS server for authorization and accounting functions. The RADIUS client can be located on the corporate LAN or at a remote site.

RADIUS servers

The RADIUS server provides all AAA services, but communicates with the RADIUS client rather than directly with the end-user's system. A RADIUS server can authenticate connections against a variety of information stores. These include a flat file, a proprietary RADIUS database, a UNIX password file, a Network Information Service (NIS), or even Active Directory. The RADIUS server is located on the corporate LAN.

The RADIUS authentication process

The authentication process involves actions by the user, the RADIUS client, and the RADIUS server. In general, the process works as follows:

1 The user connects to the NAS (network access server).

2 The RADIUS client (the NAS) requests authentication information via a username and password or a CHAP challenge.

3 The user supplies the logon credentials.

4 The RADIUS client encrypts the password, if necessary, and forwards the credentials to the RADIUS server.

5 The RADIUS server authenticates the user and replies with an Accept, Reject, or Challenge message.

6 The RADIUS client receives the message and acts accordingly:

  • **Accept** — The user's connection is finalized.

  • **Reject** —The user can be re-prompted for credentials, or if the maximum number of requests has been reached, the user can be disconnected.

  • **Challenge** — The user can be prompted for more credentials, which are used to further tailor the connection and the services to which the user has access.

Realms

In RADIUS, a *realm* defines a namespace. It also helps determine which server should be used to authenticate a connection request. Realm names are formatted like Internet domain names, though they have no actual relation to domains. A user's full RADIUS name might be janedoe@outlanderspices.com, where outlanderspices.com is the realm.

RADIUS defines three types of realms, which essentially define three configuration possibilities at your RADIUS client (the NAS):

  • **Named realm** — You configure your client to use a specific RADIUS server for a given named realm. For example, authentications for outlanderspices.com go to RadServerA, while those for megaspices.com go to RadServerB.

  • **Default realm** — You specify the server to be used for authentication for realms not explicitly listed in the client configuration. (In other words, the user logon name contains a realm, but that realm is not listed in your client configuration.)

  • **Empty realm** — You specify a realm to be used when a customer's login attempts don't contain a named realm. This, in effect, defines which server to use for authenticating such requests.

Named realms can be *cascaded*, meaning joined together in a chain. For example, janedoe@outlanderspices.com@megaspices.com describes a cascade. Authentication requests are sent to the servers in order: first to the server configured to authenticate for the outlanderspices.com realm, followed by the server for the megaspices.com realm.

Standards and technical details

RADIUS authentication and authorization functions are described by RFC 2865. The accounting functions are described by RFC 2866. Before those standards were developed, RADIUS authentication and authorization traffic used UDP port 1812, and accounting traffic used port 1813. Some Microsoft products still default to those values. The RFCs defined UDP ports 1645 and 1646 for those traffic streams; those ports are the defaults used by Cisco and Juniper Networks products. Most RADIUS products can use either set of ports.

RADIUS communication security

The RADIUS client and server communicate over a channel that is secured via a shared secret key. That key is never sent over the network. Instead, the installer must configure each system with that key before deployment.

Furthermore, the user station's authentication messages, which are ultimately forwarded to the RADIUS server, are encrypted via the Extensible Authentication Protocol (EAP).

- If you're configuring multiple RADIUS client/server pairs, use a unique secret key for each pair. This practice reduces the opportunity for spoofing-based attacks.

- Use a long secret key; RFC 2865 suggests at least 16 characters. Keys over 22 characters are required to provide sufficient complexity to thwart most dictionary-based attacks.

- The RADIUS server doesn't authenticate messages from the client, so the server is open to IP spoofing–based attacks. To prevent such attacks, configure your systems to use the MD5-hashed Message-Authenticator attribute in all Access-Request messages.

- Enable authentication attempt limits (the number of times a user can try to authenticate before being locked out) to prevent brute-force and dictionary-based attacks.

- By default, RADIUS uses a relatively weak stream cipher with MD5-based hashing of user passwords. You can use IPSec with Encapsulating Security Payload (ESP) to provide more secure transport of RADIUS messages.

Benefits

The distributed client/server architecture of RADIUS provides the following benefits:

- **Improved security** — Authentication is centralized on the RADIUS server and possibly integrated with your core network's authentication systems. This setup eliminates the need to configure each remote access connection point, eliminates potential duplicates, and reduces the opportunities for insecure configurations, such as short or empty passwords.

- **Scalable architecture** — A single RADIUS server can authenticate requests for many RADIUS clients. Users can therefore connect to various clients as they travel, but can still be authenticated by the same server.

- **Interoperability** — The RADIUS architecture is defined by widely accepted and long-established Internet standards. You can therefore mix and match products from various vendors. The standards also enable vendor-specific customizations that don't break core functionality. For example, you can get a product integrated with Active Directory that authenticates Windows, Macintosh, and Linux user stations.

Do it!

A-1: Examining RADIUS authentication

Questions and answers

1 Name the benefits of using RADIUS authentication compared to configuring your network access servers to perform authentication.

2 True or false? A RADIUS client is the end-user's computer connecting to your network.

3 When configuring multiple RADIUS clients, you should use a unique _____ with each client-server pairing.

4 Because RADIUS uses a relatively weak stream cipher with MD5-based hashing of user passwords, you should use _____ to provide secure message transport.

5 What is a realm?

   A   A domain

   B   A name space

   C   A scope of authority

   D   An MD5 hash key

LDAP and remote access

Explanation

LDAP (Lightweight Directory Access Protocol) is the industry-standard protocol for network directory services. LDAP systems store information about users, network resources, file systems, and applications. Applications and services can use an LDAP data store to locate and store such configuration information.

Many RADIUS servers enable you to use LDAP as your remote access configuration repository. FreeRadius, for example, is one RADIUS server solution that features LDAP integration. Such a solution is possible because RADIUS is an AAA protocol. Servers that implement this protocol typically provide a database component and tools for managing the configuration data. However, you can just as easily use your existing LDAP repository instead.

LDAP security

LDAP is a critical network service and is thus a prime target for internal and external attacks. Such attacks can be categorized in a number of ways. Perhaps most useful is to consider attacks against the LDAP systems themselves, typically for the purposes of shutting down or destroying the services, and attacks against the data cataloged within the LDAP database.

An attack against the LDAP data would enable a hacker to:

- Gain unauthorized access to data.
- Gain unauthorized access to network resources.
- Modify or delete the LDAP data.
- Impersonate LDAP functions to gain further and more privileged access to the network or its resources.

Often such attacks are carried out by spoofing, by hijacking valid sessions, or by brute-force attacks against the authorization mechanisms.

An attack against the LDAP services would enable a hacker to:

- Prevent legitimate users from accessing resources (denial-of-service attack).
- Redirect access requests to imposter resources (trick a user into using the wrong shared folder).
- Hide his or her attempts to attack (or hide successful attacks on) the data stored in the LDAP system.

Commonly, such attacks would take the form of attacks against the LDAP server's operating system or attacks against the LDAP control software. An attacker could also attack support servers, such as the database server that stores the data managed by the LDAP system.

LDAP authentication and authorization

To access the LDAP directory service, the client must first authenticate itself to the LDAP server by performing a Bind operation. LDAP supports three Bind methods:

- Simple Bind
- Simple Authentication and Security Layer (SASL)
- Anonymous Bind

In a Simple Bind, the client sends its *distinguished name* (DN) along with a plaintext password. Such connections should be protected through TLS (Transport Layer Security). During the Bind operation, the client specifies the LDAP protocol version to be used. This is typically LDAPv3, though other versions are possible.

Strong authentication methods are supported in a SASL Bind operation. For example, the client and LDAP server can use Kerberos authentication, or the client can send its security certificate over a TLS link.

In an Anonymous Bind, the client sends a message with an empty DN and password. This resets the connection to a non-authenticated, or anonymous, state.

Do it!

A-2: Examining the role of LDAP in a remote access environment

Questions and answers
1 Why would you use LDAP in conjunction with a RADIUS system?
2 Name at least two goals a hacker might have when attempting to access your LDAP data.
3 Describe the functional differences between LDAP Simple Bind and Anonymous Bind operations.
4 To improve password security in LDAP Simple Bind messages, you should implement _____.

The Terminal Access Controller Access Control System

Explanation

The *Terminal Access Controller Access Control System* (TACACS) is a proprietary authentication protocol developed by Cisco Systems. Like RADIUS, it is designed to provide centralized and scalable authentication. TACACS+ also provides authorization and accounting functions.

TACACS+ is the current version of the protocol, and while it shares the name with earlier versions, it is not compatible with them. TACACS and Extended TACACS (XTACACS) are older protocols and are no longer supported.

Comparing TACACS+ and RADIUS

TACACS+ uses TCP rather than UDP for messages. TCP is connection-oriented, providing acknowledgements that requests have been received. Such acknowledgements provide, at minimum, an indication that a client or server might have failed if it doesn't respond within a predetermined period of time.

In TACACS+, unlike RADIUS, the message body is fully encrypted to provide greater security without resorting to IPSec or other means. TACACS+ uses TCP port 49.

Unlike RADIUS, TACACS+ can provide its services independently. This means that a TACACS+ server can use separate databases for each AAA function. It can interface with various services on a function-by-function basis. You can even use individual TACACS+ servers for each function.

TACACS+ supports usernames and passwords, ARA, SLIP, PAP, CHAP, and Telnet authentication messages by default. The protocol is also extensible so that vendors can add extra functionality, such as supporting Kerberos authentication messages.

Finally, TACACS+ offers multiprotocol support. In addition to TCP/IP, it supports AppleTalk Remote Access, NetBIOS Frame Protocol Control, Novell Asynchronous Services Interface, and X.25 PAD connections.

Do it!

A-3: Examining TACACS+ authentication

Questions and answers
1 Name the benefits of using TACACS+ authentication compared to RADIUS.
2 Name the authentication message types supported by TACACS+.
3 TACACS+ uses TCP port _____.

The 802.1X protocol

Explanation

The 802.1X standard is an extensible authentication protocol designed to let you control which devices have access to your network. By using 802.1X, you can prevent unauthorized workstations from connecting to your network. Furthermore, you can prevent users or attackers from attaching hubs and wired or wireless routers to your network (which they might do to extend your network or create unsecured access points).

The 802.1X protocol adds strong authentication services to wired and wireless networks. It works in conjunction with a dedicated authentication server, such as a RADIUS or TACACS+ server. In wireless networks, it enables you to provide strong authentication even when using WEP encryption.

802.1X device roles

According to the 802.1X protocol, devices have one of three roles:

- **Supplicant** — The end-user's PC or network device.
- **Authenticator** — A switch between the supplicant and the remainder of the network.
- **Authentication server** — The RADIUS or TACACS+ authentication server that grants or denies access to the network.

When a supplicant tries to connect to the network, it sends an authorization request, which is passed from the authenticator to the server. The authentication server exchanges messages with the supplicant to establish an authenticated session. If the request is granted, the server notifies the authenticator, which then allows network traffic to and from the supplicant.

If a supplicant tries to transmit data without first authenticating, the authenticator (switch) blocks the traffic. It returns a message to the supplicant, demanding that the device authenticate. This system prevents unauthenticated access to your network.

Although the system generally works well, engineers at Microsoft have discovered a flaw. Basically, after a session has been authenticated, further traffic is permitted without any checks. So, in theory, a hacker can insert his station into the network by hijacking an authenticated session. Adding IPSec encryption to the system would prevent such physical injection attacks. Of course, the rogue user would also need physical access to your network to accomplish this attack—but with a wireless network, that could mean simply being close enough to make radio contact.

The 802.1x protocol is an IEEE standard based on the EAP (Extensible Authentication Protocol). EAP is defined under RFC 3748. The 802.1X protocol is part of the larger 802 group of protocols.

Do it!

A-4:   Examining how 802.1X adds security to your network

Questions and answers

1 In 802.1X, the client's PC is known as the _____.

2 What happens when a new end-user station connects to an 802.1X-protected network?

3 To prevent physical injection attacks, you should use _____ in conjunction with 802.1X authentication.

4 True or false? 802.1X works only with wired network access points.

Network Policy Server

Explanation

The Windows Server 2008 implementation of a RADIUS server is called *Network Policy Server* (NPS). In earlier versions of Windows Server, this product was known as the Internet Authentication Service (IAS). These services are generally well regarded as capable and secure implementations of RADIUS authenticators.

NPS is not installed by default, so you must add a server role to enable this service.

NPS is integrated with the Microsoft Network Access Protection system, which enables you to enforce "health" requirements on network nodes. Basically, you can define a set of requirements to which clients must adhere: operating systems patched to a specified level, antivirus software enabled and updated to current definition files, and so forth. NPS acts as a *health policy server* (HPS) to evaluate the state of clients that authenticate via your NPS server.

Some of the features offered by NPS are listed in the following table.

Feature	Description
Generator of RADIUS shared secret keys	NPS can generate strong shared secret keys (longer than 22 random alphanumeric characters), which you can use to configure your RADIUS clients.
Server Manager Integration	You can install, configure, and manage NPS via the Server Manager console.
Configuration data stored in XML files	Because configuration data is stored in easily exportable XML files, that data can be more easily shared between NPS servers.
IPv6	NPS now supports IPv6 traffic.
EAPHost support	NPS supports EAPHost, Microsoft's new architecture for EAP authentication methods. This change means that NPS is also compatible with Cisco's Lightweight EAP (LEAP) architecture in addition to Microsoft Protected EAP (PEAP). Both systems can coexist on the same network.

Do it!   **A-5:   Installing Network Policy and Access Services**

Here's how	Here's why
1 On your ##secplus server, log on as Administrator and open Server Manager	
Select **Roles**	
2 Under Roles Summary, click **Add Roles**	To start the Add Roles Wizard.
Click **Next**	
3 In the list of roles, check **Network Policy and Access Services**	To select the NPS and NAP server role.

Click **Next** twice	
4 On the Select Role Services page, check **Network Policy Server**	
Check **Routing and Remote Access Services**	To select the two services you will install.
Click **Next** and click **Install**	To install the services.
5 Click **Close**	To close the wizard.
Close Server Manager	This computer is now a Network Policy Server (NPS).

Do it!

A-6: Configuring an NPS network policy

Here's how	Here's why
1 On your NPS computer, click **Start** and choose **Administrative Tools, Network Policy Server**	To open the MMC with the NPS snap-in.
2 Under Getting Started, in the Standard Configuration list, select **RADIUS server for 802.1X Wireless or Wired Connections**	To select a configuration scenario for your Network Policy Server.
Click **Configure 802.1X**	
3 Select **Secure Wireless Connections**	
Click **Next**	
4 Click **Add...**	To begin adding a RADIUS client (an access point).
5 In the Friendly Name box, enter **My AP##**	Where ## is the same ## assigned to the server's name.
In the Address box, enter the IP address of the classroom wireless access point	Your instructor will provide this information.
6 Select **Generate**	The radio button.
Click **Generate**	To generate a strong secret key.
Point to ⚠	The message warns you that not all access points support very long keys. You might need to use a subset of the generated key both here and at the AP.
Click **OK**	
7 Click **Next**	
8 From the list, select **Microsoft: Protected EAP (PEAP)**	To select the EAP type to use with this server.
Click **Next**	

9 Click **Add...**	To begin adding users or groups who will be permitted or denied access.
Type **Domain Users**	To permit all domain users to use the network.
Click **OK**	
10 Click **Next**	
Click **Next**	To skip past the VLAN configuration page of the wizard.
Click **Finish**	To finish and close the wizard.
11 In the console tree, expand **Policies**	
Select **Network Policies**	Your new policy is listed with a green checkmark, indicating that it is active.
Select **Secure Wireless Connections**	To select your network policy. Your policy grants access to members of the Domain Users group over wireless network connections.
12 What would be your next step in configuring NPS and 802.1X on your network?	

Do it!

A-7:   Configuring NPS accounting

Here's how	Here's why
1 In the console tree of the NPS console, select **Accounting**	
2 Click **Configure Local File Logging**	NPS is configured to log accounting and authentication requests, as well as periodic status information.
Click the **Log File** tab	By default, NPS will create a log file in a database-compatible format every month.
3 Click **OK**	
Observe the SQL Server option	You could log your accounting data directly in a database. You would need to specify which data to log and select a database in which the information would be saved.
4 Close the Network Policy Server console	

Topic B: Virtual private networks

This topic covers the following CompTIA Security+ objectives for exam SY0-301.

#	Objective
1.1	**Explain the security function and purpose of network devices and technologies** • VPN concentrator
1.3	**Distinguish and differentiate network design elements and compounds** • Remote access
1.4	**Implement and use common protocols** • IPSec • TLS • SSH • SSL

VPN technologies and security models

Explanation

A *virtual private network* (VPN) is in essence a network transmitted across another network. VPNs enable the secure transmission of data over insecure networks. For example, employees can securely access corporate network resources via the Internet by using a VPN. This sort of VPN would be called a *remote-access VPN*. You could also use a VPN to link the networks at two locations via the Internet. This VPN would be described as a *site-to-site VPN*.

VPN technologies

VPNs use authentication, encryption, and tunneling technologies to create a secure communications channel across the public network. These technologies are used as described in the following table.

Technology	Role in a VPN
Authentication	Many VPNs use RADIUS, Diameter, TACACS+, or proprietary remote access authentication technologies to ensure that only authorized users can access the network.
Tunneling	Packets sent to and from the end-user can be bundled within the packets of the public network. Consider a packet originating at a client's workstation. Equipment or software at her location inserts the packets into Internet packets and sends them via the Internet to the corporate VPN server. On the corporate LAN side of the connection, the interior packets are removed and forwarded onto the LAN. The process is reversed for data being transmitted to the client's station. In effect, the private network "tunnels" through the public network.
Encryption	VPNs can encrypt the entire client packet before putting it into the data field of the public network packet. This encryption ensures that hackers and unintended recipients cannot decipher any valuable information. Various encryption technologies can be used, depending on your VPN solution.

VPN security models

VPNs typically follow one of these three security models:

- Authentication before connection
- Trusted delivery network
- Secure VPNs

With *authentication before connection*, clients, network devices, and even servers must authenticate to the VPN system before being able to complete a connection. This type of system is often used to give a subset of users access to additional resources over a LAN. Tunneling is not typically used with this sort of system.

Trusted delivery networks are third-party private networks protected by various means. Clients and servers connect to this network, rather than connecting to the LAN via a public network. Security mechanisms on the provider's network provide assurance that data can be transmitted safely. Tunneling is not typically used on this sort of network.

Secure VPNs are the typical sort of networks that enable secure connections to be made over insecure public networks. Secure VPNs rely on tunneling, authentication, and encryption to protect private data. Secure VPNs are the focus of the remainder of this section of the course.

VPN protocols

Secure VPNs use various protocols for transmitting data securely. The most common protocols are described in the following table.

Protocol	Information
PPTP	(Peer to Peer Tunneling Protocol) A VPN protocol developed by Microsoft. Once a link has been established, the client is added as a virtual node on the LAN, and packets between the two are encrypted using Microsoft Point-to-Point Encryption (MPPE). In general practice, L2TP is preferred over PPTP.
L2F	(Layer 2 Forwarding) An obsolete Cisco VPN protocol.
L2TP	(Layer 2 Tunneling Protocol) A standardized tunneling protocol described under RFC 3931. L2TP generally combines the best features of PPTP and L2F to provide tunneling over IP, X.25, Frame Relay, and ATM networks. L2TP relies on IPSec for encryption and on RADIUS or TACACS+ for authentication. Currently at version 3, called L2TPv3.
IPSec	(IP Security) A standardized network protocol that encrypts data at the Network layer (OSI layer 3) of the protocol stack. Because it operates at the IP level, IPSec can provide security for both TCP and UDP traffic. Furthermore, applications do not need to be specially designed to work with this form of security.

Protocol	Information
SSL/TLS	(Secure Sockets Layer/Transport Layer Security) While SSL is commonly used in Web-based e-commerce, many vendors use this technology for secure VPN communications. SSL/TLS can either encrypt the entire protocol stack or be used to provide a proxy between the client and the network.
OpenVPN	An open-source VPN project that uses a variant of the SSL/TLS protocol to provide transmission security. With OpenVPN, the entire protocol stack is encrypted.
MPVPN	(Multi Path Virtual Private Network) A proprietary and trademarked protocol developed by Ragula Systems Development Company.

The following table compares PPTP and L2TP.

Feature	PPTP	L2TP
Encryption	Native PPP encryption encrypts data, but negotiations are sent in plaintext.	Relies on IPSec or other encryption protocols.
Authentication	PPP authentication using PAP, CHAP, or MS-CHAP protocols. PAP is the Password Authentication Protocol. It isn't very secure because it transfers ASCII passwords as plaintext. CHAP is the Challenge-Handshake Authentication Protocol. It's more secure than PAP because it requires the authenticating server to send a challenge to the connecting computer, requiring it to calculate a hash value based the challenge and a shared secret, such as a user password. This challenge is repeated at random intervals during the connection. The shared secret is never sent in plaintext. MS-CHAP is Microsoft's implementation of CHAP.	Relies on RADIUS or TACACS+ for authentication.
Data protocols	IP	IP, IPX, SNA, NetBEUI
Port	1723 (TCP)	1701 (UDP)

IPSec

The IPSec protocol suite is made up of four protocols:

- **Authentication Header (AH)** — Ensures authenticity by signing packet data with MD5 or SHA-1 hashes and a shared secret key.
- **Encapsulating Security Payload (ESP)** — Ensures confidentiality by encrypting the packet, using the DES or Triple-DES (3DES) cipher.
- **IP Payload Compression Protocol (IPComp)** — Compresses packet data before transmission.
- **Internet Key Exchange (IKE)** — Negotiates the shared secret keys.

All four are typically used, but systems could implement each sub-protocol independently.

IPSec encryption modes

IPSec enables two modes of encryption: transport and tunnel.

- *Transport mode* encrypts only the packet's data (not the header). It is used in host-to-host (peer-to-peer) communications.
- *Tunnel mode* encrypts the entire packet (data and header). In this mode, source and destination addresses are hidden so that eavesdroppers cannot glean information about your internal network configuration. This mode should be used in a VPN.

Secure Shell (SSH)

Programs such as Telnet and FTP send logon information in plaintext. For better security, you can use Secure Shell (SSH), which uses public key encryption to establish an encrypted and secure connection from the user's machine to the remote machine. By default, a server would listen on port 22 (TCP) for SSH connections.

SSH is a popular tool for remote command-line system access and management. Current implementations also support secure file transport (over Secure FTP, or SFTP). To implement SSH, you will need both a server service and a client program. Most Linux distributions include an SSH daemon (service), but Windows does not. Go to http://sshwindows.sourceforge.net/download/ to download a free open-source Windows SSH server service.

For the client, there are a number of popular free tools for Linux and Windows systems. These tools include PuTTY (www.chiark.greenend.org.uk/~sgtatham/putty/) for Windows, and Open SSH for Linux, BSD-variants, and Windows (by using the Cygwin POSIX-over-Windows framework).

The current protocol version, SSH-2, divides functionality into three primary layers:

- The Transport layer, as defined in RFC 4253, manages the key exchange process.
- The User Authentication layer, as defined in RFC 4252, manages client authentication through various methods (public key, password, "keyboard interactive," Kerberos, and so forth).
- The Connection layer, as defined in RFC 4254, manages communication channels. Each client-server connection can support multiple channels over which distinct operations can proceed—for example, you could have multiple command-line shells and a file transfer session over a single connection by using multiple channels.

Do it!

B-1: Comparing VPN protocols

Questions and answers

1 Give at least two reasons to choose L2TP over PPTP.

2 Name at least two obsolete or antiquated VPN protocols.

3 Which IPSec mode should be used for a VPN? Why?

4 Name an advantage and a disadvantage of SSH, compared to Telnet and FTP.

VPN solutions

Explanation

To create a VPN, you will need to select and set up two categories of components:

- Remote access communication options
- VPN hardware and software

Communication options

Remote-access VPNs are most often implemented via the Internet nowadays. This means that users will need a way to connect to the Internet, such as DSL, cable, or even dial-up. They will need an ISP account and the equipment required by the ISP for their connection—a cable modem, DSL router, or analog telephone-style modem.

Site-to-site VPNs are again most often implemented via the Internet. Few other shared public networks remain since access to the Internet became widespread. Thus, your remote offices will need a communications line to the Internet. Most often, this line would be provided through an always-on connection. DSL, cable, ISDN, and T/E dedicated circuits are all common ways that companies provide Internet connectivity, though dial-up access is doable.

VPN hardware and software

VPN solutions are offered by many vendors. Some solutions require dedicated access hardware, most commonly on the corporate LAN side of the connection. Many solutions require special software to be installed on the client workstation.

A *VPN concentrator* is a networking device that is built specifically for creating a VPN, using the latest technology to encrypt communications and authenticate users, and that is usually placed behind the network device that faces the internet. VPN concentrators provide a high level of scalability and availability and are best deployed when a single device has to handle a large number of VPN tunnels. You can configure a VPN concentrator as a RADIUS client to provide authentication services. Most concentrators provide administrative access through a command-line interface or a Web interface.

Microsoft's VPN solution uses standard Windows components on the client side. Under Windows Server 2008, you can install the Routing and Remote Access Service (RRAS) components of the Network Policy Server (NPS) to create the server to which clients connect.

Cisco, Juniper Networks, and OpenVPN provide commercial or open-source VPN solutions to businesses and end-users. Some solutions are software only; others require specialized hardware components.

Third-party service providers offer VPN solutions that work like this: The business creates a secure connection to the VPN provider's systems; the client connects to the provider's network via the Internet or dial-up. Such solutions eliminate the need to purchase, install, and maintain VPN systems. However, communications from the client to the provider are not secure (though communications over the provider's network are secure).

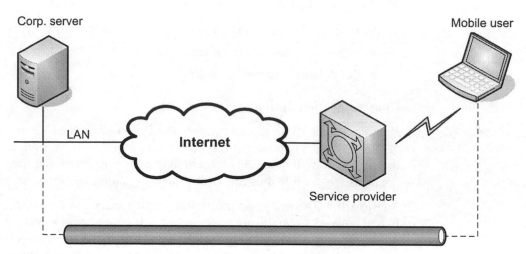

Exhibit 11-1: Service provider tunneling

Microsoft Routing and Remote Access Service (RRAS)

The Windows Server operating systems include VPN software in the form of the *Routing and Remote Access Service* (RRAS) component. With RRAS, you can enable VPN clients to connect to your network. The server on which you run RRAS should have two network adapters: one connected to the Internet and one connected to your LAN.

Do it!

B-2: Installing Routing and Remote Access Services

Here's how	Here's why
1 On your ##secplusRAS server, log on as Administrator and open Server Manager	
2 Select **Roles**	
Click **Add Roles**	To begin the Add Roles Wizard.
Click **Next**	
3 From the list of roles, select **Network Policy and Access Services**	To select the NPS and NAP server role.
Click **Next** twice	
4 Check **Routing and Remote Access Services**	Leave Network Policy Server unchecked.
Click **Next**	
Click **Install**	To install the services.
5 Click **Close**	To close the wizard.
Close Server Manager	

RRAS and NPS configuration

Explanation

You can use RRAS to manage authentication. You can also integrate RRAS with a RADIUS server, such as that enabled by NPS (Network Policy Server). To integrate RRAS with NPS, you need to configure NPS first, and in the process, generate a strong shared encryption key. Then, configure RRAS. If these services are running on the same system, you will need to configure both services at the same time.

Client connections

Windows 7, Windows Vista, and Windows XP include VPN client software. For other platforms, or to work with third-party VPN systems, you will need to install dedicated VPN client software.

To configure a VPN client connection, open the Network and Sharing Center and create a new network connection. Select the VPN connection type. You'll need to enter your VPN server's Internet domain name or IP address. You might need to specify encryption and protocol options. You can enter user credentials when you set up the connection, or you'll be prompted when you attempt to use the connection object.

Do it!

B-3: Enabling a VPN

Here's how	Here's why
1 On ##secplusRAS, click **Start** and choose **Administrative Tools**, **Routing and Remote Access**	
2 In the console tree, right-click **##secplusRAS** and choose **Configure and Enable Routing and Remote Access**	
Click **Next**	
3 Click **Next**	Remote Access (dial-up or VPN) is selected by default.
4 Check **VPN**	To enable the VPN configuration rather than a dial-up configuration.
Click **Next**	
5 Select **RRAS Network Interface**	Your computer has two network adapters installed. During class setup, the connection simulating an external IP address was renamed as "RRAS Internet Interface." However, due to classroom constraints, the IP address assigned to this card is not a valid routable Internet address and you won't be able to create the connection in a following activity.
Record the IP address associated with this interface	IP: _____

6 Observe the "Enable security on the selected interface" option	By default, RRAS will enable a static packet filter that will permit only VPN traffic to access your server via this network adapter.
Click **Next**	
7 Select **From a specified range of addresses**	Your network doesn't have a DHCP server installed, so you'll have to specify a range of IP addresses for RRAS to assign to its VPN clients. If you had a DHCP server, your VPN server could pass address requests to that server and have it automatically assign IP addresses to VPN clients.
Click **Next**	
8 Click **New**	
In the Start and End IP address boxes, enter the IP addresses assigned by your instructor	
Click **OK**	
9 Click **Next**	
10 Select **Yes, setup this server to work with a RADIUS server**	
11 Click **Next**	
12 In the Primary RADIUS Server box, enter **##secplus.secplus##.class**	This is where you installed NPS.
In the Shared secret box, enter **security+**	You should use longer shared secrets, but for simplicity's sake in class, you'll use this simple string.
Click **Next**	
Click **Finish**	To finish the configuration wizard and start RRAS.
13 Click **OK**	To acknowledge the DHCP relay agent message.
14 In the Routing and Remote Access console, in the console tree, observe your server	There is a green arrow next to it, indicating that it is configured and running.
15 Close the Routing and Remote Access console	

Do it!

B-4: Configuring NPS to provide RADIUS authentication for your VPN

Here's how	Here's why
1 On your ##secplus server, click **Start** and choose **Administrative Tools**, **Network Policy Server**	
2 In the console tree, select **NPS (Local)**	If necessary.
3 In the Standard Configuration list, select **RADIUS server for Dial-up or VPN Connections**	
Click **Configure VPN or Dial-Up**	To open the configuration wizard.
4 Select **Virtual Private Network (VPN) Connections**	
Click **Next**	You could change the connection name before clicking Next.
5 Click **Add**	To begin configuring the RADIUS client connection.
In the Friendly name box, enter **##secplusRAS**	Where ##secplusRAS is the Windows Server 2008 member server where RRAS is installed.
In the Address box, enter the RRAS server's IP address	You recorded this address in the previous activity.
In the Shared secret and Confirm shared secret boxes, enter **security+**	You should use longer shared secrets, but for simplicity's sake in class, you'll use this simple string.
Click **OK**	
Click **Next**	
6 Check **Extensible Authentication Protocol**	
From the Type list, select **Microsoft: Protected EAP (PEAP)**	To specify the type of authentication protocol to be used.
Click **Next**	

7	Click **Next**	To leave the user groups list empty, so the policy will apply to all users.
8	Click **Next**	To bypass the IP filters configuration page.
9	Click **Next**	To accept the encryption settings.
10	In the Realm name box, enter **Outlander**	
	Click **Next**	
11	Click **Finish**	To complete the configuration wizard and enable the VPN-RADIUS connection.
12	Right-click **NPS (Local)**	
	Choose **Register server in Active Directory**	When a Network Policy Server is a member of a domain, it uses Active Directory to authenticate. It must be authorized to do so by registering.
	Click **OK** twice	
13	Close the Network Policy Server console	
14	Close all open windows	

Unit summary: Remote access security

Topic A

In this topic, you learned that authentication, authorization, and accounting (**AAA**) are the three phases of remote access. You learned that **RADIUS** and **TACACS+** are two popular systems for implementing an AAA infrastructure. You also learned that **802.1x** is an extensible protocol that enables you to control which devices connect to your network. You installed **Network Policy Server**, Microsoft's RADIUS server.

Topic B

In this topic, you learned that **virtual private networks** enable you to extend secure network connections across insecure networks. VPNs use tunneling, authentication, and encryption to provide secure connections. You learned about the popular VPN protocols, including PPTP, L2TP, and IPSec. Finally, you installed **RRAS** (the Routing and Remote Access Services) and used it to create a VPN.

Review questions

1 True or false? To enable remote access to your network, you must provide services for authentication, authorization, and accounting.

2 In RADIUS terminology, what is the name given to the system that provides authentication services for remote computers?

3 In RADIUS terminology, what is the name given to the system that provides connectivity services for remote computers?

4 After authenticating, the RADIUS client will receive a message that will be one of three message types; these types are _____, _____, and _____.

5 What is a RADIUS realm?

6 What are the three LDAP Bind methods?

7 True or false? TACACS+ is backward-compatible with TACACS and XTACACS.

8 TACACS+ uses _____ rather than UDP for messages.

9 TACACS+ provides better message security than RADIUS because it encrypts _____.

10 For Windows Server 2008, Microsoft's RADIUS server is called _____.

11 VPNs generally use _____, _____, and _____ to enable secure remote connections to be made across insecure networks.

12 What are the three VPN security models?

13 Name two VPN protocols.

14 What are the two IPSec encryption modes?

15 _____ is a popular and free SSH client for Windows-based systems.

Independent practice activity

In this activity, you will use SSH to create a secure connection to a server.

1 On the Windows Server 2008 domain member computer (the Remote Access Server), verify that the Internet Zone is set to Medium-high:

    a In Internet Explorer, open Internet Options.

    b On the Security tab, verify that the zone is set to Medium-high.

    c If you can't drag the slider, turn off IE ESC in Server Manager. If the slider is still in the incorrect position, click the Advanced tab and click Reset. Click Reset again, click Close, and click OK twice. Close and reopen IE. Use Internet Options to set the Internet Zone security to Medium-high.

2 On the same Windows Server 2008 computer in your lab station:

    a Visit **http://www.freesshd.com/** to download freeSSHd for Windows. (Turn on the Phishing Filter if prompted. Turn off IE ESC in Server Manager, if necessary.)

    b Install the service onto the server, using the default settings for a Full Installation.

    c Create keys when prompted.

    d Install the program to run as a system service.

    e View any messages, and close any open windows.

3 Start the SSH server:

    a Double-click the freeSSHd icon (on the desktop). Wait for its icon to appear in the system tray.

    b Right-click the service's icon in the system tray and choose Settings.

    c Click the SSH tab and specify **2200** for the port number. Apply the change.

    d Click the Server status tab and start the SSH server.

4 Configure login information:

    a Click the Users tab.

    b Click Add.

    c In the Login box, type **Administrator**.

    d In the Domain box, type **secplus##.class** (where ## is your lab station's assigned domain number).

    e Check Shell.

    f Click OK. Click OK again.

5 Configure a firewall exception for freeSSH on the server:

    a Open the Control Panel and then Windows Firewall.

    b Click "Allow a program through Windows Firewall."

    c Click Add port.

    d In the Name box, type **freeSSHd**.

    e In the Port number box, type **2200**.

    f Click OK twice.

    g Close the Windows Firewall and Control Panel windows.

6 On your Windows 7 computer, download and install the PuTTY client from **www.chiark.greenend.org.uk**. Close IE when done.

7 Use PuTTY to connect to your SSH server:

    a Open PuTTY.exe. In the Host Name (or IP Address) box, enter your SSH server's IP address.

    b In the Port box, enter **2200**.

    c Click Open. Click Yes.

    d When prompted, next to "login as," type **Administrator** and press Enter.

    e Next to administrator@*serverIPaddress*, type **P@$$word** and press Enter.

8 Display a directory listing of the C:\Windows directory. You have command-line access to your server via SSH at this point.

9 On your SSH server, view the online users:

    a In the system tray, right-click the freeSSHd icon and choose Settings.

    b Click the Online users tab. Your connection as Administrator should be listed in the window.

10 On your Windows 7 computer, enter **exit** to close the PuTTY window. Close all other open windows.

11 On your SSH server, stop the SSH server. Close the freeSSHd settings window.

12 On your SSH server, right-click the freeSSHd icon in the system tray and choose Unload.

Unit 12

Vulnerability testing and monitoring

Unit time: 90 minutes

Complete this unit, and you'll know how to:

A Perform vulnerability and penetration testing.

B Monitor application and security logs.

C Use intrusion detection and prevention systems.

D Perform forensic analysis after a security incident.

Topic A: Risk and vulnerability assessment

This topic covers the following CompTIA Security+ objectives for exam SY0-301.

#	Objective
3.7	**Implement assessment tools and techniques to discover security threats and vulnerabilities**

- Vulnerability scanning and interpreting results
- Tools
- Risk calculations
  - Threat vs. likelihood
- Assessment types
  - Risk
  - Threat
  - Vulnerability
- Assessment technique
  - Baseline reporting
  - Code review
  - Determine attack surface
  - Architecture
  - Design reviews

#	Objective
3.8	**Within the realm of vulnerability assessments, explain the proper use of penetration testing versus vulnerability scanning**

- Penetration testing
  - Verify that a threat exists
  - Bypass security controls
  - Actively test security controls
  - Exploiting vulnerabilities
- Vulnerability scanning
  - Passively testing security controls
  - Identify vulnerability
  - Identify lack of security controls
  - Identify common misconfigurations
- Black box
- White box
- Gray box

Assessment types

Explanation

When you conduct a risk and vulnerability assessment of your organization's network and data security, there are three overall assessment types you need to consider.

Type	Description
Threat	A threat assessment is meant to list and describe every possible threat your organization might face. Threats include not just intentional, unauthorized acts to access or destroy data, but also natural threats, such as storms, floods, or earthquakes, and the loss of utilities, such as electricity or water.
Vulnerability	This assessment is performed after the threat assessment, using the results of the threat assessment to determine your level of vulnerability for each threat. By ranking the threats, you can determine how you want marshal your security resources.
Risk	Risk assessment is the process of determining the likelihood of a threat against your network or assets, the possible impact of such a threat, and your organization's tolerance for accepting the risk. To perform this type of assessment, you must identify your assets; determine the likelihood of a threat against one or more of those assets; and determine what your organization's tolerance level is for those threats.

Vulnerability assessments

While the exact method of vulnerability assessment depends on your specific organization and its assets, an overall procedure for assessing vulnerability is outlined in the following steps:

1   **Establish a baseline** — The baseline-reporting step establishes a starting point for minimum system settings, including the base operating system and any installed applications.

2   **Review the code** — During this step, you review the code in the applications you've deployed to determine if it's the best it can be given the technology currently available. Just assuming that the code is acceptable isn't enough; you must review it to determine its technological soundness based on current standards.

3   **Determine the attack surface** — The *attack surface* is the combination of code and services available in each application to all users, including unauthorized users. The more services and ports available to unauthorized users, the larger your attack surface. The larger the attack surface, the greater the vulnerability of your system.

4   **Review the architecture** — This step requires you to examine the system components and how they interact with the operating system and applications. A review of the architecture can reveal vulnerabilities in the way applications address the system components, such as memory, which can be exploited in an attack.

5   **Review the design** — After you've gathered all the information, you must review the design of your systems, from operating system to applications, to determine the vulnerabilities you can remove through tighter security settings or the reduction or removal of unnecessary code.

Vulnerability testing provides you with the opportunity to passively test security controls and identify security issues, after which you can decide how you want to address the vulnerabilities, either through a tightening of security controls or with further penetration testing (described later in this topic). You can use readily available tools to scan your network and assets to identify any lack of security controls and common incorrect configurations that can leave you open to attacks.

Vulnerability testing tools include:

- Port scanners
- Network mappers
- Password crackers
- OVAL-compliant tools
- Nessus and other dedicated scanning applications

Port scanners

A *port scanner* is a tool that examines a host or network to determine which ports are being monitored by applications on that host or network. Open ports—particularly those for insecure services—could be a point of vulnerability. For example, an attacker might check to see what service is listening on the FTP port, hoping to find that you're running an FTP server with known vulnerabilities.

Network administrators often run port scanners to find vulnerabilities before attackers find them. Most vulnerability scanners, such as OVAL and Nessus, include port scanning features. You can also use dedicated scanners, such as the free Angry IP Scanner (http://www.angryip.org).

Network mappers

A *network mapper* is a tool you use to scan your network and to build a map (or inventory) of the systems, open ports, running services, operating system versions, and so forth. In many ways, a network mapper is like a port scanner that also looks for additional details about each system.

Vulnerability scanners often include network mapping functions. Additionally, you can use a dedicated network mapper, such as the free Nmap (http://nmap.org/).

Password crackers

Password crackers are applications that you use (or attackers use) to attempt to determine or decipher the passwords associated with user accounts. Crackers use various techniques to determine or guess passwords. These techniques include:

- Brute-force decryption
- Dictionary-style password guessing
- Decryption based on known weaknesses or vulnerabilities

Examples of password crackers are Elcom System Recovery and pwdump (available in various versions). Visit www.openwall.com/passwords/microsoft-windows-nt-2000-xp-2003-vista for an extensive list of Windows-based password crackers.

OVAL

The *Open Vulnerability and Assessment Language* (OVAL) is a project sponsored by the U.S. Department of Homeland Security and managed by Mitre Corporation. OVAL standardizes the way systems and applications are tested for vulnerabilities and how those vulnerabilities are described and reported. OVAL also provides a central repository of vulnerability information.

Before the development of OVAL, operating system and security software vendors created proprietary and incompatible vulnerability assessment systems. Each system had its own way to discover, describe, and report vulnerabilities. This made enterprise-wide testing difficult, time-consuming, and error-prone.

The OVAL project publishes a standard XML schema that supports a common method to describe systems configurations. The schema standardizes the way vulnerabilities are discovered. It also provides a common method to describe and report vulnerabilities so that law enforcement authorities, system administrators, and software developers can quickly and easily understand and act upon the reports.

OVAL is not a specific product. It is a combination of a language, an XML schema, and a repository. Commercial and open-source systems implement the OVAL standards to ensure interoperability. Mitre has released a "reference implementation" called the OVAL Interpreter. The Interpreter is meant to demonstrate how information can be collected from systems and reported in a unified manner. It is also intended to enable OVAL developers to test their implementations of the specification.

Nessus

Nessus is a free security scanner published by Tenable Network Security (www.nessus.org). With it, you can scan one or more computers on your network to determine operating system and patch levels, the security state, and vulnerability to known exploits. By using Tenable's commercial products, you can centrally gather security statistics and dynamically reconfigure systems to match your baseline security specifications.

With Nessus, you can determine the state of your computers to see if they match the risk assessment plan you have created. You can also perform ongoing monitoring to make sure systems remain in compliance with your baseline specifications.

Penetration testing

Penetration testing is essentially the process of attacking your own systems. Using the same tools and techniques an attacker might use, you try to breach the security of your network or hosts. Penetration testing can be a powerful way to test any vulnerabilities to determine an actual threat level.

When you perform penetration testing, you generally follow this process:

1 Verify that a threat exists. You can do this by using numerous techniques, including vulnerability testing, which can show you where security settings are poorly configured or missing on a variety of systems, such as firewalls, mail servers, and domain controllers. You can also perform a manual vulnerability test by watching how secure employees are with their passwords (are they on sticky notes?), what information they keep on their desks (proprietary information, or employee names and phone number lists), and how they use their security badges (do they keep doors propped open, or do they allow several people through the door on one badge?).

2 Bypass and actively test security controls, and exploit vulnerabilities. After you've identified threats, try to bypass and test the security controls in place and exploit vulnerabilities. For example, use simple passwords on a user account, use a network sniffer to grab user account information, contact servers on unsecured ports, or enter the building without a security card. You can also use social engineering to try to gain information about user accounts, network configuration, or employee names and phone numbers.

When you perform your penetration testing, you should approach it using the methods described in the following table. Each method assumes a different level of knowledge about your infrastructure, and the method you choose will depend on the level of threat you want to protect against.

Method	Description
Black box	This level simulates a casual hacker who knows nothing about your organization or network. Often this type of attack is merely an exercise in gathering information about a target.
Gray box	This next level of attack assumes an attacker who has gained some knowledge of the organization and its infrastructure, either after a period of information gathering or after receiving some basic level of insider knowledge from within the organization.
White box	This final level simulates an attacker with extensive knowledge of the organization and its infrastructure and security controls. The knowledge would come either from independent research and information gathering or from a trusted inside source with full knowledge of the network and its defenses.

You can use the results of your testing to increase security throughout the organization—not just computer or network security, but also physical security—and even to help increase awareness of social engineering vulnerabilities.

If you plan to engage in penetration testing, make sure that you document your intentions. Preferably, you should obtain permission from senior managers before making any such attempts. Failure to do that could result in your dismissal if other staff catch you in the act—you will need to prove your good intentions once you're caught, or they'll think you're just another malicious attacker!

Penetration testing vs. vulnerability scanning

Penetration testing can be used in addition to vulnerability scanning, but it should generally not replace it. Most vulnerability scanners check for dozens or hundreds of potential security weaknesses. Many scanners are also well vetted, so you can be assured that the tests they perform are thorough and comprehensive. Unless you are a master hacker, you might not be able to test as thoroughly as a vulnerability scanner can.

However, a vulnerability scanner can tell you only that a weakness is there, or potentially there. Only by attempting to exploit the weakness can you be sure that a hole in your security truly exists. For example, just because your server is listening on a particular port does not mean that the port is a means of attack on that server.

Vulnerability scanning is also unable to test the human factors of security. Your scanner cannot, for example, check to see if users have posted passwords on sticky notes on their monitors or will give out passwords to purported technicians over the telephone. You could test for such weaknesses in your system, however, by engaging in a penetration test that included such attack vectors.

Do it!

A-1:   Examining vulnerability and penetration testing

Questions	Answers
1 Distinguish between threat, vulnerability, and risk assessments.	
2 Why is it important to establish a baseline before determining the attack surface?	
3 Describe the difference between vulnerability testing and penetration testing.	
4 What level of insider knowledge distinguishes gray box and white box penetration testing?	

Do it!

A-2: Scanning the network

Here's how	Here's why
1 Obtain the Nmap setup file from your instructor	
Install Nmap, using the default installation options	Enter Administrator credentials, if necessary.
2 Start Nmap	If necessary, navigate to C:\Program Files\Nmap and doubleclick Zenmap. Zenmap is the GUI front end to Nmap.
In the Target box, type **##secplus**	The host name for your domain controller.
In the Profile box, verify that **Intense Scan** is selected, and then click **Scan**	To scan your domain controller.
3 Observe the Nmap Output tab	You can see the tests that Nnap is running while scanning the domain controller.
4 After the scan is complete, observe the Nmap Output tab	You can see the open ports and services, as well as the computer's MAC address, OS detail, uptime statistics, and network distance in hops.
5 Click the **Ports/Hosts** tab	To see a list of ports, protocols, and services.
6 Click the **Topology** tab	To display the network map that's being built. You can use this tab to begin gathering host names, IP addresses, and a general view of the network configuration.
7 Click the **Host Details** tab	To display the status of the computer and detailed information about it.
8 Observe the left pane	Nmap builds a list of hosts and services. You can start to gather information about the network and its configuration.
9 Perform an intense scan of your RAS server	To gather information about another host on your network.
Observe the information on the tabs	You can see how a potential attacker can begin to gather information about your network and its hosts.

10 Assuming that you're using Nmap
to begin collecting information
about the network as an attacker,
what method of penetration
testing are you using: black box,
gray box, white box?

Topic B: Auditing and logging

This topic covers the following CompTIA Security+ objectives for exam SY0-301.

#	Objective
1.2	**Apply and implement secure network administration principles** • Log analysis

3.6	**Analyze and differentiate among types of mitigation and deterrent techniques**
	
	• Monitoring system logs
	    – Event logs
	    – Audit logs
	    – Security logs
	    – Access logs

Event Viewer

Explanation

The Windows logging tool is called Event Viewer. This application is available in most versions of Windows, though the way you access it varies. In Windows Server 2008, open Server Manager and expand the Diagnostics node.

Log files

Event data from Windows and various applications are stored in log files. Which logs are available depends on your version of Windows and on the components, roles, and applications you have installed.

Event Viewer in Windows Server 2008 includes many log files, categorized as follows:

Log type	Description
Windows	The "traditional" Windows log files, including the Application, Security, and System logs. Windows Server 2008 also includes a Setup and Forwarded Events log, which might not be available in other versions of Windows.
Applications and Services	Log files for each of the roles installed on your server, plus a hardware events log. For example, installing the DNS server role adds the DNS Server log.
Microsoft / Windows	Log files for each Window component. For example, the stock list includes a TaskScheduler log, which records events generated by the Windows Task Scheduler component. Found under the Applications and Services Logs category.

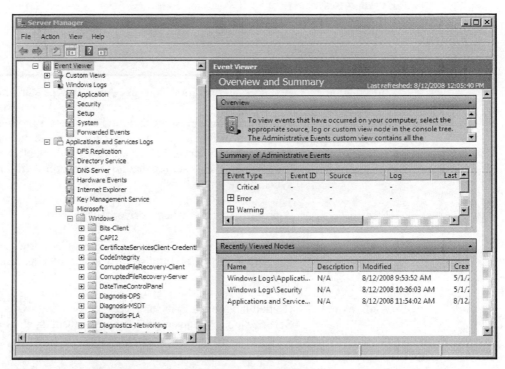

Exhibit 12-1: Windows Server 2008 Event Viewer

Events

In each log, Windows records events—the details associated with something of significance that happened on your system. For example, when you log on, Windows records a number of events associated with your action; notably, a success or failure event is saved in the Security log.

Windows records the many details for each event, summaries of which are listed in the following table:

Item	Description
Type	The event type: Information, Error, Warning, and so forth.
Date and time	The date and time the event occurred.
Source	The program, component, or service that generated the event.
Event ID	An ID number that specifically identifies the event type. For example, a "success" informational event is typically given an event ID of 1.
Category	A descriptor used to classify events. Not all events are assigned a category. Events in the Security log are often assigned a category, such as Logon or Logoff, to describe the general classification of the action that generated the event.
User	The user or process associated with the event.
Computer	The computer on which the event occurred.

Event types

Windows classifies events into the following types:

Type	Description
Information	A successful operation, such as when a service starts normally.
Warning	An informational message that might indicate a problem that you should investigate or fix. A warning might also indicate that only part of an operation has finished. For example, when the DNS Server starts, you might see warning events stating that it is waiting for Active Directory synchronization to finish.
Error	A problem, such as when a driver fails to load.
Audit Success	(Called Success Audit in some versions of Windows; appears only in the Security log.) A successful security event, such as when you log on successfully.
Audit Failure	(Called Failure Audit in some versions of Windows; appears only in the Security log.) An unsuccessful security event, such as when you mistype your password and thus cannot log on.

In the list of events, you can double-click an event to see the full details about it. Exhibit 12-2 shows the details you would see if you double-clicked a Logoff event in the Security log.

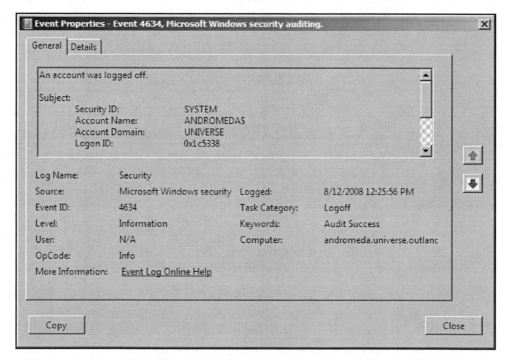

Exhibit 12-2: Event details

Do it!

B-1:   Viewing event logs

Here's how	Here's why
1 On your Windows domain controller, open Server Manager	
2 In the console tree, expand **Diagnostics**	
Select **Event Viewer**	The details pane shows an overview and summary of the event logs.
3 In the console tree, expand **Event Viewer**, **Windows Logs**	
Select **Security**	To view the Security log.
4 Double-click the first **Audit Success** event associated with a Logon event	This type of event is recorded each time a user or service successfully logs onto your computer or domain.
Click **Close**	
5 In the System log, locate an **Error** event and display its details	Such an event might not be listed if your system has not logged any error conditions. If that's the case, skip to the next step.
Close the details dialog box	If necessary.
6 In the console tree, expand **Applications and Services Logs**	
Select **DNS Server**	
7 Select the first **Warning** event	
View the general summary in the lower pane	To determine if the warning indicates a condition you should investigate or if it indicates a temporary state, such as the service waiting for another event to occur.
8 Close Event Viewer	

Device and application logging

Explanation

In addition to using the logging enabled by Windows and the Reliability and Performance console, you should consider enabling logging on your servers and network devices. For example, your router or wireless access point probably provides logging capabilities. Examine its logging capabilities and enable those that will help you capture needed information without adversely affecting performance.

Component	Information to log
Antivirus software	Signature version and update date, last scan date and time, positive detections, date and time the software is disabled or shut down.
Firewall	Blocked access requests, blocked application requests, malformed packets, invalid requests, management actions (such as opening ports).
Wireless access point and RADIUS	Failed logon attempts, NPS (RADIUS) access rejections, malformed packets, invalid requests.
DNS server	DNS record update, update request failures, zone transfer requests, zone transfer failures.
Domain controller	Failed access attempts, failed and successful administrator logons, requests for privilege escalations.
Applications	Version information, dates and times of updates, security-related events.

Do it!

B-2: Discussing device and application logging

Questions and answers

1 Identify a challenge associated with enabling logging on devices and remote servers. Then speculate on solutions to that challenge.

2 Speculate on information you should log that isn't included in the preceding table.

3 Let's say you enable the logging of data on users' personal firewall software. Why would you want to monitor management actions, such as opening ports?

Topic C: Intrusion detection and prevention systems

This topic covers the following CompTIA Security+ objectives for exam SY0-301.

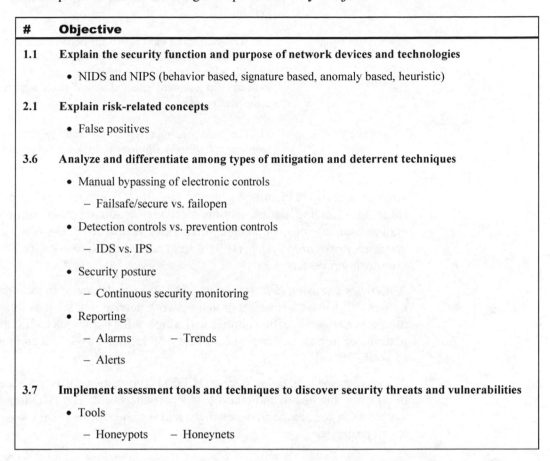

#	Objective
1.1	**Explain the security function and purpose of network devices and technologies**
	• NIDS and NIPS (behavior based, signature based, anomaly based, heuristic)
2.1	**Explain risk-related concepts**
	• False positives
3.6	**Analyze and differentiate among types of mitigation and deterrent techniques**
	• Manual bypassing of electronic controls
	– Failsafe/secure vs. failopen
	• Detection controls vs. prevention controls
	– IDS vs. IPS
	• Security posture
	– Continuous security monitoring
	• Reporting
	– Alarms – Trends
	– Alerts
3.7	**Implement assessment tools and techniques to discover security threats and vulnerabilities**
	• Tools
	– Honeypots – Honeynets

Intrusion detection and prevention

Explanation

Intrusion detection is the process of detecting and possibly reacting to an attack on your network or hosts. *Intrusion detection systems* (IDSs) monitor key network points, network devices, and important hosts for anomalous activity. For example, a pattern or volume of network traffic might indicate an attack on your network.

Intrusion detection and monitoring systems can generally be classified as follows:

Classification	Description
Anomaly-based, or heuristic	The IDS compares the current state of your system to a baseline, looking for differences that would signal an attack or compromised system.
Behavior-based	The IDS monitors your system for behaviors that would be typical of a compromised system. For example, if a client workstation begins sending a large volume of e-mail messages, the IDS may flag that as indicative of a system infected with a virus, which is sending itself to unsuspecting users.
Signature-based	The IDS monitors your system based on signatures, much like antivirus scanners use virus definitions to look for infected files.

After an activity is identified as malicious, the IDS can take either passive actions (logging, sounding alarms, sending alerts) or proactive actions (dropping packets, ending user sessions, stopping applications). A proactive IDS is often called an *intrusion prevention system* (IPS), a term coined by NetworkICE, a maker of intrusion monitoring products.

A *network intrusion detection system* (NIDS) is a device or system designed to monitor network traffic on a segment or at a network entry point, such as a firewall. The NIDS monitors network traffic volumes and watches for malicious traffic and suspicious patterns or trends. Depending on where you located a NIDS, it can monitor some or all of your network.

A *host intrusion detection system* (HIDS) is typically a software-based system for monitoring the health and security of a particular host. The HIDS monitors operating system files for unauthorized changes and watches for unusual usage trends and failed logon requests.

Event analyses

When analyzing an event, an IDS can make one of four possible determinations:

- True negative
- True positive
- False positive
- False negative

A true negative determination indicates that the IDS has correctly identified the event as a normal, non-threatening action. In other words, the IDS correctly determined that normal network or system activities occurred. A true positive indicates that the IDS has correctly identified an attack or breach of security.

A false positive means that the IDS has incorrectly identified normal or benign activity as being a sign of an attack or breach. The pattern of activity has fooled the IDS into "thinking" that malicious acts are being carried out, when in fact normal user activity is occurring.

A false negative is the worst situation: the IDS has misidentified an attack or breach as normal or benign activity. In this case, your network or host is under attack, and the IDS is not detecting this situation.

The administrator of an IDS will typically spend considerable time at first tuning the system to correctly identify the many events that it will monitor. As time goes on, if the administrator correctly tunes the system, fewer false positive and negative readings will be made. During the initial tuning time, you will need to be diligent not only in tuning the IDS but also in following up on each potential attack to be sure your system is not actually being breached.

Do it!

C-1:   Discussing IDS characteristics

Questions and answers

1   Considering a network protected by a firewall, why would you want to implement an intrusion detection system (either a network or host intrusion detection system)?

2   You want to detect and thwart attacks against the server in your perimeter network. Would you implement a network intrusion detection system, a network intrusion prevention system, or a host intrusion detection system?

3   Describe an example of a false positive event.

4   Describe an example of a false negative event.

5   Which of the IDS classifications—anomaly-based, behavior-based, and signature-based—requires the least ongoing interaction by a network administrator?

Does that make it the best system?

Network intrusion detection systems

Explanation

NIDSs (network intrusion detection systems) are typically dedicated devices or single-purpose hosts running specialized software. A NIDS often uses two network interfaces. One is placed in promiscuous mode, meaning that it reads all packets that pass by, rather than reading only those for its specific MAC address. This interface analyzes the network traffic to look for patterns of suspicious behavior. This interface does not have a network address and cannot be used for normal networking activities.

The second network interface connects to the network so that the NIDS can send alerts, communicate with management ports on network devices, and so forth. Through this port, you can also remotely administer the NIDS if it supports such actions.

Network location

Where you place a NIDS determines what portion of your network it can monitor. This does not imply that you should choose the location to maximize the extent of coverage. Instead, you should place a NIDS where it can monitor the most crucial or valuable network resources. For example, you might put a NIDS on the segment on which your primary corporate servers are also located. Network intrusion detection systems might also be placed on your perimeter network segment or integrated with your firewall to monitor incoming traffic.

Indicators of malicious activity

Network intrusion detection systems can be configured to watch for various anomalous conditions that might indicate an attack. These conditions include:

- **String signatures** — The NIDS watches for text, within the packet's payload, that matches specific patterns. For example, this might include watching for strings that contain command-line entries that might compromise a password file. String signatures are system-dependent and are subject to change as new vulnerabilities are discovered and exploited.

- **Port signatures** — The NIDS monitors connections to specific ports on selected hosts. For example, you might configure a NIDS to monitor for attempted connections to TCP port 23, which is the Telnet service port number. Such attempts might represent an attempted attack.

- **Header signatures** — The NIDS watches for specific patterns of header fields that are known to be dangerous or are simply illogical (possibly representing a new type of attack).

For such signature-based monitoring, you must regularly update the NIDS. For example, you might need to enter new string signatures and update monitored ports. Some commercial systems offer subscription services to make such updates simple or automatic. (However, such subscriptions would not include port signatures because those depend on your specific network configuration.)

Not all malicious activity is indicated by the contents of the packets analyzed by the NIDS. A large quantity of packets targeting a specific host or coming from a single address might indicate a denial-of-service attack. *Profile-based detection* builds a statistical profile of normal activity and considers activities that fall outside that profile to be potential attacks. Successful profile-based detection does not depend on up-to-date signature files.

Active reaction options

A NIDS can take various actions to respond to an indicator of malicious activity.

- **TCP reset** — The NIDS sends a TCP reset packet to the victim host, thereby terminating all current sessions. This will often stop an attack that is in progress. TCP resets do not block the initial packet sent to the victim, so they are not effective in halting all forms of attack.

- **Shunning** — Also called blocking, shunning involves automatically dropping packets from the attacker. Typically, the NIDS would connect to the firewall and create a temporary rule that would drop all packets coming in from the attacker.

- **Antivirus scanning and cleaning** — The NIDS examines packet contents to detect virus-infected payloads. When appropriately configured, this NIDS can also try to remove the virus from the payload before transmitting the packets.

- **Failsafe/secure or failopen** — A *failsafe* or *secure reaction* shuts down a component or network connection, such as a network card or a server, if an intrusion has been detected. A *failopen reaction* opens the component or device to all access—the opposite reaction to failsafe. Although a failopen reaction on a firewall or a server might seem counterintuitive, in a situation with locking doors, it provides a way to access or exit a secure area.

Passive reaction options

In addition to active responses, a NIDS can also take these passive actions during an attack:

- **IP session logging** — The NIDS logs some or all of the traffic between the attacker and the victim hosts for later forensics and investigations.

- **Alerts and alarms** — The NIDS can send various alerts, including console messages, e-mail messages, and pager messages, to in essence request human intervention.

NIDS examples

Examples of commercial network intrusion detection systems include Cisco's IOS NIDS (www.cisco.com) and Computer Associates' eTrust Intrusion Detection (www.ca.com). Examples of free or open-source NIDSs include Snort (www.snort.org) and Untangle (www.untangle.com).

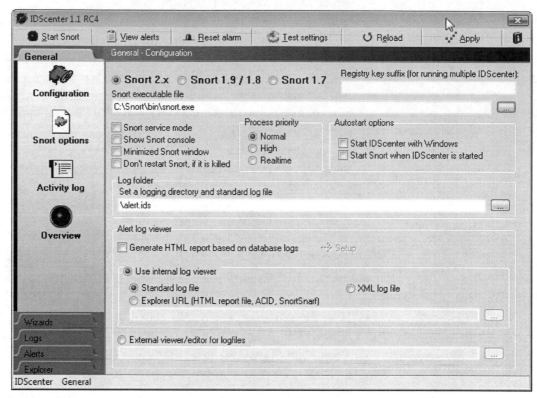

Exhibit 12-3: The IDScenter front-end for Snort

```
alert icmp any any -> any any (msg: "ICMP traffic alert";sid:2;)
```

Exhibit 12-4: A sample Snort rule

Host-based intrusion detection systems

A host-based intrusion detection system is software that runs on a host computer, monitoring that system for signs of attack. A HIDS typically relies on operating system logging features to gather the data it analyzes. By relying on the OS to gather data, the HIDS places less of a resource burden on the host than it would if it added its own monitoring functions to those already included in the operating system.

Host-based intrusion detection systems monitor only the hosts on which they are installed. However, many HIDS products enable you to install agents on various hosts, each of which sends reports of events to a central monitoring server. In this way, you can create a centrally managed network-wide infrastructure of HIDS monitors.

HIDS operation

A HIDS will use one or more of these techniques to watch for suspicious activity:

- Auditing system, event, and security logs
- Monitoring files to watch for modifications
- Monitoring application, system process, and resource requests
- Monitoring incoming packets from the network interface

Logs

A HIDS monitors log entries, looking for patterns that match attack signatures. As with NIDS signatures, you must keep your HIDS software up-to-date with current signatures to detect ever-evolving forms of attack.

File modifications

A HIDS monitors operating system and application executable files, watching for changes that might indicate an attack. Typically, a HIDS will do so by recalculating file checksums, which are hashes of the file's contents, and comparing the new checksums with archived checksum values.

Application and resource monitoring

Modern HIDS products monitor requests for system resources and applications. For example, they can watch for attempts to access restricted files, or watch for users' attempts to take administrative actions or elevate their privilege levels.

To perform such monitoring, the HIDS product must be tightly integrated with the operating system. Such products must be able to intercept software requests at the driver and kernel levels. You will need to carefully evaluate such software to be confident that it will effectively monitor your system without interfering with normal operations or slowing performance unacceptably.

OS-integrated HIDSs have several advantages; they can:

- Prevent files from being modified, deleted, or even opened.
- Prevent registry changes.
- Prevent system services from being stopped or modified.
- Prevent changes in user-level configuration settings.
- Prevent users from performing administrative actions or escalating their permission levels.

A HIDS that provides log, file, application, and resource monitoring does so through agents. Host-based agents are essentially services (or daemons) that you install atop the operating system.

Network traffic monitoring

A HIDS can monitor packets as they arrive and before they are processed by the operating system. It can also monitor connection requests. In either case, the HIDS can detect a malicious network action before the operating system receives the communication, and the HIDS can then block the connection. Host-based intrusion detection systems provide network monitoring capabilities through *host wrappers*, which are in essence a type of personal firewall.

Advantages

HIDS monitoring offers a number of advantages over NIDS monitors. These advantages include the following:

- A HIDS can determine whether an attack failed or was successful by analyzing logs and comparing checksums.
- A HIDS monitors individual user actions and thus can identify the exact user account and location being used by an attacker. A HIDS can also take immediate actions to stop such actions.
- A HIDS can monitor attacks in which the attacker has direct physical access to the system.
- Host-based intrusion detection systems do not rely on a particular network location, topology, or network device. Thus, they can be easier to set up than a NIDS.

In general, however, NIDS and HIDS products are complementary. You will likely find advantages to using both to protect your networked systems.

HIDS examples

Examples of commercial HIDS products include Computer Associates' Host-based Intrusion Detection System (CA HIPS, www.ca.com), IBM Internet Security Systems' Proventia IPS (www.iss.net), and McAfee's Entercept (www.mcafee.com).

OSSEC (www.ossec.net) is an open-source HIDS product. Although components are available for Linux, Windows, Macintosh, and other operating systems, OSSEC requires one Linux server to act as the central management and reporting console.

WinSNORT (www.winsnort.com) is free HIDS which implements the SNORT intrusion detection application on a Windows system. WinSNORT relies on various third-party add-on products, including WinPcap, MySQL, PHP, and the Apache Web server.

Tripwire is sometimes described as a HIDS solution, and it is available in both open-source (http://sourceforge.net/projects/tripwire/) and commercial (www.tripwire.com) versions. However, it is primarily a configuration-change monitoring product. In other words, it will monitor systems for configuration changes but will not necessarily perform other HIDS operations, such as monitoring log files, detecting attacks, and so forth.

Do it!

C-2: Comparing host-based and network intrusion detection systems

Questions and answers

1 Considering the following diagram, what portion of the network would be protected by the NIDS?

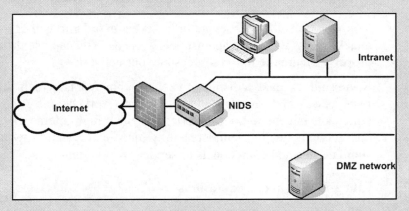

2 Considering the diagram in the previous step, would the NIDS detect internal or external attacks?

3 Is the location of the NIDS in the preceding diagram optimal?

4 In this example, would the server on the perimeter network be better protected by a HIDS than by the NIDS as shown?

Honeypots and honeynets

Explanation

Honeypots are systems specifically designed to deceive or trap attackers. A honeypot appears to be a vulnerable system offering legitimate data and resources, when in fact it is simply a decoy. When an attacker compromises the honeypot, a log of all actions is recorded for later forensics. A *honeynet* is a network that's been designed to deceive or trap attackers. The same principles apply, but they apply to a network, not to a single device.

You would deploy a honeypot or honeynet in order to gather information on the types of attacks being attempted against your systems. You can use the information you gather to properly secure the real resources on your network.

Some sources make a distinction between honeypots, which simulate servers, and client honeypots, which simulate end-user (client) workstations or applications. Furthermore, honeypots in general are categorized as either high-interaction or low-interaction. High-interaction honeypots simulate a fully functional system; low-interaction honeypots simulate selected components or services of a system.

Ethics and legal considerations

Honeypots and honeynets are not commonly used in corporate networks, in part over fears of the legal and public relations implications. Some people believe that deploying a honeypot or honeynet is a form of entrapment. Others believe that the presence of a honeypot or honeynet doesn't cause an innocent person to launch an attack, but instead simply attracts the attention of someone already intent on attacking your network. Therefore, these people regard these devices not as entrapment but more like a "speed trap," used by the police to catch unlawful drivers.

Honeypots and honeynets are more commonly used by security researchers. Specifically, firms that monitor security and develop security products use both devices to learn of new attack techniques.

Honeypot and honeynet examples

Much information about honeypots and honeynets is available. Selected commercial and open-source honeypots are listed in the following table.

Honeypot	License	Description
HoneyPoint	Commercial, closed source	The HoneyPoint family of products from MicSolved, Inc., offers various honeypot configuration options. For more information, see www.microsolved.com.
Symantec Decoy Server	Commercial, closed source	Part of Symantec's Intrusion Detection package, Decoy Server is a commercially supported honeypot system. For more information, see www.symantec.com.
Specter	Commercial, closed source	Specter, from Network Security Software, runs on a Windows host and simulates servers running Windows, Linux, Macintosh, and other operating systems. For more information, see www.specter.com.
PacketDecoy	Commercial, closed source	PacketDecoy is a honeypot system from Palisade Systems, Inc. For more information, see www.palisadesys.com.
HoneyBot	Free, closed source	HoneyBot is a free but closed-source honeypot from Atomic Software Solutions (www.atomicsoftwaresolutions.com). Unlike many of the other options, HoneyBot runs on Windows.
Honeyd	Free, open source	This is a Linux daemon that runs on a single host yet simulates multiple virtual computers, each of which can be configured as a distinct honeypot.
Project Honey Pot	Free, open source	This is an anti-spam project that seeks to identify spammers by tracking which systems are gathering e-mail addresses from Web pages. This organization also provides software tools. For more information, see www.projecthoneypot.org.

In addition to those listed in the table, you can use virtualization products, such as VMWare or Citrix XenServer, to create virtual hosts that you configure as honeypots. User Mode Linux can likewise be configured to simulate systems for the purpose of creating honeypots.

To read and share information about honeynets around the world, visit honeynet.org. The Honeynet Project is a global security research project that seeks to discover new forms of attacks and to share information about the attacks and how to prevent them.

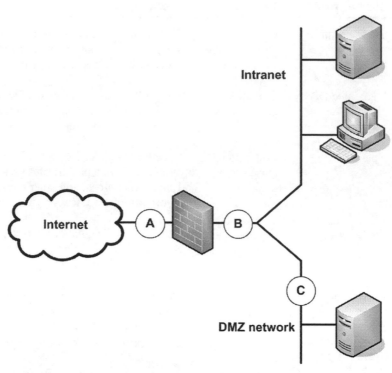

Exhibit 12-5: Honeypot deployment

Deployment

Where you install a honeypot or honeynet determines what types of attacks it will intercept. Depending on your needs, you might install a honeypot or honeynet outside of your firewall to capture attack attempts coming from the Internet. Such placement would not capture attacks from within your network, however.

You could put both a honeypot and a honeynet on your perimeter network, hoping to capture attacks targeting servers on that network. With this location, though, you would not capture attacks aimed at your external firewall, nor would you capture internal attacks against resources not part of your perimeter network.

There is no perfect location for either a honeypot or a honeynet. Where you put them will depend on where you think attacks are most likely to originate and what they will target.

Honeypots and honeynets need to be populated with enticing data, something that will attract an attacker. Additionally, they must attract without alerting the hacker to their true purpose. Some attackers might be wary of a system with absolutely no security. Surveillance components must be sufficiently hidden to avoid detection by the attacker.

Finally, you want to make sure that your honeypots and honeynets are not staging grounds for attacks against the real systems on your network. You must take care to configure the system such that when it is compromised, the attacker does not gain privileges that would give him access to legitimate systems on your network. You must monitor your honeypots and honeynets frequently to detect and act upon attacks.

Do it!

C-3:   Examining the role and use of honeypots and honeynets

Questions and answers

1 Why might you choose a commercial versus open-source honeypot system?

2 Consider this scenario: The servers on your network have been repeatedly attacked by unknown hackers in recent weeks. You have applied various patches and reconfigured security settings. But based on log entries, it's obvious that attackers are still gaining access to the systems. How would a honeynet offer advantages over an intrusion detection system to thwart future attacks?

3 Where would you locate a honeypot in your network?

Topic D: Incident response

This topic covers the following CompTIA Security+ objectives for exam SY0-301.

#	Objective
2.3	**Execute appropriate incident response procedures**
	• Basic forensic procedures
	– Order of volatility
	– Capture system image
	– Network traffic and logs
	– Capture video
	– Record time offset
	– Take hashes
	– Screenshots
	– Witnesses
	– Track man hours and expense
	• Damage and loss control
	• Chain of custody
	• Incident response: first responder
3.6	**Analyze and differentiate among types of mitigation and deterrent techniques**
	• Security posture
	– Remediation

Computer forensics

Explanation

Forensics is the science of investigating an event in the context of a legal action. Computer forensics is typically taken to mean an investigation of a security incident, typically for the purpose of taking legal or procedural actions following an attack.

For example, you might use forensics to gather the information necessary to prosecute an attacker or to discipline an employee who attacked your systems. You might also use the information gathered during forensics to improve the security of your systems.

The goal of forensics is to create a record of the facts that can be used in a legal or procedural action. In other words, you must gather all the facts in an unbiased manner. You must preserve logs and other records in such a manner that these facts can be used in legal or civil proceedings. And finally, you must gather information in a timely manner—before it is overwritten or becomes legally unusable (for example, due to a statute-of-limitations deadline).

The forensics process

There are generally four stages to computer forensics:

1 Preparation
2 Collection
3 Analysis
4 Reporting

Preparation

This stage refers to the preparation of the examiner, not of the specific investigation at hand. This stage would include training, certification, and ongoing learning about the forensics tools and procedures used within your industry for the specific incident under investigation.

Security teams sometimes include "first responders," who react to alarms or alerts set off by an IDS. Their responsibilities are to quickly stop an ongoing attack and to implement damage and loss control measures. Such investigators must be properly trained in forensics techniques so that they are aware of the implications of their actions. Whenever possible, their goal should be to preserve data so that it can be used as part of a forensics investigation.

Additionally, you should track the number of hours expended during the incident response and any expenses involved. This information will help assess the total impact to the organization and help in budgeting for future incident responses.

Collection

The collection stage is also an ongoing process, usually accomplished by the recording of log files, screenshots, system images, video images, network traffic data, and system state data and the gathering of reports from intrusion detection systems and honeypots or honeynets. This stage can also include the collection of data from other forms of hardware, including RFID tags, "black box" recording devices like those used in airplanes, and environmental monitoring devices, such as shock sensors and recording thermometers.

When collecting data, you should apply the principle of *order of volatility*, which states that you should focus your collection efforts first on the data that is most volatile, because it will disappear quickly. Generally speaking, the following list outlines the order of volatility of some common elements, from most volatile to least volatile, from nanoseconds to years:

1 Memory and caches
2 Swap files
3 Network state
4 System state of individual computers (including processes)
5 Hard disks
6 Floppy disks, USB drives, tape drives
7 CDs, DVDs, printed documents

Another valuable source of information will be the people involved in the incident. Interviews should be conducted in an open environment, with witnesses, and you should record the interview for later examination and verification.

When possible, timestamps, hashes, witness statements, and other ways of authenticating the collected data should be used. Your goal is to create a legally defensible claim that the data you have collected is complete and unaltered. Also, when you're dealing with systems in multiple time zones, record time offsets to get an accurate timeline in a specific time zone, usually one that encompasses the location of your investigation.

Analysis

Analysis is the active stage of examining the evidence to determine the means and scope of an attack. This is the stage most people probably think of when they envision a forensics investigation.

Analysis can be carried out through "manual" means, such as reading log files, examining Registry settings, and so forth. You can also use various tools to automate the process and generate a more easily understood format for non-technical investigators.

Attacks often leave traces in altered files or log entries. Sometimes, though, the only evidence of an attack exists in volatile storage locations, such as a computer's memory or temporary files. "Dead" analysis refers to analyzing stored data, such as log files. "Live" analysis refers to examining an in-use system so that you can access information in volatile memory locations.

Reporting

Reporting is the final stage of the process. You might generate a written report describing the incident and evidence, along with the money and person-hours spent on the investigation, as part of the calculation of the total financial impact of the incident. You could also consider the presentation of evidence to law enforcement and regulatory agencies and court testimony to be part of the reporting phase.

Evidence-gathering principles

You should not engage in forensics or investigations unless you have the legal authority to do so. Furthermore, forensics should be performed only by specially trained personnel if you intend to use the results in any legal actions. Investigations by untrained or uncertified personnel might not be legally admissible in court.

In general, you should following these guidelines when investigating an incident:

- "Touch" (access or manipulate) the original evidence as little as possible to minimize the chances that your actions will change that data. When possible, work on a copy of the original evidence rather than the original.

- Before an investigation, establish procedures that clearly define who will do the investigation, who will "own" the data, what steps will be taken, and what information will be documented.

- Document everything that you do during the investigation.

- Use only techniques and tools that have been tested and accepted for use in forensics within your industry.

The chain of custody

The chain of custody is a process used to track and document who has handled evidence, when, and why. You should generate and record a chain of custody with all information gathered during your investigation. This information would typically include:

- The person or persons who discovered the evidence and the precise time they made the discovery.

- The location from which the information was collected. You should be specific, including not only the computer or device from which you gathered the data, but also the specific log file, memory location, temporary file name, and so forth.

- The precise time the information was collected.

- The names of any and all individuals who accessed and had access to both the original evidence and any copies of it during the investigation.

- The names of the people who "owned" the evidence at every stage of the investigation, and a record of precisely when such ownership changed. A legally admissible signature (a written signature or a digital certificate) should be associated with each custody change.

Remediation

After the investigation is completed and you've created a report, it's the perfect time to create a remediation plan, which will incorporate ways to enhance your organization's security and help prevent any further security incidents. The plan can include any of the security measures you learn about in this course, including:

- Installing and updating antivirus software on clients, servers, and other network devices

- Disabling unused ports and services on servers and devices

- Instituting strict controls on wired and wireless access and on remote network access

- Updating the operating systems with security patches

- Tightly controlling access to resources through user, group, and role-based access control

- Continuous monitoring, using logs and intrusion detection systems

- Enhancing physical security by using alarms, security guards, fencing, locks, access control systems, lighting, and video surveillance

Although security incidents can have a big impact on your organization, you need to take the opportunity they present to learn where to enhance security to prevent any further attacks. Security incidents can provide valuable learning experiences.

Do it! **D-1:** **Examining the forensics process**

Questions and answers

1 Of the stages of the forensics process, is any one stage more or less important than the others?

2 Speculate on various types of devices or systems from which you could collect data for a forensics investigation and that are not listed in the preceding concepts.

3 Your IDS alerts your first-response team that an attack is underway against one of your file servers. List at least one action this team should take to both limit loss and preserve evidence for a forensics investigation.

4 Whom should you report an attack to?

5 What is the purpose or significance of maintaining a chain of custody during a forensics investigation?

6 What steps should you take after a security incident?

Unit summary: Vulnerability testing and monitoring

Topic A   In this topic, you learned how to perform vulnerability and penetration testing. You learned about **assessment types**, and the procedure you should employ for **vulnerability testing**. You learned about different types of vulnerability testing tools, including **port scanners** and **network mappers**. You then learned about **penetration testing** and how to approach it in your organization.

Topic B   In this topic, you learned how to read **log files** to look for events that might indicate a security incident. You learned about different types of log files, and you read some sample logs and alerts.

Topic C   In this topic, you learned about **intrusion detection systems**, including host-based and network intrusion detection systems. You learned that these systems monitor events on your devices and the network to alert you to security intrusions.

Topic D   In this topic, you learned how to investigate security incidents by using standard **forensics procedures**. You learned about what type of information to gather, how to gather it, and how to preserve a **chain of custody** for possible criminal prosecutions. You also learned how to create a **remediation plan** to enhance security and help prevent future security breaches.

Review questions

1   Name a free vulnerability scanner.

2   The Mitre Corporation manages the _____ project, which is sponsored by the U.S. Department of Homeland Security.

3   Which is worse, a true positive or false negative event?

4   During a computer forensics examination, you should maintain a clear and documented _____ for all information you gather.

5   True or false? You have to place a NIDS on your perimeter network.

6   List at least one action that a HIDS can take when it detects an attack.

7   When performing computer forensics, you should _____ the original evidence as little as possible.

8 Describe the essential differences between a network intrusion detection system (NIDS) and a host-based intrusion detection system (HIDS).

9 What are the differences between high-interaction and low-interaction honeypots?

10 True or false? All organizations have the same tolerance for risk and loss.

11 If you placed a honeypot outside your firewall, what types of attackers might you catch?

12 Name the four steps of the computer forensics process.

13 List at least five devices from which you could collect useful information for a computer forensics examination.

Independent practice activity

In this activity, you will perform a penetration test by using Nmap.

1 From your instructor, obtain the necessary computer name or IP address information for a computer to scan.

2 On your Windows client, start Nmap and initiate an intense scan of the system.

3 Create a report detailing the information you've discovered, including open ports, services, and any details about the computer.

4 What recommendations would you make for creating a more secure computer?

5 Close Nmap.

Unit 13

Organizational security

Unit time: 60 minutes

Complete this unit, and you'll know how to:

A Create organizational policies.

B Identify the educational and training needs of users and administrators.

C Properly dispose of or destroy IT equipment and data.

Topic A: Organizational policies

This topic covers the following CompTIA Security+ objectives for exam SY0-301.

#	Objective

2.1	**Explain risk-related concepts**
	• Control types
	  – Technical
	  – Management
	  – Operational
	• Importance of policies in reducing risk
	  – Privacy policy
	  – Acceptable use
	  – Security policy
	  – Mandatory vacations
	  – Job rotation
	  – Separation of duties
	  – Least privilege
	• Risk calculation
	  – Likelihood
	  – ALE
	  – Impact
	• Quantitative vs. qualitative
	• Risk avoidance, transference, acceptance, mitigation, deterrence

2.2	**Carry out appropriate risk mitigation strategies** • Implement security controls based on risk • Change management • Incident management • User rights and permissions reviews • Perform routine audits • Implement policies and procedures to prevent data loss or theft
2.8	**Exemplify the concepts of confidentiality, integrity, and availability (CIA)**
5.2	**Explain the fundamental concepts and best practices related to authentication, authorization, and access control** • Least privilege • Separation of duties • Time-of-day restrictions • Mandatory vacations • Job rotation

The CIA triad

Explanation The core principles of information security are confidentiality, integrity, and availability (CIA). This group of three principles has been called the CIA triad.

- **Confidentiality** — The systems you implement to ensure that information is not disclosed to unauthorized people or systems.

- **Integrity** — The systems you implement to ensure that data and programs cannot be altered without that modification being detectable.

- **Availability** — The systems you implement to ensure that information is available when needed.

Modern security professionals have extended the triad to include three additional principles. These are:

- **Possession** — The systems you put in place to ensure that you remain in possession of information. The loss of possession might not indicate a security breach, but it would lead to the potential for a breach.

- **Authenticity** — The systems you implement to ensure that information can be traced back to its originator. This principle includes non-repudiation, meaning that the creator cannot disclaim ownership.

- **Utility** — The systems you implement to ensure that information remains useful and accessible. For example, you might have a key management server that helps make sure you don't lose encryption keys. Without these keys, you might still have your original information, but it would be useless.

The original triad plus the three new facets make up the *Parkerian hexad*. Not all security professionals agree with all components of the hexad. Other than introducing them here, we won't cover them.

Exemplifying the CIA triad

The systems and techniques you have learned about during this course can generally be classified as implementing one of the three CIA principles. Many such systems cover more than one component of the triad. The following table describes one possible way to correlate those systems with the three CIA principles.

Principle	Systems you use to implement this principle
Confidentiality	User accounts, file permissions, access control lists, data encryption, privacy policies, and so forth.
Integrity	File hashes and checksums, digital signatures, encryption, and so forth.
Availability	Backups, server clusters, cloud computing, RAID drives, failover network links, backup power supplies, and so forth.

Control types

Another way to look at security and systems is to examine control types. *Control types* are the systems you put in place to prevent loss, minimize risks, or prevent a breach. These controls can be categorized in various ways.

CompTIA defines three control types, described in the following table:

Control type	Generally encompasses...
Technical	Authentication systems, anti-malware tools, encryption, firewalls and network controls, and so forth.
Management	Management oversight, security awareness and training, policies and the systems you use to review or create policies, and so forth.
Operational	Procedures for day-to-day actions and for responding to incidents; procedures for data retention and destruction; records, reports, and audits; and personnel identification and security vetting.

Risk assessment

Before putting any controls in place, you should calculate your risks and tailor your responses accordingly. You should consider both the likelihood of an incident and its impact. Your response to an unlikely but devastating breach will be different from your reaction to a likely but minor incident. Within reason, you should be prepared to handle both extremes.

Some security professionals make a distinction between qualitative and quantitative assessments. In practical terms, the biggest distinction is that quantitative assessments attempt to assign financial values to assets (information, equipment, personnel, reputation, and so forth) and to their loss or damage. Qualitative assessments might simply describe the downtime that could occur or the reputation loss that might happen. Qualitative assessments are useful, but they probably won't help you justify the budget expenditures needed to reduce security risks.

Some organizations attempt to calculate an *Annual Loss Expectancy* (ALE) value. (Another term for this valuation is the Estimated Annual Cost, or EAC.) The ALE value is the product of the costs of individual incidents times their annual rate of occurrence. If you examine the math, you can see that a high-cost, infrequent incident could have the same ALE as a low-cost, frequent incident. Calculating your ALE will help you justify the expense of implementing security controls.

Having quantifiable values associated with losses is critical to stressing the importance of security within your organization. For example, you should attempt to place dollar costs on such factors as downtime, lost productivity, lost market opportunities, and even employee consequences (loss of morale or maybe even loss of key employees). Some such costs will be difficult to calculate. Others, such as the cost of downtime, can be as simple as multiplying staff salaries by the number of hours of downtime slipping away while employees sit idly by, watching a hacked system being rebuilt.

Risk avoidance

You might think that the most logical way to reduce the costs associated with security is to prevent all incidents. However, your risk assessment calculations (whether qualitative or quantitative) will likely lead you to conclude that other strategies can be more cost-effective.

Instead of avoiding all risks, you might implement one of these other strategies:

Strategy	Description
Transference	You transfer the risks, costs, or responsibilities to another party. For example, you might place the burden of security on your business partners, customers, or service providers.
Acceptance	Perhaps the most obvious strategy is to simply accept the risks. For incidents with a low risk or low cost, you might simply want to deal with the consequences if they arise.
Deterrence	You can impose consequences that would discourage potential security breaches. HR policies that include termination clauses are a great example of a deterrence technique. Employees are discouraged from taking certain actions because of the threat of job loss.
Mitigation	You can make plans to minimize the impact and costs of a loss or security breach. For example, backups of critical data minimize the impact of a failed hard drive.

Do it!

A-1: Examining CIA, controls, and risk assessment

Questions	Answers
1 What techniques have you learned so far during this course that would enable you to implement the CIA triad?	
2 Describe the differences between technical, management, and operational controls.	
3 Give an example of a likely breach that has minimal consequences.	
What might your mitigation strategy and responses be to this type of incident?	
4 Give an example of an unlikely but significant breach.	
What might your mitigation strategy and responses be to this type of incident?	
5 Give an example when transference is a better strategy than risk avoidance.	

Security policies

Explanation
Every organization should have a well-defined security policy, as well as a human resources policy that outlines and defines the organization's commitment to information security. Working together, the Information Technology staff and senior management create the security policy. It defines rules and practices the organization puts in place to manage and protect information within the organization.

The security policy document defines the security program's policy goals and identifies who is responsible for making sure those goals are achieved. The security policy document should include sections covering:

- Acceptable use
- Due care
- Privacy
- Separation of duties
- Need-to-know information
- Password management
- Account expiration
- Service-level agreements
- Methods of properly destroying or disposing of equipment, media, and printed documents

Part of a sample security policy is shown in Exhibit 13-1.

XYZ, Inc., Security Policy

Each individual employee of XZY, Inc., has the responsibility to protect the informational assets of the organization, along with all intellectual property of the organization. These assets need to be protected to reduce the potential negative impact on XYZ's clients. The security of information is critical and should be integrated into all facets of XZY's operations.

To ensure that these objectives are met, policies and procedures have been developed to ensure that secure practices are used at XZY. Information security is a high priority at XZY, and detailed procedures have been developed to secure the information.

XZY is required to abide by specific privacy laws and regulations defined by state and federal laws. Failure to abide by these regulations might result in fines, legal actions, or audits, and customer confidence could be affected; this could result in direct financial losses to the organization. Every employee of XZY must therefore be responsible for obeying all pertinent laws and regulations.

Exhibit 13-1: A sample security policy

Acceptable use

Acceptable-use policies define how an organization's computer equipment and network resources can be used. The main goal is to protect the organization's information and to limit the potential liabilities and legal action against the organization and its employees. This policy also might address employee productivity as it relates to Internet use.

The misuse of computer resources and its impact on business activity can affect the productivity of an organization and its staff. Many people use their employer's Internet connection for personal use, and it is important that they not use this connection to access resources that might reflect poorly on the organization. The time spent on personal Internet use can have a big impact on productivity and lead to loss of revenue for the organization. Furthermore, proprietary information might be compromised if users share sensitive information with external parties or visit sexually explicit or socially unacceptable Web pages. An organization could be held legally responsible for agreements made by someone using an e-mail address from the organization.

The acceptable-use policy needs to identify whether specific actions are appropriate uses of company resources and time. Reading and signing the policy document should be required when employees are hired. A copy of the signed document should be retained. Employees should be required to periodically re-sign the policy to refresh its importance in everyone's minds. If there is reason to believe that a violation has occurred, this document will help absolve the organization of responsibility in the matter. The measures for enforcing the policy also need to be documented so that all employees are aware of the consequences of their actions.

Due care

The exercise of judgment or care in a given circumstance is known as *due care* or *due diligence*. It identifies the risks to the organization and assesses those risks and the measures employees need to take to ensure the security of the organization's information.

If a major security incident occurred within the organization, the organization might be sued by customers, business partners, shareholders, and others who were negatively affected by the incident. Creating and abiding by a strong security policy helps an organization prove that due care was exercised and thus can help protect the organization from legal actions against it.

Privacy

Security policies also need to address the privacy and protection of customer and supplier information. Trust between the organization and external entities can be strengthened when both parties know that the information is secure. Because the external entities' information could be highly sensitive, it is imperative that the organization show its respect for this information. It might include contracts, sales documents, financial data, or personally identifiable information. If the information is compromised, then not only might the entities lose trust in an organization, but they might also take legal action against it for exposing their information.

Separation of duties

In any situation in which too much responsibility for a process falls to one person, there is the potential for abuse. If the function is too valuable to do without, as with protecting an organization's information assets, then it is imperative that no one person is given the power to abuse the trust that others place in the information's security.

No one in the organization should be irreplaceable, because eventually, people leave, and the smoother the transition, the better. Sometimes employees purposely document their work poorly so that it will be harder to replace them. The company might face a dilemma: pay this person what he or she demands, or face possible problems when this person leaves. The best strategy is to make sure the next person does not leave you in such a predicament.

Another reason to separate duties is that if the person with all of the knowledge of a certain area or function suddenly leaves the company or dies in a tragic accident, then that knowledge is gone with the person. Someone else would have to quickly take over the position, possibly without adequate training, leaving the information vulnerable to attack while the new person learns the job.

Distributing security tasks throughout the IT staff and documenting all procedures can help prevent such problems. Job rotation is another means to distribute knowledge and competence. For example, some companies require employees in critical positions to rotate assignments every couple of years. Mandatory vacation policies force organizations to manage the problems that can arise when knowledge and competence must be shared.

Time-of-day restrictions prevent employees from using accounts and systems during their non-standard work hours. Such restrictions can help separate duties, blocking people from doing the jobs that others should be doing, and prevent the burnout that comes from working long shifts. Of course, you'll need a mechanism for exceptions, such as when an administrator switches shifts to help a fellow employee meet the mandatory vacation requirements.

The security function should be separated into multiple elements. Each of those elements is part of making the whole security structure work, and each element can be assigned to a different person or group of persons. This strategy helps prevent the abuse of power and ensures that you have someone in place if one person suddenly becomes unavailable.

Need to know

In the case of very sensitive information, only those who absolutely must have access to the data should have it. This kind of data is referred to as *need-to-know information*. The goal is to make unauthorized access highly unlikely, without unduly hassling users who do have authorized access.

Giving employees on the IT team just enough permissions to perform their duties is an example of where this strategy might come into play. This *least privilege* basis of access prevents an employee from putting the company at risk. Users should be given permission to access only the information they need to do their jobs. For example, not every employee needs access to the organization's marketing plan, and certainly most employees don't need access to HR or IT databases. Those employees who do need access to that information should be given explicit access.

Password management

Passwords can be used on workstations, networks, Web sites, and even on entry doors. If passwords are compromised, the company's information and network assets are at risk. Implementing a strong password policy should be an important part of your organization's security policies. The policy must be clear to users so that they can adhere to it and create strong passwords.

Password policies should address several attributes, including:

- Minimum password length
- Required characters (minimum number of alphabetic, numeric, and/or special characters)
- Password reset interval (how long the password is valid before it must be changed)
- Reuse of passwords, including variations of existing passwords

The policy should also address users' handling of their passwords. The policy should state the consequences of revealing a password to someone, under what circumstances it can be done, and what to do after it has been revealed. For example, if the IT technician needs the password to troubleshoot a user's e-mail problem, then using a secure method, the user can give the technician the password; when the technician is finished, the user needs to immediately change the password.

When feasible, use group policies to set domain password policies in Active Directory. The network administrator or security management team should routinely check for weak passwords. Administrators can use password cracking tools to locate any weak passwords. If any are found, the users should be notified immediately, and measures should be taken to reset the passwords and to teach the users how to create strong passwords.

Account expiration

Unneeded user accounts must be deleted, or at least disabled, soon after they become unnecessary. Some systems enable you to automatically disable unused accounts. For example, if a user doesn't log on for 30 days, the account is automatically disabled. You should implement such a feature, if available, or routinely scan for unused accounts, especially those associated with former staff.

Obviously, your expiration period will need to take into account vacations, holidays, sabbaticals, maternity leave, and so forth. However, it is not uncommon for accounts to be disabled (but not deleted) during extended leaves.

Service-level agreements

A *service-level agreement* (SLA) is a contract documenting the level of service that a provider is expected to deliver to end-users. This binding document specifies the service levels for support and documents any penalties to be incurred if the services are not provided. Disaster recovery plans also need to be documented in the SLA.

In addition, contingency plans are needed in case the provider is unable to meet its obligations. This might happen if the entire area is in the midst of a weather-related event that is preventing local service providers from responding. Plans for ensuring business continuity during the initial recovery period should be covered as well.

Disposal and destruction

It is just as important to secure discarded and unused documents and equipment as it is to secure them while they are in use. Simply deleting files or reformatting disks doesn't eradicate all of the information.

Magnetic media should be *degaussed*, which demagnetizes the media and thus makes anything on them unreadable. An alternative approach is to overwrite all of the data with zeros; this process is referred to as *zeroization*. If neither of these methods is enough to ensure the safety of your organization's information, you can physically destroy the media by breaking them apart and making them unusable. Sometimes all of these techniques are used together to ensure that nobody will have a chance to read data on those media ever again.

Paper copies of important information also need to be destroyed. Documents should be placed in locked recycle bins and then shredded or burned, or both. Document shredding companies can be hired to do the shredding. Under the supervision of someone from the organization, a bonded and insured technician shreds the documents on site. The documents are shredded into the smallest possible pieces so that the documents have no chance of being pieced back together.

Not all data deserves the same level of protection. Some data is simply not that critical or secret. Likewise, not all obsolete data and equipment deserve the same disposal treatment. You should classify data and equipment according to their protection and disposal needs.

Those items that contain sensitive or secret information warrant more thorough destruction practices. For example, you might be able to get away with simply erasing less-sensitive information from a hard drive. But you would need to physically destroy obsolete hard drives containing your company's financial records. Handling disposal according to your classifications can save money and ensure that you have the resources to properly dispose of the most sensitive items.

Do it!

A-2: Creating a security policy

Questions and answers

1 What is the purpose of acceptable-use policies?

2 Why is the separation of duties an important measure to consider when developing a security policy?

3 What is the purpose of due care?

4 A password policy should include which of the following attributes?

    A   Minimum length

    B   Allowed character set

    C   Disallowed strings

    D   Duration of use of the password

    E   All of the above

5 When you're setting an account expiration policy, what factors should you consider?

6 What is the purpose of an SLA, and what are the typical contents?

7 Why is it important to classify information?

8 List some types of sensitive or secret personal information that the company and employees should not divulge.

Human resources policies

Explanation
Redundant knowledge is as important as redundant hardware. If staffing places all of the knowledge about the organization's security policies in one person's hands, and something happens to that person, then nobody else will know what to do. The knowledge should be shared by several staff members through cross-training of the technology staff.

Another thing to consider is how to manually perform the duties that are usually automated. Whenever possible, manual procedures should be documented for business continuity in case an incident renders hardware unavailable. These manually performed duties might need to be added to the job descriptions of IT staff.

The HR policy should also address such issues as the use of ID badges, keys, and restricted-access areas. Security personnel not only need to follow such policies, but also must be able to help enforce them to ensure the security of the organization and its information.

Three aspects of personnel management should be considered. The HR policy should document the procedures for hiring, employee review and maintenance, and employee termination. The employee's status on the security team should be thoroughly checked at each of those stages.

Hiring

When you're hiring for a network administrator or security team staff position, it is imperative that you perform a complete background check on the potential candidate. This includes doing reference checks (including character references), checking with past employers, doing criminal checks, and verifying certifications and degrees the candidate claims to possess.

Employee review and maintenance

Periodic reviews should be conducted for all employees, and especially for those who are responsible for the security of your organization's network and information. The employees' performance can be evaluated, and any potential security risks arising from their performance can be identified. Security clearances should be evaluated and any necessary changes should be made immediately. An employee might need higher or lower security access, depending on the job duties.

Policies regarding job rotation, time off, and separation of duties should be implemented. At review meetings, a supervisor can determine which jobs an employee has knowledge of, which jobs need to be learned, and whether any skills need to be refreshed. Another thing to check during reviews is whether the employee has been using her vacation time, as outlined in the HR policies, to get periodic breaks.

It is important that employees not get burned out, which would make them less effective in carrying out their duties. Mandatory vacations can ensure that employees take the time off that they should. Maintaining a separation of duties can help ensure that one person doesn't have too much power, which could be abused.

Post-employment

The HR policy should document the procedures to be taken when someone's employment is terminated. Part of the process should be an exit interview with an HR staff member. This meeting should be conducted in a friendly, professional manner.

Angry employees might act out against the company and could threaten the security of the network and of proprietary information. For this reason, security badges, keys, and other access devices should be retrieved from any employee leaving the organization. After the exit interview, a manager, security guard, or HR representative should escort the employee to clean out his or her personal belongings and then escort the person from the premises.

All of the employee's accounts should be disabled at this time as well. Any shared passwords need to be changed immediately.

The code of ethics

A code of ethics helps define the organization's information security policies. The code of ethics requests that all personnel be responsible, act legally, and be honest; these actions help protect the organization. The code of ethics should also document certain aspects of conduct, such as employees providing proficient service to all persons they come into contact with while performing their professional duties. By being ethical in the performance of their duties, the employees help prove the reliability of the organization to customers, suppliers, and other employees.

Do it!   **A-3:   Creating a human resources policy**

Questions and answers

1   Why should periodic reviews be part of a human resources policy?

2   How does job rotation help minimize security risks?

3   What is a benefit of the separation of duties?

4   Why would forcing staff members to take a vacation benefit an organization, particularly from a security standpoint?

5   Identify the tasks that your human resources policy should address when an employee is terminated.

6   Explain why a code of ethics in a human resources policy can help maintain information security.

Incident response policies

Explanation
A security breach or disaster should be dealt with by following the plans described in the *incident response policy*. An incident is an event that adversely affects the network. Incidents might include viruses, system failures, unauthorized access, service disruptions, and any attempts to violate the organization's security policies.

There can be significant legal consequences, depending on how people and automatic processes respond to an incident. Client information must be handled with due care so as not to compromise privileged information. An incident that isn't quickly brought under control can quickly turn expensive and complicated. A rise in incident occurrences can sometimes be linked to the incompetent handling of an initial incident.

By developing and implementing a solid incident response plan, the organization increases the probability that incidents will be handled properly. A well-thought-out incident response plan helps the organization exercise due care.

A solid incident response policy addresses six areas:

1 Preparation
2 Detection
3 Containment
4 Eradication
5 Recovery
6 Follow-up

Preparation

It is important that you have steps in place to cope with an incident before it occurs. Resources need to be made available to quickly and efficiently respond to an incident.

It is equally important to balance easy access to system resources with effective system controls that help prevent incidents. Having resources in place to balance these two diverse conditions is part of the preparation phase. Resources used to respond to an incident need to be resistant to attacks as well.

The preparation section of the incident response document needs to identify the steps to be taken by the incident response team and in which circumstances the steps should be taken. The document should also list the team members, their contact information, and the information that needs to be shared with each team member.

Acceptable risks should be documented in the preparation section. The document should also identify the dedicated hardware and software to be used for analysis and forensics after the incident. All incident response team members need to be trained in handling incidents.

Doing due diligence as part of the preparation phase will help the organization carry on if an incident occurs. A documented contingency plan will help the organization get through the trying time a data disaster brings. Determining tolerable risk levels will also help the organization plan for a successful incident response if the time comes when it must be implemented.

Preparation can also include preventative measures, such as routine security audits. You should routinely review technical controls, such as user rights and permissions and system security. You should also routinely review management and operational controls, such as updating your security policies and incident response procedures.

Detection

The first action the incident response team needs to take when an incident occurs is to assess the state of affairs and then try to figure out what might have caused the incident. Next, the team needs to estimate the scope of the incident in order to figure out how to deal with it. The team needs to ask questions and document the responses to questions, such as:

- How many systems were affected?
- How many networks were affected?
- How far did the intruder get into the internal network?
- What level of privileges was accessed?
- What information and/or systems are at risk?
- How many paths of attack were available?
- Who has knowledge of the incident?
- How extensive is the vulnerability?

The response team needs to document information about the incident. The document needs to be shared with the Chief Information Officer, any personnel affected by the incident, the public relations department, the rest of the incident response team, the legal department, and, if appropriate, any law enforcement or government agencies. The incident response policy should identify what needs to be reported, such as incident details that need to be included in the report, the incident type, the resources being used to deal with the incident, the source of the incident, consequences of the incident, and the sensitivity of any compromised data. The policy should also specify when and how information about the incident is shared.

Containment

For each incident that occurs, you will need to determine which containment techniques to implement. For example, you might need to shut down a system to prevent further damage from occurring. A piece of hardware or a file system might need to be taken offline. You might need to change firewall filtering rules. Login accounts might need to be suspended until the incident is under control. File transfers should be disabled as well.

Monitoring levels should be increased. After an intruder has gained access to your network, it is even more important to keep an eye on what is happening. Doing so will help you determine how deeply into the network the intruder has penetrated.

If the incident is the result of a malicious attack, any compromised equipment or data should not be used until the incident has been resolved. The response team should alert the appropriate people to analyze the incident. Information gathered at this point in the process can be used to identify the perpetrator and to help prevent additional attacks.

Eradication

After the incident has been contained, the incident response team needs to eradicate whatever caused the incident. If the incident was related to viruses or malicious code, the affected files need to be cleaned or deleted. If you need to restore data to drives, first verify that the backups are free of viruses and malicious code.

Recovery

After the incident has been eradicated from the network or system that was compromised, the recovery step of the process can occur. The incident response policy should document where new equipment should be ordered from if any equipment was damaged or compromised. Procedures for quickly replacing equipment should be documented and worked out with suppliers. The organization might make arrangements to obtain borrowed or vendor-sponsored equipment if mission-critical equipment was affected so that the organization can function as close to normally as possible during recovery.

If the file system was affected, you should consider doing a full system restore. This is time-consuming, but it's the best assurance that the network is back to its normal state. Data should be restored from the most recent full backup after you have made sure that it is free of viruses and malicious code. If you use a RAID system, you can attempt to recover data from the redundant drives.

Passwords should be changed after an incident. It is difficult to determine whether an attacker was able to obtain passwords, thus compromising them.

Follow-up

Your incident response policy should include a follow-up step to help the recovery team learn from what happened. The entire process should be documented; this can justify the expense the organization incurs in implementing the security policy and help the incident response team. The incident response documents can be used as training material for new members of the recovery team. The documentation can also be used for any legal proceedings that result from the incident.

Do it!

A-4:   Considering incident response and reporting policies

Questions and answers
1 What are some of the actions that should be part of the incident response preparation phase?
2 Which step comes first: containment or eradication? Why?

3 Identify containment methods that might need to be considered during an incident response.

4 What needs to be done during the recovery phase?

5 What are the benefits of completing the follow-up phase?

6 How might your help desk software, or a specialized incident management application, help you manage incident responses?

Change management

Explanation

Whenever a network change is made, a set of procedures called *change management* is followed. These procedures are developed by the network staff. All changes in the IT infrastructure need to be documented.

The change management process is initiated with a *request for change* (RFC) document. This records the proposed change, the category that the change falls into, and any items the change might affect.

Next, the RFC is sent through an approval process for review. A priority is set, and the task is assigned to whoever will make the change. If the organization decides not to make the change, this decision is documented. Depending on the scope of the RFC, it will be evaluated by an IT manager or by a *change advisory board* (CAB). CABs are formed with representatives from various departments affected by the change, possibly including HR. All of the discussions related to the RFC are documented.

The RFC is scheduled and a proposed completion time is set. The change is then planned, developed, tested, and implemented by the person or team to which the RFC was assigned. All of this is documented in the RFC log.

The change is complete when both the change owner and the requester verify that the change has been successfully implemented. The RFC is reviewed by all parties involved, and the change is closed.

Achieving security through consistency

Develop a change management process for your network. Whenever there are network upgrades—whether patches, the addition of new users, or an updated firewall—you should document the process and procedures. If you are thorough in documenting the process, you limit your security risks. When you add new users to the network, do you always do the same thing? What if you forget a step? Is your security breached? Be methodical and follow a written process.

Change documentation

In addition to architecture documentation, each individual system should have a separate document that describes its initial state and all subsequent changes. This document includes configuration information, a list of patches applied, backup records, and even details about suspected breaches. Printouts of hash results and the system dates of critical system files can be pasted into this document.

System maintenance can be made much smoother with a comprehensive change document. For instance, when a patch is available for an operating system, it typically applies only in certain situations. Manually investigating the applicability of a patch on every possible target system can be very time-consuming; however, if logs are available for reference, the process is much faster and more accurate.

Do it!

A-5:   Examining change management software options

Questions and answers

1   Using your browser and favorite search engine, search for
   change management software

   Example sites you might find include:

   www.sunviewsoftware.com
   www.elite-is.com
   www.tripwire.com
   www.hansky.com

2   What benefits do the publishers claim for their software, compared to using standard office tools (for example, using Microsoft Word documents and e-mail for distribution)?

3   What are the downsides to using a dedicated change management tool instead of standard office tools?

4   Of the tools you examined, is there one or more that you would consider using in your organization?

Topic B: Education and training

This topic covers the following CompTIA Security+ objectives for exam SY0-301.

#	Objective
2.4	**Explain the importance of security-related awareness and training**
	• Security policy training and procedures
	• Personally identifiable information
	• Compliance with laws, best practices, and standards
	• User habits
	– Password behaviors
	– Data handling
	– Clean-desk policies
	– Preventing tailgating
	– Personally owned devices
	• Threat awareness
	– New viruses
	– Phishing attacks
	• Use of social networking and P2P

Education

Explanation

Educating staff about security risks is a cost-effective investment in the organization's protection of information assets. Network administrators and end-users all need to be educated about systems and security to create an environment that prevents the accidental loss of data. Knowledge about the security procedures in place in the organization enables all network users to be part of the organization's security team. This knowledge might also enable a regular user to spot a potential security problem or even a security violation.

As long as they are properly secured, making security policy resources and references available to all employees might give them access to information that wasn't covered during formal training sessions. If the resources and references aren't properly secured, however, an attacker could gain access to the policies and get information on how to bypass security blocks.

The training should be customized to provide the level of knowledge needed by different groups of users. A big-picture level of knowledge of security policies is appropriate for end-users. A detailed level of knowledge is required for administrative users. An exhaustive level of knowledge, including detailed knowledge of all policies and procedures, is required for employees who are in charge of security.

Communication

One of the things users should learn in their security training is what information can be shared and who they can share that information with. Employees also need to know what information should never be shared, such as usernames and passwords.

If a technician needs to help a user troubleshoot a problem, and needs access to the person's username and password, the user should be taught the importance of immediately changing his or her password after the work is completed. Users should also learn that the technician needs to show proof of identity in order to prevent someone posing as a technician from gaining system access. While the technician is working on the system, the user should stay with him or her to make sure that the technician isn't looking through data on the user's computer or on the network.

The training should also include information about social engineering threats, including how they are conducted and what kinds of information attackers are usually seeking. In addition, user training should cover the types of information that might inadvertently be revealed through casual conversation and that an attacker could use to guess a username or password.

User awareness

All staff members should have security training so that they know what measures they should take to help ensure the security of the organization's information. The training should be based on and reflect the policy objectives of the organization.

The following items should be included in user security training:

- The reason for the training
- Whom to contact if people suspect or encounter a security incident, and what actions they are expected to take (or not take) in response to an incident
- Policies regarding the use of systems, information assets, and accounts
- Ways to maintain the security of system accounts (including password policies that dictate complexity, change frequency, prohibitions against sharing, and so forth)
- Policies regarding the installation, removal, and use of applications, databases, and data
- Policies regarding the use of personally owned software and devices, such as cell phones, PDAs, and tablet computers
- Policies regarding the disclosure and sharing of private, personal, and sensitive information, including personally identifying information, financial data, and corporate secrets
- Compliance with laws, best practices, and standards
- Policies regarding use of the Internet, e-mail, social networks, peer-to-peer (P2P) systems, and so forth
- Policies related to the access, labeling, handling, and control of media and data
- Approved techniques for sanitizing (degaussing, overwriting, or destroying) media and paper documents
- Threat awareness, including such threats as viruses and social engineering attacks, such as tailgating and phishing

To reinforce formal training, users can be kept aware of the information presented in the training sessions. You can remind users of the security policies through such means as logon banners, system access forms, and departmental bulletins.

Do it!

B-1: Identifying the need for user education and training

Questions and answers
1 How important is it that end-users are educated about security issues?
2 How can training about security help users keep information secure?
3 List some of the topics that should be covered in end-user targeted security training.
4 Identify some of the ways users might be reminded periodically of the information learned in formal security training.

Types of training

Explanation

There are a variety of ways that personnel can be trained. Some training might be delivered on the job, in a classroom, or in an online training format. Different kinds of information might be best delivered in different ways. Some people might find one format more beneficial to their learning style than other formats.

On-the-job training

Nobody wants to have to deal with a security incident, but when one does occur, you should take advantage of the experience to learn all you can about it. You need to know how to detect the incident, how to respond, how to clean it up, and how to recover from it. The next time a similar incident occurs, you'll have learned how to deal with it.

Documenting the steps taken in response to the incident serves as training as well. The act of recording this information helps reinforce it, and you have the information in case the incident happens again. The information can also be used as an example in other training, such as classroom or online training sessions.

An advantage of on-the-job training is that it lets new personnel get hands-on experience in dealing with incidents. Without some additional training, however, it will sometimes be difficult for new staff members to be effective.

Classroom training

A course such as the one you are taking right now is a good investment in training administrative personnel in how to keep the network secure. A course based on incidences that have occurred in your organization is also beneficial. It can be difficult to fit such classroom training into a busy IT person's schedule, but the time and investment will pay off with people knowing how to secure the network and how to react when an incident does occur.

An advantage of classroom training is that students can share their experiences. Especially in a public class with students from various organizations, one or more students might have experienced a security incident and could share how they dealt with it.

Online resources

Because it can be difficult to gather personnel together to deliver classroom training, online delivery can be an effective training method. Policy and procedure training can also be delivered online.

You might have someone create training documents and store them in a network location to which users and/or IT personnel have access. You could also consider storing the organization's security and disaster recovery policies and procedures on an internal website (intranet site). This site could include both text and multimedia content, such as audio and video files. To make sure that all personnel who need to review these documents have done so, you could create tests that students have to turn in to management.

You could also enroll personnel in online courses created and presented by training organizations. Many of these courses are facilitated by online instructors, and sometimes students can earn continuing-education credits by taking the courses.

IT personnel should also use resources on the Internet, such as knowledge bases and manufacturers' support websites, to troubleshoot problems and get software updates and fixes.

Do it!

B-2: Identifying education opportunities and methods

Questions and answers

1 List advantages of on-the-job, classroom, and online training.

2 List disadvantages of on-the-job, classroom, and online training.

3 Which type of training would work best in your organization? Why?

Topic C: Disposal and destruction

This topic covers the following CompTIA Security+ objectives for exam SY0-301.

#	Objective
2.2	**Carry out appropriate risk mitigation strategies**
	• Implement policies and procedures to prevent data loss or theft
2.4	**Explain the importance of security-related awareness and training**
	• Information classification: sensitivity of data (hard or soft)
	• Data labeling, handling, and disposal
	• Compliance with laws, best practices, and standards
	• User habits
	– Data handling

Disposal of data and equipment

Explanation

Disposal considerations must include both the decommissioning of equipment and the proper disposal or destruction of data. Usually, the data contained within a device is worth more than the device itself. The cost of the loss of a hard drive is nearly entirely determined by the value of the data it held.

When you are disposing of equipment, your first concern should be to determine the value of the data it contains. Such a valuation should consider:

- Actual data, such as files that the device might store, and the hard (monetary) and soft (qualitative) costs of that data
- Configurations or settings that might reveal your security controls, network topology, and so forth
- Intrinsic properties, such as the brand or model of device uses. Such characteristics could reveal business partnerships, characteristics of product prototypes, or other technical details about your business.

Data disposal

When disposing of equipment, you should destroy the data it contains. When deciding how to destroy data, take into account the actual data, configuration data, and intrinsic properties.

Data slated for storage or disposal should be categorized and clearly labeled. For example, you might adopt government-like labels, such as sensitive, secret, top-secret, and so forth. If industry-specific terms exist, you should use them. Such labels help users decide how to properly handle, store, and dispose of the information. For example, you want to be sure that secret data is destroyed in a secure manner, but you don't want users to opt for that handling with non-secret data because it's more expensive to securely dispose of an item than to toss an item in the trash.

Data destruction

Erasing or formatting the drive isn't sufficient to destroy data. Unerasing and unformatting utilities abound, and services exist that recover old data from the traces left over, even after new files are written to the disk.

To truly destroy data, you need to use a utility designed to repeatedly write random data to the media. Only by writing data several times, perhaps hundreds of times, can you be sure that all traces of the old data are destroyed. Some utilities that include this capability are:

- OnTrack Data Eraser, www.krollontrack.com (commercial)
- Norton System Works, www.symantec.com (commercial)
- Eraser, www.tolvanen.com/eraser/ (open source)
- Wipe, sourceforge.net/projects/wipe (open source for Linux and UNIX platforms)

Removable media devices can be bulk-erased with large magnets. Optical media, tapes, and removable cartridges should be physically destroyed. Options include shredding, melting, chemical destruction (using solvents to dissolve magnetic coatings), cutting or smashing, and so forth.

Sensitive paper records should be shredded, burned, or chemically destroyed, depending on the value of the data they contain. You might consider hiring a professional data destruction service for very secret and confidential information.

Configuration destruction

When the configuration of equipment could reveal secrets about your organization, you should take steps to "de-configure" the equipment prior to disposal. You might restore equipment to its default settings by using its software interfaces. You might remove add-on components and change physical jumpers and wires. Generally, it's cheaper to physically destroy the equipment than to take the time to undo configuration settings.

Intrinsic properties destruction

If the intrinsic properties of a device would reveal sensitive information, then your only choice is to physically destroy the device. Crushing, pulverizing, and other techniques can be used to destroy equipment beyond recognition. It is unlikely that you'll need to worry about this level of disposal very often unless your business is involved with national defense, intelligence, or similar industries.

Disposal of electronics

It's often more cost-effective to replace a component or even an entire computer than to fix it or upgrade it. Home users and companies alike often end up with large piles of broken or outdated computers and other electronic equipment that needs to be disposed of properly. When calculating the cost of repairing or upgrading versus replacing equipment, be sure to consider all factors, including disruption to the user, the cost of the IT person's time, and any other factors unique to your organization.

Electronic components and equipment can't just be sent to the landfill along with the rest of the trash. They contain many hazardous materials, a number of which can be reclaimed. To help prevent environmental damage, you need to remove hazardous materials before sending items to the landfill. Be sure to check the material safety data sheets (MSDSs) for information on how to handle and dispose of the equipment.

Hazardous materials

Hazardous materials in electronic equipment often include lead. Lead is used in the solder joints in electronics. CRT monitors contain phosphorous. Both of these materials must be disposed of by following OSHA and EPA guidelines. The MSDS lists any hazardous materials in equipment, along with measures to take when disposing of it.

Disposal of computer equipment

Many batteries contain heavy metals that can't be sent to the landfill. Batteries in the equipment might contain nickel, mercury, or cadmium. Battery recyclers remove the heavy metals from the batteries and sell the metals to industries that can use them in products. The rest of the battery can then safely be disposed of. You can find battery recyclers by searching the Web. They often offer collection containers in which you can ship them batteries for recycling.

CRTs contain phosphorous and sometimes mercury switches, as well as lead and other precious metals, in their components. These materials can't be thrown into the landfill; they must be disposed of properly. When you are sending CRTs for recycling, make sure they're packaged so the screens won't break. Most recyclers can't reclaim anything from a CRT with a broken screen.

LCD monitors also contain materials that shouldn't be thrown in the landfill. Recyclers can reclaim components from these as well.

The computer itself has many components that can be reclaimed. Precious metals can often be extracted from circuit boards. The case can be recycled. The metals can then be sold back to manufacturers for use in new products. If you're disposing of a storage disk, it's important that you physically destroy the area where data is stored. Otherwise, even if you use software to erase the disk, the data could be retrieved by a savvy thief.

Companies specializing in the disposal of electronic and computer equipment are now available. They sort the equipment by type and then begin manually dismantling the equipment. They divide it into plastic, metal, and electronic components and CRTs. The electronics boards are then sent on for recapturing precious metals. A breakdown of the materials found in one ton of electronics boards can be found at thegreenpc.com.

Reusing equipment

When your computer equipment no longer meets your needs, the best option is to donate it to an organization that can use it. This might be a local school or other charitable organization. Many PC recyclers attempt to send usable equipment back out for use rather than dismantling it for materials reclamation.

Methods of disposal

Some municipalities offer local electronic equipment recycling services. These services might be available year round or offered periodically. There's often a small fee for disposing of the equipment. Considering the amount of manual labor involved in recycling these materials, the fees aren't exorbitant.

If no local service is offered, you can check the Web for recyclers. If you have pallet upon pallet of equipment, a recycler might be able to pick it up from you or arrange to have it picked up.

Do it! **C-1: Deciding whether to destroy or dispose of IT equipment**

Here's how	Here's why
1 The paper sensor on an inkjet printer is damaged	
Determine the cost of repairing the printer	When calculating the repair cost, be sure to include the cost of the employee's salary.
Determine the cost of replacing the printer	
Determine the cost of recycling the printer	
2 The company is replacing all of the CRT monitors with LCD monitors	
Determine the cost to recycle the monitors	
3 Several computers in your organization do not meet the requirements for Windows 7, to which your organization is upgrading	
Determine how to redeploy the computers within the organization or donate them to a charitable organization	
4 Create the basic outline of a policy on how to deal with outdated and non-functioning computer equipment	
Include information in the policy about how to deal with media	

Unit summary: Organizational security

Topic A

In this topic, you learned about creating **organizational policies**. First, you examined the information covered in security policies, such as acceptable use, due care, privacy, separation of duties, and password management. Next, you learned about human resources policies and how they apply to the security of the organization. You then examined the six steps to be documented in incident response policies: preparation, detection, containment, eradication, recovery, and follow-up.

Topic B

In this topic, you learned that **education and training** help all users perform their jobs more efficiently. You learned that when all users are aware of potential security problems, users and IT personnel can identify possible security threats and problems. You also learned about various options for training, including on-the-job, classroom, and online training.

Topic C

In this topic, you learned about the **secure disposal and destruction of computers** and components. You examined options, such as reuse or recycling, and methods of disposal. You also learned about the need for and ways of destroying data on old equipment.

Review questions

1 What kind of policy addresses the use of computer equipment and network resources for personal reasons or for uses that don't benefit the organization?

2 _____ means that reasonable precautions are being taken, indicating that the organization is being responsible.

3 "Least privilege" refers to employees having only the information that they _____.

4 Why is it necessary to have a policy regarding the proper disposal and destruction of computer equipment?

5 How does the code of ethics in a human resources policy relate to computer security?

6 What kind of policy details how a security break or disaster shall be dealt with?

7 What kind of policy describes the set of procedures to be followed whenever a network change is made?

8 True or false? When users are being trained, it's important to alert them to ways that attackers try to gather personally identifiable information and information about the organization's network.

9 Why can't computer equipment just be thrown in with the regular trash?

Independent practice activity

In this activity, you will practice creating organizational security policies. You will record only the high-level outline of the topics to be included in each policy. If time permits, you can add more information about what the policies should include.

1 Outline the topics to be covered in a security policy for your organization.

2 Outline the topics to be covered in a human resources security policy for your organization.

3 Outline the topics to be covered in an incident response policy for your organization.

Unit 14
Business continuity

Unit time: 90 minutes

Complete this unit, and you'll know how to:

A Create a business continuity plan and prepare for natural disasters.

B Create and store backups.

C Explain the importance of environmental controls.

Topic A: Business continuity planning

This topic covers the following CompTIA Security+ objectives for exam SY0-301.

#	Objective
2.5	**Compare and contrast aspects of business continuity**
	• Business impact analysis
	• Removing single points of failure
	• Business continuity planning and testing
	• Continuity of operations
	• Disaster recovery
	• IT contingency planning
	• Succession planning
2.7	**Execute disaster recovery plans and procedures**
	• Backup/backout contingency plans or policies
	• High availability
	• Cold site, hot site, warm site
	• Mean time to restore, mean time between failures, recovery time objectives, and recovery point objectives

Business impact analysis

Explanation

Performing a business impact analysis helps you identify the mission-critical functions in your organization and the impact a disaster would have on those functions. Part of the assessment is analyzing the time frame of the recovery process. The organization needs to compare the recovery costs with the revenue lost because of a disaster. Determine the time frame that the organization can accept for downtime and then determine the feasibility of the recovery plan and the acceptable costs. The costs of disaster recovery might be less than the costs of lost revenue. Another cost to consider is the cost of damage to the organization's reputation if a sound business continuity plan is not in place and effectively carried out.

Your organization might benefit from categorizing business functions. You might categorize functions as:

Category	Description
Critical	Functions to be restored immediately for normal operation.
Essential	Functions that will be restored as quickly as resources are available.
Necessary	Functions that will be restored when normal processing has been restored.
Desirable	Non-critical functions that will be suspended during the incident.

Many organizations express their availability as a "number of nines." For example, a "five nines system" has 99.999% availability. They also give the equivalent amount of downtime per year for that percentage of availability—five minutes. Minimizing downtime is critical now for companies that rely solely on the Internet to attract customers and take orders. However, the more nines (using the number-of-nines system), the greater the cost to keep everything running.

Planning and testing

Several items should be included in a disaster recovery plan. We'll cover all these items in the following sections.

Covered disasters and threats

Business is most often interrupted due to equipment failure or user error, but you need to be prepared to deal with other types of incidents as well. Different disasters and threats might need to be dealt with in different ways. Some incidents might require a relocation, and others might just require switching over to backup or redundant systems.

The threats can be categorized into several types:

Threat	Examples
Natural disasters	Flooding, earthquakes, tornadoes, snowstorms, wildfires
Accidents	Power disruption, vehicular accidents, chemical spills, fires
Internal	Sabotage, employee violence, theft
External	Industrial espionage, hacker attacks
Armed conflict	War, terrorism, civil unrest

For each of these threats, you need to analyze what needs to be done so that the organization can continue operating without interruption, or as close to that as you can get. You need to identify the mission-critical information and equipment needed to continue working. You also need to document the process for restoring data and systems. The network managers should contribute to the documentation of the disaster recovery plan so that they can establish the best way to get mission-critical information systems back online. The disaster plan needs to be thoroughly thought out and tested to ensure business continuity in the event of a disaster.

Business continuity teams

The business continuity team should contain members from each department in the organization. This prevents any department's needs from being overlooked during the incident. The team should include members to represent:

- Senior management
- The IT department
- Facilities management
- Users

The disaster recovery documentation should describe each team member's function during the incident and the succession plans for any critical team members who are unavailable during the incident. It's important to remember that you will have employees with business needs throughout the incident. Supervisors or senior managers—who can approve expenditures for food, housing, or replacement parts— must be available, or a designated replacement or "second-in-command" should be on site or available by phone or video conference.

Team members need to coordinate the recovery effort with the personnel from their department. External emergency services might need to be contacted; the documentation should identify who should do this. The documentation should also list any outside vendors that would need to be contacted and who should do that.

To be successful in managing crises, the team must contain the appropriate members. They need to be trained and be ready to respond immediately when the need arises.

Contingency plans

The contingency plan documents the procedures needed to keep the organization's business going during the failure of a crucial component. This document identifies team members responsible for the recovery process and describes what they need to do, which functions to restore first, and how to restore those functions.

The contingency plan should include the following information:

Item	Describes...
Responsibility checklist	The responsibilities of each member of the recovery team, and contact information for team members. Any "second-string" personnel should also be listed in case a primary team member is unavailable.
Emergency contacts	The people and organizations to notify, such as upper management, the fire department and police, and utility companies.
Warning system	When and how to contact employees and customers to tell them that an incident has occurred and tell them how the contingency plan will be carried out.
Procedures	Damage assessment, damage control and containment, and the procedures for recovering critical systems. You must also document the minimum threshold to be met before the contingency plan goes into effect, as well as the following: • Recovery time objectives — How long the planned recovery is expected to take. This estimate includes the time needed to assemble the necessary employees and prepare the equipment at the planned recovery sites, and the *mean time to restore* (the amount of time needed to restore the minimum defined business functions). • Recovery point objectives — The minimum threshold for determining that business has resumed and you've recovered from a disaster. These objectives can be expressed in terms of the number of orders placed, the number of employees performing daily duties, or the number of phone calls taken at a call center. This condition is specific to your organization.
Alternative sites	The location of and access procedures for off-site facilities and remote backup facilities.

Item	Describes...
Backup/backout contingency plans and policies	Plans for rolling back the disaster recovery effort when you've met your goals for business continuity and the disaster has passed. These plans should address how you're going to resume normal business operations at your primary location (including switching IT and phone operations), who is in charge of these efforts, and how to determine when to return to normal business operations.

Each part of the disaster recovery plan needs to be thoroughly documented. The wording of the documents needs to be clear and concise so that anybody can follow the procedures without requiring additional information.

Proper documentation enables you to rapidly respond to a disaster and to minimize the challenges faced during that response. All of the documentation should be stored in both electronic and paper formats. If the server is unavailable, the hard copy will become essential. Copies of the documentation should be stored on site and off site. The documentation should be stored securely so as not to compromise the network if the information were to fall into the wrong hands.

The following documents need to be included in the disaster recovery plan as part of IT contingency planning:

Document	Description
System configuration	The configuration for all key network devices, including servers, routers, and firewalls; all changes made since the devices were originally deployed; and passwords and login names for the devices.
Diagrams	Network and facilities diagrams, including blueprints of the entire network and facilities infrastructure. This information will allow the infrastructure to be re-created at an alternative site if needed.
Vendor and supplier lists	Contact information for any vendors or suppliers whom you might need to contact during the disaster to obtain new equipment to replace what has been damaged or compromised. Document any procedures that you work out ahead of time with the vendor or supplier to obtain equipment quickly.
Backup plan	The backups to be used to rapidly restore business functions. This plan should include the steps taken to perform backups, when the backups are performed, and the data backed up on each set of backup media.

Among other things to cover for IT contingency planning, you will need to consider:

- **Backup generators and UPSs** — Gas-powered generators and battery-powered UPS devices can keep systems up and running. This allows work to continue or an orderly shutdown to be performed, depending on the length of the power outage and the amount of time the device can provide power. Using a generator or a battery-powered UPS can prevent catastrophic damage to hardware and help keep the business running. This can be especially important when customers need to be able to use your site or your customer service representatives need to take and fulfill orders.

- **Single point of failure, redundancy, and spare parts** — If a server's network adapter fails, even though the server is still running, the server will be unavailable. This is just one example of a single point of failure occurring, which would need to be dealt with. Your server might be equipped with a redundant adapter, which would take over immediately if a failure occurred. Your disaster recovery plan should include information on which components need to be redundant. Also, it should stipulate that spare parts are kept on site or verify that they will be available immediately from your vendor if components fail.

- **Data backup and restore** — The data from the compromised system needs to be transferred to the replacement system. In the case of a natural or man-made disaster, you might need to be able to access the backups from a remote location.

Utility services

Utilities such as electricity, Internet connections, and phone service are essential to the functioning of an organization. If these fail, business can come to a standstill. You need to have contingency plans for dealing with the failure of these services.

Power outages can be recovered from by using *uninterruptible power supplies* (UPSs), which can switch to battery power. The switch-over timing is essential to preventing the server from going down. A UPS can give the administrator time to shut down the server in an orderly manner, or some units can keep the server running for several hours. Gas-powered generators can often keep the power going for a long period of time if needed.

If a natural disaster or an act of war occurs, blackouts might occur and lead to equipment failure. People might not be able to reach the office, and critical jobs would be left without someone to perform them. This is where cross-training comes into play so that someone who is in the office will know how to do the jobs that need doing. If possible, planning should include mechanisms for personnel to perform some critical duties from a remote location to deal with this particular contingency.

Communication and Internet connections might fail during a storm or be cut by a crew installing new lines or by a construction company, even though they should have called the utility companies to get the exact location of the lines before digging. Having redundant lines into the building (following a different route than the main lines) offers protection for such problems. For essential communication needs, your continuity plan might include the use of cell phones and cellular broadband connections.

Redundant locations

In addition to redundant systems, your plan might also call for a redundant location. The alternate location can be set up ahead of time, fully or partially configured, or it might be just a space where equipment can be set up with all required services. These alternate locations are known as hot sites, warm sites, and cold sites.

- A *hot site* is an alternative site that is fully configured and will be ready for operation within just a few hours of an incident. This high-availability solution has several advantages, including exclusive use of the site by your organization. Because it is your own private site, you can be flexible in the configuration and can perform periodic testing. The major disadvantage of a hot site is the expense, which might increase data center costs by over 50 percent.

- A *warm site* is an alternative location that is only partially configured for operation. It contains some computer equipment that is partially configured, and it provides some peripherals, but it does not include everything on the original network. Although this solution is less expensive than maintaining a hot site, it won't be ready for operation quite as quickly. It is usually reserved for exclusive use by the organization that set up the site, but because it is only partially configured, periodic testing of it will be difficult or impossible.

- A *cold site* is an alternative location that provides only the most basic environment in which to operate the business. The site provides wiring, ventilation, plumbing, and possibly raised flooring for routing cables. This relatively low-cost site does not include the hardware needed to carry on the organization's business, so you will need time to set up hardware. Because no hardware is set up ahead of time, it cannot be tested before the site is needed. This site might or might not be reserved for the exclusive use of a single organization.

Disaster recovery exercises

Finally, no matter how well you plan, you cannot be sure that your disaster recovery strategy will work until you put it to the test. You should conduct regular disaster recovery exercises. For the most realism, you should stage a simulation at your hot or warm site.

1 Simulate a disaster.

2 Implement your recovery plan.

3 After normal operations are restored, assess the effectiveness of your plan, documentation, and personnel.

4 Adjust your plan, documentation, and training to address any shortcomings you identified.

Because business requirements change, it might be useful to meet before a testing session to determine if the documented business needs have remained the same.

Assessing the recovery effort

After you've experienced at least one actual recovery effort (not just a planned exercise), you must document the success of your efforts. This assessment can provide critical documentation that describes the nature of the disaster, the success or failure in reaching business resumption goals, and how recovery efforts must proceed in the future in order to meet defined goals, if those goals were not met.

Over time, you can collect data on the *mean time between failures*, which is the number of hours or days elapsed between the repair or remediation of a disaster and the time of the next failure that requires a disaster recovery effort. You can use this information to plan ahead for the next failure and ensure that your resources are ready to handle it.

Do it!

A-1: Creating a business continuity plan

Questions and answers

1 Compare features, advantages, and disadvantages of hot, warm, and cold sites.

2 List some of the measures you can take to prevent a catastrophic data disaster.

3 List documents that should be included in your business continuity plan.

4 Performing a _____ helps you identify the mission-critical functions in your organization and the impact a disaster would have on those functions.

5 List topics that should be included in the documentation for IT contingency plans.

6 A disaster recovery exercise is likely to be expensive and time-consuming. For the greatest effectiveness, you should perform the exercise at your hot, warm, or cold site. Given these concerns, what good can come from a disaster recovery exercise?

Topic B: Disaster recovery

This topic covers the following CompTIA Security+ objectives for exam SY0-301.

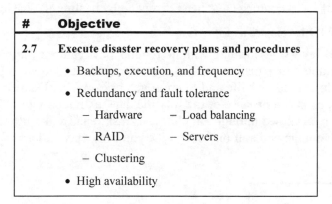

#	Objective
2.7	**Execute disaster recovery plans and procedures**
	• Backups, execution, and frequency
	• Redundancy and fault tolerance
	– Hardware – Load balancing
	– RAID – Servers
	– Clustering
	• High availability

The importance of disaster recovery plans

Explanation

Disaster recovery plans define exactly what to do when disaster strikes. The plan spells out the actions and resources needed to restore mission-critical processes damaged or put out of action as a result of the disaster. The plan needs to cover every aspect of what needs to be done for the organization to continue operating throughout the disaster and how the recovery plan will be implemented. If there is a gap of time between the disaster and the implementation of the recovery plan, the plan should specify what should be done during that time to continue the operation of the organization's business.

An effective disaster recovery implementation should, if possible, smoothly transition to redundant systems so that nobody even notices the switch. When this isn't possible, the switch to redundant or replacement systems should be done as quickly and effectively as possible so that the organization's systems are down for as short a time as possible.

Fault tolerance

Fault tolerance is essential in keeping your server up and running. The fault-tolerant system immediately switches to a redundant component or subsystem when the main part fails. You can add fault tolerance to a server by adding additional hard drives, CPUs, power supplies, network adapters, or other components. Having a fault-tolerant server is critical for *high-availability systems* (systems that must always be available).

Redundant systems for all components are needed for high availability. If an organization needs to claim 99.999% availability, then they need duplicate components to deal with any malfunctions. This redundancy is also known as a *failover* system. Such a system enables service to continue without interruption until the primary system or component can be brought back online.

For this process to be successful, the data on the failover system must be synchronized with the data on the main system. This ensures that the information is up-to-date. This synchronization can be accomplished through server clusters and with RAID systems. In *server clustering*, multiple servers jointly perform each task. Most current operating systems are able to use clustering so that failover systems can be used.

Load balancing, which can be used to improve performance by spreading critical business applications over multiple servers, can also provide a level of redundancy. If one server in a server farm fails, the other servers in the farm can pick up the workload.

RAID levels

RAID is a technique for adding redundancy, lengthening disk life, improving performance, and enabling relatively uninterrupted access to data. There are various basic levels of RAID, which have been extended by nesting the basic types.

The basic RAID levels are as follows:

- **RAID level 0** — Striping with no redundancy features. *Striping* works by spreading data equally over two or more drives, as shown in Exhibit 14-1. It is used to extend disk life and to improve performance. Data access on striped volumes is fast because of the way the data is divided into blocks that are quickly accessed through simultaneous disk reads and multiple data paths. The disadvantage is that if one disk fails, you can expect a loss of all data on the volume.

Exhibit 14-1: RAID level 0, two disks in a striped volume

- **RAID level 1** — Disk mirroring. Data is duplicated onto multiple drives (a "mirror" set), typically two disks. If one of the disks fails, data can be read from the secondary disk (or disks). Disk mirroring is illustrated on the left in Exhibit 14-2.

  Disk duplexing, illustrated on the right in Exhibit 14-2, is similar to disk mirroring, but each disk is managed by a separate adapter.

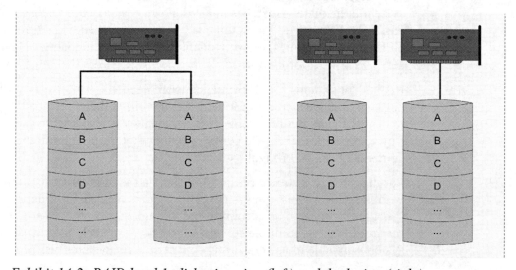

Exhibit 14-2: RAID level 1, disk mirroring (left) and duplexing (right)

- **RAID level 2** — Bit-level striping with dedicated parity. Data is striped, bit by bit, across all disks in the array. Parity (error detection) information is stored on one or more dedicated disks in the array. RAID 2 is rarely used.

- **RAID level 3** — Byte-level striping with dedicated parity. Data is striped, byte by byte, across the disks in the array. Parity is stored on a dedicated parity disk. RAID 3 offers high-read performance, but write performance can suffer because of the bottleneck caused by the single parity drive.

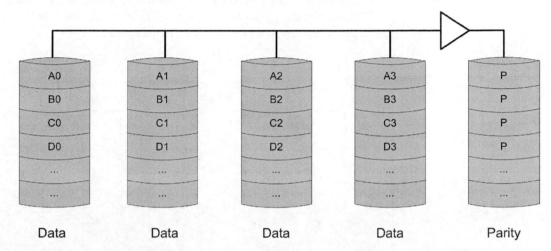

Exhibit 14-3: RAID 3 stripes data and stores parity on a dedicated drive

- **RAID level 4** — Block-level striping with dedicated parity. Data is striped, block by block, across the disks in the array. Parity is stored on a dedicated parity disk.

- **RAID level 5** — Block-level striping with distributed parity. Data is striped block by block across the disks in the array. Parity is distributed across all of the disks rather than being stored on a dedicated parity disk. Distributing the parity data removes the single-drive bottleneck that limits write performance in lower-numbered RAID levels.

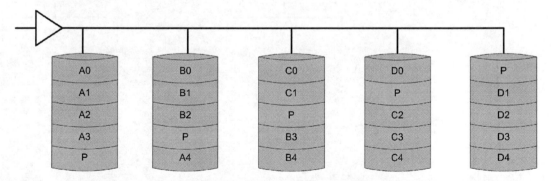

Exhibit 14-4: RAID 5 stripes data and parity across a set of drives

- **RAID level 6** — Block-level striping with double distributed parity. RAID 6 is essentially identical to RAID 5, except that the parity information associated with each block of data is stored twice (on separate drives). This enables the array to continue operating if two drives fail.

Nested RAID levels

Often, the drives in an array can themselves be arrays. Such a configuration creates a *nested array*, in which one whole array takes the place of a single drive in a larger array. This arrangement was originally called a "hybrid array," but is now generally called "nested."

The most common nested RAID levels are:

- **RAID 0+1 (or RAID 01)** — A mirrored set of striped disks. At a minimum, this arrangement requires four drives. For example, two drives are striped and then mirrored with another pair of striped drives.

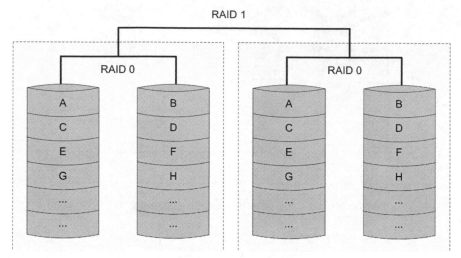

Exhibit 14-5: RAID 0+1 is a mirrored set of stripes

- **RAID 1+0 (or RAID 10)** — A striped set of mirrored disks. For example, two mirrored drives are striped with another pair of mirrored drives.

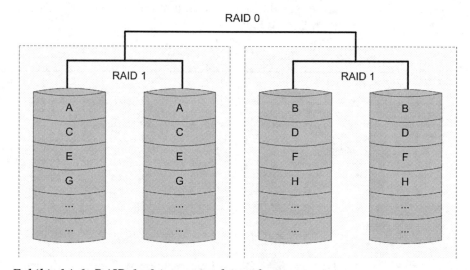

Exhibit 14-6: RAID 1+0 is a striped set of mirrors

Many other nested RAID combinations are possible. Each one offers a mix of benefits, such as greater redundancy or higher performance, and disadvantages, such as higher costs and greater complexity.

Considerations for using RAID

When considering a RAID solution, keep the following factors in mind:

- RAID 0 (striping) doesn't provide any redundancy. Its only benefit is speed.
- Windows Server 2000 and newer and Windows Vista and 7 natively support RAID levels 0, 1, and 5 via dynamic disks. You must install, partition, and convert each drive to dynamic disks first. Then you can use Disk Management to join them into a single volume based on one of the three listed RAID levels.
- You can place the boot and system files onto a RAID 1 volume when using Windows Server, but not with the client operating systems. You cannot place these files on a RAID 5 volume.
- There is a minimum number of required physical disks for each RAID level. For example, RAID 1 requires at least two disks. RAID 5 requires at least three disks, though typically more are used.
- On a per-gigabyte (or per-megabyte) level, RAID 1 is more expensive to implement than RAID 5. The reason for this is that with RAID 1, half of your total disk space is used for redundancy, whereas that value is one-third or less for RAID 5. The amount of disk space used for parity in RAID 5 is $1/n$ times the capacity of your smallest drive, where n is the number of drives in the array.
- Reading from disk is faster than writing with both RAID 1 (duplexing) and RAID 5. This difference results from the system's being able to read files or blocks of data from multiple drives simultaneously, whereas it must write as a singular operation.

Level-specific considerations

In addition to the general considerations given in the preceding section, there are factors specific to each level that you should examine when choosing a solution.

RAID level	Benefits	Detractions
RAID 0 (striping)	Reduces the wear on multiple disk drives by equally spreading the load.	No fault tolerance other than that gained through reduced wear.
	Increases disk performance compared to a single disk.	A loss of a single disk in the stripe set destroys the data on the entire volume.
	Enables you to create larger volumes than a single physical drive might permit.	
RAID 1 (mirroring or duplexing)	Increases read performance over a single-disk solution.	With mirroring, write performance can be degraded, because a single adapter manages write operations to both disks in the set.
	Can protect the boot and system volumes.	Depending on the software and hardware implementation, read performance might not be enhanced. For example, older IDE adapters could read from only one of the drives in a set. Software might compare data read from each drive to check for errors, thus reducing performance to a single-drive level.
	You can "split the mirror" to back up one drive while the other one services ongoing disk requests.	
RAID 5 (striping with distributed parity)	Read and write performance can be better than that provided by a single drive as long as writes, on average, involve the amount of data that would fit in a single stripe, or more data than would fit.	When writing chunks of data smaller than a single stripe, the overhead for calculating parity can reduce performance below that of a single disk (or mirror or stripe).
	Lower cost-per-gigabyte compared to RAID 1.	The performance of random write operations, such as those associated with databases, is slower than with a single disk (or mirror or stripe).
		Mean time between failures (MTBF) can theoretically be worse than that of a single disk.

Software RAID and hardware RAID

Two approaches to RAID can be implemented on a computer: software RAID and hardware RAID. Software RAID implements fault tolerance through the computer's operating system (such as by using the Disk Management tool in Windows) or through third-party software. Hardware RAID is implemented through hardware in the server or a dedicated storage subsystem and is independent of the operating system.

Some manufacturers have implemented hardware RAID on the adapter, such as a SCSI adapter, to which you connect multiple drives. You can also purchase dedicated storage appliances, such as a *storage area network* (SAN) or *network attached storage* (NAS), that might implement one of the RAID levels. (Not all SAN and NAS devices implement RAID.)

Hardware-based RAID is more expensive, but offers the following advantages over software-based RAID:

- Read and write performance can be better with hardware-based RAID. The hardware might use caching or optimization techniques. Even without caching, RAID hardware manages striping or mirroring operations or calculates the parity, removing that burden from the operating system.

- Depending on the hardware system, you might be able to place boot and system files on volumes with RAID levels different from those supported by Windows software-level RAID.

- Typically, you can hot-swap a failed disk without shutting down the server when using hardware-based RAID. (This option can vary by manufacturer.)

- Manufacturers might offer additional redundancy features that cannot be matched by software. For example, a built-in battery backup can prevent data corruption that might occur if the power goes out in the middle of a write operation.

Do it!

B-1: Discussing RAID levels

Questions and answers

1 How many hard disks are required to implement a RAID-5 volume at a minimum?

  A Two

  B Three

  C Four

  D Five

2 What term is used to describe disk mirroring when each drive is connected to its own hard disk controller?

  A Disk mirroring

  B Disk duplexing

  C Shadowing

  D Controller mirror

3 Which of the following RAID levels provides no fault tolerance?

  A RAID 0

  B RAID 1

  C RAID 4

  D RAID 5

Data backups

Explanation

You can anticipate that your hardware will eventually fail. Having backups of the data on your network is a critical part of disaster recovery. How often you back up the data and the rotation method you use for those backups will depend on the data needs of your organization. Although some organizations can make do with daily backups, other organizations might need hourly backups in order to fully protect mission-critical data. Some other information, such as static tables, might only need to be backed up weekly.

In addition to backing up data, you might also want to create an image of the entire network hard drive. Image backups copy the hard disk sector by sector, making a "snapshot" of the disk that can be restored to another disk at a later time.

Backup tools

You can back up your Windows Server 2008 server by using Windows commands or third-party programs. Research the features of each to determine the needs of your organization. For Windows Vista and Windows 7, you can use the Backup and Restore Center or a third-party program.

You install the Windows Server Backup utility from within Server Manager. You can perform a full system backup or a custom backup. The backups are performed on a per-volume basis. This utility doesn't allow you to back up individual folders within the volume.

Another tool you can install is the command-line tool Wbadmin. To back up system state data, you need to use Wbadmin because this capability is not included in the Windows Server Backup snap-in. The system state data cannot be written to a removable drive or to the system drive; a secondary drive must be available to record this data. System state data includes boot files, the Active Directory database, Sysvol, Certificate Services, cluster databases, the Registry, performance counter configuration information, and the Components Services Class registration database.

Backup types

You should determine how often to back up your information as well as which information to back up. Three common backup types are full, incremental, and differential. Archive bits are used to indicate when files have been modified and need to be backed up.

Type	Archive bit	Description
Full	Cleared	Backs up all files on the selected drive. Slowest to complete, but only one set of backup media is needed for a full restore.
Incremental	Cleared	Backs up just the files that were modified since that last backup was performed. Faster than performing a full backup, but when restoring, you must first restore the full backup and then restore each incremental backup set.
Differential	Not cleared	Backs up only the files modified since the last full backup. Each differential backup takes more room than the previous one. When restoring files, you need to restore the full backup and only the most recent differential backup.

You can also perform image backups by using the Volume Shadow Copy Service. With this service, you can create a complete copy (known as a full copy or clone), or copy only those changes on the volume made since the last full copy (known as a differential copy or a copy-on-write). This service creates two images; one is the original volume, and the other is the shadow copy volume. The original volume has full read and write capabilities; the shadow copy is read-only.

Backup media

There are several options for backup media. Some organizations still use the traditional magnetic tape. It's getting more and more common for companies to use removable hard disks for backups because the prices on hard disks have become fairly competitive with the prices on magnetic tapes. Other options include writable CDs and DVDs, another computer's hard drive, a removable hard drive, and floppy discs or flash drives (for small amounts of data). Remote backup services are available for backing up to off-site servers via the Internet.

Backups can be manual or automatic. When doing a manual backup, you will be prompted if the medium runs out of room, and you can insert another medium to continue the backup. Automated backups or unattended backups, which don't require user intervention, need to have enough room for the backup to complete. In this case, you might consider using a jukebox device with an automatic loader to insert the medium or add another medium if the first is full.

The data might be backed up to another server across a WAN connection, which often uses public networks. These connections are usually open conversations, with each file sent as clear text over the network. A VPN can be used to help protect the data. You can also encrypt the data so that only authorized users can decrypt the files.

Backup storage

Backups should be stored at a secure off-site location to protect them in case a disaster occurs at the primary location. You might also consider having a set of backups on site for immediate access in case a file is accidentally deleted or corrupted. Any on-site backups should be securely stored, preferably in a fireproof safe. The off-site location might be a bank vault, another location at which your organization does business, or with a company whose service is that of providing secure storage for backups and documents.

Do it!

B-2: Selecting backup schemes

Questions and answers

1 Should you use the Windows Server Backup utility or a third-party backup application to perform your system backups?

2 Describe the differences between incremental and differential backups.

3 Speculate on reasons that backups don't provide companies with the data protections they expect to get from the regimen.

Media rotation

Explanation

There are several methods you can use for media rotation, which allows you to have more than one set of backups. If you need to restore data from a file that was overwritten on a later date, you can use one of the older backups to recover the earlier version of the file.

The Grandfather method

The Grandfather rotation method is probably the most commonly used backup rotation method. Some organizations might also use other methods. Each of the generational methods is described in the following table.

Rotation method	Description
Son	The same set of media is used for the backup each day. No archives are created; only the last backup is available to restore from. If the backup is unsuccessful or damaged, there is no other set of media from which to restore the data.
Father-Son	A full backup is combined with differential or incremental backups each week. At the end of the week, a full backup is performed; on other days, either an incremental or differential backup is performed. This method creates an archive from which you can restore files from the previous day. You can do a full system restore by restoring the full backup and then restoring the daily backups.
Grandfather	The Father-Son rotation is used each week. The full backup is retained for a month, using a different set of backup media for each full backup for the month. At month's end, another full backup is created, which is archived for a year. The next month, the weekly full backup media are reused, and the daily media are reused each week.

The Tower of Hanoi

Another backup rotation scheme you might encounter is the Tower of Hanoi rotation. In this rotation scheme, there are at least three sets of backup media; some organizations use four or five sets. This method enables you to have more sets of media in your archive from which you can restore data. Three media sets allow you to have eight days' worth of data before the final media set is reused. Four sets allow 16 days of backups, and five sets provide for 32 days of backups.

In the following table, each backup set is given a letter. Each lettered backup set is reused as shown. For example, in a three-media-set-rotation, Set A is used on the first, third, fifth, and seventh days of the cycle, Set B is used on the second and sixth days of the cycle, and Set C is used on the third and eighth days of the cycle. If you want a permanent archive, you can keep the final set from the cycle and replace it during the next cycle.

	Set A	Set B	Set C	Set D	Set E
Days used in 3-media set rotation	1, 3, 5, 7	2, 6	4,8	N/A	N/A
Days used in 4-media set rotation	1, 3, 5, 7, 9, 11, 13, 15	2, 6, 10, 14	4, 12	8, 16	N/A
Days used in 5-media set rotation	1, 3, 5, 7, 9, 11, 13, 15, 17, 19, 21, 23, 25, 27, 29, 31	2, 6, 10, 14, 18, 22, 26, 30	4, 12, 20, 28	8, 24	16, 32

Incremented media backup schemes

In the incremented media backup scheme, a numbered set of media is used throughout the cycle. When the cycle is repeated, the media are numbered as in the last cycle, but the numbering is incremented by one. The lowest-numbered medium from the last cycle is kept as a permanent archive. This method gives you access to every backup for one cycle, and one backup for the previous cycle. This method ensures even wear of the media, but it requires a calculated schedule because it can be difficult to figure out when the next medium is to be used.

Backup storage

Each of the media rotation methods, except for the Son method, leaves you with a set of media for archiving. You might want to have the most recent backup on site for immediate access in case a file is deleted or corrupted, but you should also make sure that a verified set is securely stored off site so it will be available if a disaster occurs at your location.

Data restoration

Part of the disaster recovery plan is the procedure to restore data. In order to ensure that the backup is usable, you need to restore a file from it. You can have the backup software perform a verification that the files were successfully written, but the best test of whether the files were backed up successfully is to delete a file and restore it from the backup.

One way to test the backup, and practice following the disaster recovery plan, is to restore the entire backup to another server. Doing this provides the benefit of proving that the backup was effective and provides a chance for the disaster team to practice restoring data.

To restore data, you will need to use the same program that you used to back it up. Therefore, if you used a third-party program to create the backup and you want to restore the data set to another server, you will need to install the backup software before performing the restore. You might also need to restore the data to a different, identically configured server if the original server could not be saved.

Verification

Most backup utilities allow you to select an option to verify the backup either as it is performed or when it is completed. This process verifies the integrity of the file as compared to the original file on the server.

Do it!

B-3: Identifying appropriate media rotation and storage plans

Questions and answers
1 Which media rotation scheme does not provide any archival copies?
2 When is the full backup retained in a Grandfather rotation scheme?
3 Which media set is used most often in a Tower of Hanoi backup rotation scheme?
4 Why might you want to leave a backup on site and store another set at a remote location?

Topic C: Environmental controls

This topic covers the following CompTIA Security+ objectives for exam SY0-301.

#	Objective
2.6	**Explain the impact and proper use of environmental controls**
	• HVAC
	• Fire suppression
	• EMI shielding
	• Hot and cold aisles
	• Environmental monitoring
	• Temperature and humidity controls
	• Video monitoring

Explanation

The environment in which the computer network is located needs to be secure in order to prevent damage to data or hardware. Among the factors to be taken into account to provide protection are fire suppression, HVAC control, and shielding.

Fire suppression

Your environment should have appropriate types of fire detection and suppression systems. The fire detection systems might be manual buttons or levers, or they might be automatic sensors that are activated by heat or smoke, or both. The building in which your organization operates must meet local and national standards. Fire marshals carry out inspections periodically to ensure that the standards are being met and followed.

Fixed fire suppression systems

A fixed fire suppression system is combined with fire detection systems so that the fire suppression system is automatically activated when a fire is detected. The system could consist of water sprinklers installed in the ceiling, but because water and computer equipment aren't compatible, more likely, a fire-suppressing gas would be released from ceiling-mounted nozzles to extinguish the fire.

Fire suppression systems are described in the following table.

System	Description
Gas discharge	Halon or an EPA-approved Halon replacement gas or CO_2 gas is released.
Wet pipe	Water is immediately sprayed when the fire suppression system is activated.
Dry pipe	A valve holds back the release of the water so that you can shut down the fire suppression system if the fire has been contained or the system was accidentally activated.
Pre-action	This system combines wet- and dry-pipe features. An alarm is sounded before the system distributes water.

Fire extinguishers

Some fire extinguishers use chemicals that shouldn't be used on certain types of equipment. Each fire extinguisher lists the types of combustible materials it's designed to handle. The material safety data sheets (MSDSs) for materials and equipment list the type of fire extinguisher that should be used for fires involving that equipment or material. Newer fire extinguishers have pictures on them that indicate the types of fires they're designed to put out. Older fire extinguishers use color-coded shapes with letters to designate which types of fires they're for.

Some fire extinguishers are made to put out fires on multiple types of flammable materials. The following table describes them.

Class	Use for...	Designed to...	Labeling
A	Ordinary combustibles	Put out fires involving wood or paper.	Either a green triangle with an "A" inside it, or a wastebasket and a pile of logs on fire.
B	Flammable liquids	Put out fires involving grease, oil, gasoline, or similar liquids.	Either a red square with a "B" inside it, or a gas can on fire.
C	Electrical equipment	Put out fires involving electrical equipment.	Either a blue circle with a "C" inside it, or a plug and cord on fire.
D	Flammable metals	Be used on certain types of flammable metals.	A yellow star with a "D" inside it. There's no picture label for this class of extinguisher.

Fire extinguishers are filled with one of four substances for putting out fires. These substances are described in the following table.

Type	Description
Dry chemicals	These are designed for putting out fires from multiple types of flammable materials by using an extinguishing chemical along with a non-flammable gas propellant.
Halon	Halon gas interrupts the chemical reaction of burning materials. It's designed for use on electrical equipment. However, its use has been banned due to ozone layer depletion and to its danger to humans at a concentration above 10%. The EPA recommends using FM-200, NAF-sIII, Inergen, Argon, or Argonite instead of Halon.
Water	Class A fire extinguishers use water, along with compressed gas, as a propellant.
CO_2	Carbon dioxide fire extinguishers are designed for Class B and Class C fire extinguishers. CO_2 cools the item and the surrounding air.

Exhibit 14-7 shows a sample label for a fire extinguisher.

Exhibit 14-7: Fire extinguisher label

Fire prevention

Whenever possible, servers and other network equipment should be installed in fireproof rooms to help prevent fires started in other areas from reaching critical systems. The server room should have a gas-based fire suppression system so that if a fire does reach the server room, the fire can be extinguished without damaging the servers and network equipment.

Preventing fires should be a high priority. For fire safety, follow these guidelines:

- Keep papers orderly so that if fire does break out, loose papers don't catch fire easily. It's best to store papers in metal file cabinets whenever possible.
- Prohibit or control the use of hot pots, coffee makers, personal heaters, and other such small appliances. If employees are allowed to use such devices, be sure they're used properly and keep combustibles away from them. Not only do these appliances produce heat that can ignite materials, but they can also catch fire themselves if left on for prolonged periods of time.
- Keep working smoke detectors in all areas of the building.
- Make sure that you have fire extinguishers suitable for each type of equipment you have and that they are readily available.

HVAC

Heating, ventilation, and air conditioning (HVAC) systems control the climate within the building. An HVAC system regulates the temperature and air flow in the building, so the system must be properly sized for the space it needs to control. The HVAC contractor will determine the right size. An HVAC system that is too big or too small can be inefficient and produce an uncomfortable environment. An air conditioning system that is oversized can result in the climate's not being properly dehumidified. A heating system that is oversized can cause temperature swings that are uncomfortable to the occupants of the building.

Electronic components operate best in cooler temperatures and in environments with 40%–60% relative humidity. If the humidity is too high, condensation will occur; moisture and electricity are not a good combination. If the humidity is too low, it leads to static electricity, which can short out electronics.

A *plenum* is an enclosure that is used to move air for heating, cooling, or humidity control in a building. A plenum can also be used to run high- or low-voltage wiring. Plenum wiring is a special cable composed of fire-resistant materials so that if the cable burns, minimal amounts of smoke and fumes will be created and carried through the building by the heating and cooling systems that use the plenum.

Large server rooms with rows of server racks can be more efficiently cooled by using a *hot aisle/cold aisle* configuration. In this setup, equipment racks are arranged in rows, creating a series of aisles. Fans bring in cool air from one aisle, the cold aisle, and pass it through the racks toward another aisle, the hot aisle, where the warm air is vented from the room. In this configuration, the hot aisle will always be warmer than the cool aisle, and the airflow through the racks can be used to more efficiently cool the equipment on the racks.

Environmental monitoring

Monitoring and scheduling changes in the indoor air temperature is one way to reduce energy consumption and ensure that the proper environmental controls are in place. Proper scheduling will ensure that the building is heated and cooled only when necessary, such as during regular business hours during the work week. Scheduling lower or higher temperatures at night or on weekends, with the ability to change the temperature if specific departments are working overtime, can reduce waste.

The careful monitoring of temperatures can prevent large temperature swings, which could require extra power to counteract (to bring temperatures back into normal ranges) and could damage equipment. Monitors can notify you when a temperature rises above or falls below a set threshold, alerting you to new problems and giving you an opportunity to fix them before they become critical.

In addition to electronic temperature monitoring, video monitoring enables you to see the rooms that are sending temperature alerts so you can determine what the cause might be.

Shielding

Properly shielded cables should be used in the network to help combat *electromagnetic interference* (EMI) and *radio frequency interference* (RFI). Higher-quality cables have better shielding capabilities. High-quality UTP cables provide some protection, but STP has shielding built into the cable to better protect the data. Coaxial cables also provide good resistance to EMI and RFI. Fiber optic cables are completely protected from EMI and RFI.

The use of fiber optic cables also prevents attackers from splicing into the cables. If the use of fiber optic cable is cost prohibitive or not possible for other reasons, you should install a conduit around the network cable, with lockboxes installed at inspection and termination points.

Do it!

C-1: Examining environmental controls

Questions and answers

1 Compare wet pipe, dry pipe, and pre-action fixed fire suppression systems.

2 Which class of fire extinguisher should be used on electrical equipment?

3 What kinds of problems can be prevented by properly sizing the heating and cooling systems?

4 Proper cable shielding helps prevent problems caused by _____ and _____.

Unit summary: Business continuity

Topic A
In this topic, you learned how to prepare for natural disasters and create a **business continuity plan**. First you identified the need for the appropriate use of redundancy, through such features as fault tolerance, high-availability systems, server clustering, and RAID. Next, you examined how to create a **disaster recovery plan**, what documents to include in the plan, and how to conduct a **business impact assessment**.

Topic B
In this topic, you learned how to create and store **backups**. You started out by backing up data. Then you learned how to **restore** a file after it was deleted. Finally, you examined various **rotation methods** and options for storing backups.

Topic C
In this topic, you learned about the importance of **environmental controls**. First, you examined fire suppression systems, including fixed fire suppression systems and fire extinguishers. Next, you examined HVAC systems and the importance of maintaining a suitable range of temperature and humidity levels. Finally, you examined the use of shielding in cables to prevent EMI and RFI problems.

Review questions

1 Fault tolerance can be achieved by installing _____ components, to which the system immediately switches when a component fails.

2 Another term for a high-availability system is a _____ system.

3 RAID _____ uses disk striping with a parity disk.

4 RAID _____ uses disk striping with parity spread over all of the disks in the array.

5 What precautions can you take to protect utility services during an outage?

6 If your organization cannot justify the cost of a hot site, what other options do you have and what disadvantages are presented by those options?

7 Who should be included on the disaster recovery team?

8 Performing a business impact analysis allows your organization to compare the _____ costs with the costs of _____ from a disaster.

9   What should be included in a contingency plan's responsibility checklist?

10   In which type of backup(s) does the archive bit get cleared?

11   List at least three types of backup rotation methods.

12   What level of humidity should you maintain for electrical components and why?

Independent practice activity

In this activity, you will examine the following scenarios and identify the steps to take to prepare for each potential disaster.

1   Your office is located in a flood plain. Several times in recent years, access to the building has been affected by the nearby flooding river. So far, none of the systems have been compromised, but there are predictions that flooding will increase in the coming years. You also have a location in the mountains that sometimes becomes inaccessible during the winter due to heavy snowstorms.

2   Your organization's offices are located in an historic building that is over 200 years old. Your organization is a nonprofit agency with a limited budget. The fire marshal has indicated that although your attempts to install appropriate fire suppression systems is impressive, the nature of this old building is that if a fire were to start, there would be little the fire department could do to save the building or its contents.

3   The recent economic downturn has resulted in the need to lay off several network engineers in your organization. All of the passwords that these employees knew have been changed, but these engineers were part of the disaster response team, so they have detailed knowledge of the workings of the company and of the organization's network infrastructure. The intrusion detection system in place in your organization has detected some activity, and this has some managers wondering if any of the ex-employees might be responsible.

Appendix A
CompTIA Security+ acronyms

This appendix covers these additional topics:

A Acronyms that appear on the CompTIA Security+ exam.

Topic A: Acronym list

Explanation   The following is a list of acronyms and abbreviations that appear on the CompTIA Security+ exam. Candidates are encouraged to review the complete list and attain a working knowledge of all listed abbreviations as a part of a comprehensive exam preparation program.

Acronym	Spelled out
3DES	Triple Digital Encryption Standard
AAA	Authentication, Authorization, and Accounting
ACL	Access Control List
AES	Advanced Encryption Standard
AES256	Advanced Encryption Standards 256bit
AH	Authentication Header
ALE	Annualized Loss Expectancy
AP	Access Point
ARO	Annualized Rate of Occurrence
ARP	Address Resolution Protocol
AUP	Acceptable Use Policy
BCP	Business Continuity Planning
BIOS	Basic Input / Output System
BOTS	Network Robots
CA	Certificate Authority
CAC	Common Access Card
CAN	Controller Area Network
CCMP	Counter-Mode/CBC-Mac Protocol
CCTV	Closed-circuit television
CERT	Computer Emergency Response Team
CHAP	Challenge Handshake Authentication Protocol
CIRT	Computer Incident Response Team
CRC	Cyclical Redundancy Check
CRL	Certification Revocation List

Acronym	Spelled out
DAC	Discretionary Access Control
DDOS	Distributed Denial of Service
DEP	Data Execution Prevention
DES	Digital Encryption Standard
DHCP	Dynamic Host Configuration Protocol
DLL	Dynamic Link Library
DLP	Data Loss Prevention
DMZ	Demilitarized Zone
DNS	Domain Name Service (Server)
DOS	Denial of Service
DRP	Disaster Recovery Plan
DSA	Digital Signature Algorithm
EAP	Extensible Authentication Protocol
ECC	Elliptic Curve Cryptography
EFS	Encrypted File System
EMI	Electromagnetic Interference
ESP	Encapsulated Security Payload
FTP	File Transfer Protocol
GPU	Graphic Processing Unit
GRE	Generic Routing Encapsulation
HDD	Hard Disk Drive
HIDS	Host-Based Intrusion Detection System
HIPS	Host-Based Intrusion Prevention System
HMAC	Hashed Message Authentication Code
HSM	Hardware Security Module
HTTP	Hypertext Transfer Protocol
HTTPS	Hypertext Transfer Protocol over SSL
HVAC	Heating, Ventilation, Air Conditioning

Acronym	Spelled out
IaaS	Infrastructure as a Service
ICMP	Internet Control Message Protocol
ID	Identification
IKE	Internet Key Exchange
IM	Instant messaging
IMAP4	Internet Message Access Protocol v4
IP	Internet Protocol
IPSEC	Internet Protocol Security
IRC	Internet Relay Chat
ISP	Internet Service Provider
IV	Initialization Vector
KDC	Key Distribution Center
L2TP	Layer 2 Tunneling Protocol
LANMAN	Local Area Network Manager
LDAP	Lightweight Directory Access Protocol
LEAP	Lightweight Extensible Authentication Protocol
MAC	Mandatory Access Control / Media Access Control
MAC	Message Authentication Code
MAN	Metropolitan Area Network
MBR	Master Boot Record
MD5	Message Digest 5
MSCHAP	Microsoft Challenge Handshake Authentication Protocol
MTU	Maximum Transmission Unit
NAC	Network Access Control
NAT	Network Address Translation
NIDS	Network-Based Intrusion Detection System
NIPS	Network-Based Intrusion Prevention System
NIST	National Institute of Standards & Technology

Acronym	Spelled out
NOS	Network Operating System
NTFS	New Technology File System
NTLM	New Technology LANMAN
NTP	Network Time Protocol
OS	Operating System
OVAL	Open Vulnerability Assessment Language
PAP	Password Authentication Protocol
PAT	Port Address Translation
PBX	Private Branch Exchange
PEAP	Protected Extensible Authentication Protocol
PED	Personal Electronic Device
PGP	Pretty Good Privacy
PII	Personally Identifiable Information
PKI	Public Key Infrastructure
POTS	Plain Old Telephone Service
PPP	Point-to-Point Protocol
PPTP	Point-to-Point Tunneling Protocol
PSK	Pre-Shared Key
PTZ	Pan-Tilt-Zoom
RA	Recovery Agent
RAD	Rapid application development
RADIUS	Remote Authentication Dial-in User Server
RAID	Redundant Array of Inexpensive Disks
RAS	Remote Access Server
RBAC	Role-Based Access Control
RBAC	Rule-Based Access Control
RSA	Rivest, Shamir, & Adleman
RTO	Recovery Time Objective

Acronym	Spelled out
RTP	Real-Time Transport Protocol
S/MIME	Secure/Multipurpose Internet Mail Extensions
SaaS	Software as a Service
SCAP	Security Content Automation Protocol
SCSI	Small Computer System Interface
SDLC	Software Development Life Cycle
SDLM	Software Development Life Cycle Methodology
SHA	Secure Hashing Algorithm
SHTTP	Secure Hypertext Transfer Protocol
SIM	Subscriber Identity Module
SLA	Service Level Agreement
SLE	Single Loss Expectancy
SMS	Short Message Service
SMTP	Simple Mail Transfer Protocol
SNMP	Simple Network Management Protocol
SONET	Synchronous Optical Network Technologies
SPIM	Spam over Internet Messaging
SSH	Secure Shell
SSL	Secure Sockets Layer
SSO	Single Sign-On
STP	Shielded Twisted Pair
TACACS	Terminal Access Controller Access Control System
TCP/IP	Transmission Control Protocol / Internet Protocol
TKIP	Temporal Key Integrity Protocol
TLS	Transport Layer Security
TPM	Trusted Platform Module
UAT	User Acceptance Testing
UPS	Uninterruptible Power Supply

Acronym	Spelled out
URL	Universal Resource Locator
USB	Universal Serial Bus
UTP	Unshielded Twisted Pair
VLAN	Virtual Local Area Network
VoIP	Voice over IP
VPN	Virtual Private Network
VTC	Video Teleconferencing
WAF	Web-Application Firewall
WAP	Wireless Access Point
WEP	Wired Equivalent Privacy
WIDS	Wireless Intrusion Detection System
WIPS	Wireless Intrusion Prevention System
WPA	Wireless Protected Access
XSRF	Cross-Site Request Forgery
XSS	Cross-Site Scripting

Course summary

This summary contains information to help you bring the course to a successful conclusion. Using this information, you will be able to:

A Use the summary text to reinforce what you've learned in class.

B Determine the next courses in this series (if any), as well as any other resources that might help you continue to learn about Security+.

Topic A: Course summary

Use the following summary text to reinforce what you've learned in class.

Unit summaries

Unit 1

In this unit, you learned about common threats and examined core system maintenance tasks. Then you examined **application vulnerabilities**, which are created by application components and add-ons. You learned that sloppy programming practices can lead to injection attacks and buffer overflows. Next, you examined application hardening, baselining, and secure coding practices, which are **countermeasures** to the most common vulnerabilities. You also learned that **physical security** is an important part of your overall security profile. Then, you learned how to protect a system from **malware** and you examined the many kinds of malware. Finally, you learned about the threats posed by **social engineering**

Unit 2

In this unit, you learned that **encryption** is a process that converts plaintext into ciphertext, and that **decryption** reverses that process. You learned about the characteristics of **symmetric cryptographic ciphers**. Then you learned that **public key cryptography**, an example of asymmetric cryptography, uses two keys. Also, you learned that **digital signatures** use hashing and public key cryptographic techniques to provide authentication, integrity, and non-repudiation. In addition, you learned about **single- and dual-key certificates**, which incorporate a user's public key, identifying information, and digital signature into a conveniently distributed package. Finally, you learned about the components of the **public key infrastructure (PKI)** and about the **trust models** for certificate chains.

Unit 3

In this unit, you identified the **components of security:** authentication, authorization, and accounting. Then you identified and compared **authentication systems**, and you examined **authentication vulnerabilities**. You also looked at **security practices**, such as password best practices, account lockout policies, and the principle of least privilege. Finally, you examined methods of cracking passwords.

Unit 4

In this unit, you **created local and group policies**. First, you created a console to manage local security policies. Then, you used the Group Policy Management Console on a domain controller to set some policies. Finally, you **secured network resources** by creating users and groups based on security needs, and then you secured file resources by setting permissions on folders.

Unit 5

In this unit, you **secured storage devices** and learned how to secure **peripherals and computer components**. You identified the security risks associated with common peripherals and then took measures to mitigate some of those risks. Finally, you examined **mobile device security** by looking at risks and vulnerabilities, including loss or theft, eavesdropping, tracking, malware, and unauthorized access.

Unit 6

In this unit, you learned about the various phases of the **key life cycle** and how **encryption key management** is used in each phase. Then you learned how to install and administer a **certificate server** and how to issue, manage, and revoke certificates. You also learned how to use certificate templates to enable a **key recovery agent**. Then, you learned how to configure your Web server to support **HTTPS** connections and how to require **SSL** connections to a Web address. You also requested a user certificate via your certificate server's Web interface and installed that certificate.

Unit 7

In this unit, you learned that **application security** involves actions by programmers, security administrators, and users. Next, you examined **e-mail security**. You identified the security risks of e-mail, including phishing, malware, spoofing, and eavesdropping. Then you examined e-mail security options, including **encrypted authentication** and secure password transmission. Finally, you examined security issues related to **social networking** and **instant messaging**. You learned that social networking risks include malware, information disclosure, impersonation, and brand or reputation disparagement.

Unit 8

In this unit, you reviewed **TCP/IP protocols** and network services, including TCP, IP, UDP, ARP, and RARP. You also examined IPv4 and IPv6 and compared their features. Then you examined **protocol-based attacks**, including denial-of-service attacks (such as SYN flood, smurf, and ping-of-death attacks), DDoS attacks, man-in-the-middle attacks, spoofing attacks, replay attacks, and TCP/IP hijacking.

Unit 9

In this unit, you learned about **networking devices**, including switches, routers, firewalls, and proxy servers. You also examined the **vulnerabilities** in these devices, chiefly those vulnerabilities presented by built-in management accounts, firmware, and operating software. Then you learned that **firewalls** and **proxy servers** are critical devices for implementing network security, and you learned why following standard, tested **network administration principles** can improve the security of your network. Next, you learned that **virtualization** saves money through better hardware utilization and improves security. Lastly, you examined **cloud computing**, which is a model for enabling convenient, on-demand network access to a shared pool of configurable computing resources,

Unit 10

In this unit, you learned that wireless networks are vulnerable to many forms of attack, and you learned that **transmission encryption**, through such methods as WEP, WPA, and WPA2, prevents unauthorized access and eavesdropping. Next, you learned that **mobile devices** can fall victim to attacks, such as bluejacking, bluesnarfing, and bluebugging.

Unit 11

In this unit, you learned that **RADIUS** and **TACACS+** are two popular systems for implementing remote access authentication. You also learned that **802.1x** is an extensible protocol that enables you to control which devices connect to your network. Then you installed **Network Policy Server**, Microsoft's RADIUS server. Lastly, you learned that **virtual private networks** enable you to extend secure network connections across insecure networks, and you installed **RRAS** (the Routing and Remote Access Services) and used it to create a VPN.

Unit 12

In this unit, you learned how to perform vulnerability and penetration testing. Then you learned how to read **log files** to look for events that might indicate a security incident. You learned about different types of log files, and you read some sample logs and alerts. Next, you learned about **intrusion detection systems**, including host-based and network intrusion detection systems. You learned that these systems monitor events on your devices and the network to alert you to security intrusions. Finally, you learned how to investigate security incidents by using standard **forensics procedures**. You learned about what type of information to gather, how to gather it, and how to preserve a **chain of custody** for possible criminal prosecutions. You also learned how to create a **remediation plan** to enhance security and help prevent future security breaches.

Unit 13

In this unit, you learned about creating **organizational policies**, and you learned that **education and training** help all users perform their jobs more efficiently. You also learned about various options for training, including on-the-job, classroom, and online training. Then you learned about the **secure disposal and destruction of computers** and components. You examined options, such as reuse or recycling, and methods of disposal. You also learned about the need for and ways of destroying data on old equipment.

Unit 14

In this unit, you learned how to prepare for natural disasters and create a **business continuity plan**. Next, you examined how to create a **disaster recovery plan**, what documents to include in the plan, and how to conduct a business impact assessment. Then you learned how to create and store **backups** and how to **restore** a file. Then, you examined various **rotation methods** and options for storing backups. You then learned about the importance of **environmental controls**, including fixed fire suppression systems and fire extinguishers. You learned about HVAC systems, the importance of maintaining a suitable range of temperature and humidity levels, and the use of shielding in cables to prevent EMI and RFI.

Topic B: Continued learning after class

It is impossible to learn Security+ concepts in a single day. To get the most out of this class, you should begin working with security principles as soon as possible. We also offer resources for continued learning.

Next courses in this series

This is the first course in this series. The next course in this series is:

- *CompTIA Certification: Advanced Security Practitioner*

Other resources

For more information, visit www.axzopress.com.

Glossary

802.11

An IEEE standard specifying a wireless computer networking technology that operates in the 2.4–2.5 GHz radio frequency (RF) band.

802.11i

A standard that defines security mechanisms for wireless networks.

Acceptable-use policy

A policy that defines how an organization's computer equipment and network resources can be used.

Access point (AP)

A device that functions as a transparent bridge between the wireless clients and the wired network.

Accounting

The process of tracking a user's network activity, including how long the user is connected and which resources the user accesses.

ACL (access control list)

A mechanism that controls the permissions to allow or deny user access to a folder or printer.

ActiveX

A loosely defined set of technologies developed by Microsoft that provides tools for linking desktop applications to Web content.

AD DS (Active Directory Domain Services)

The native directory service included with the Windows Server 2008 operating systems.

Admin Approval Mode

A Windows Vista and Windows 7 feature that requires users, even when logged on as a local administrator, to approve any task an application attempts to perform that requires administrative privileges.

AES (Advanced Encryption Standard)

A symmetric block cipher operating on 128-bit blocks of data, using a 128-, 192-, or 256-bit key and 10, 12, or 14 rounds of processing to compute the ciphertext.

AES256

The AES cipher using 256-bit keys.

ARP (Address Resolution Protocol)

A protocol that translates IP addresses and MAC addresses; requests a MAC address when the IP address of a node is known.

ARP poisoning

An attack in which the attacker sends forged ARP replies so that the compromised computer sends network traffic to the attacker's computer.

Asymmetric cipher

A cipher that uses different encryption and decryption keys.

Authentication

Positive identification of the entity, either a person or a system, that wants to access information or services that have been secured

Authorization

A set level of access granted to an entity so that it can access the resource.

Back-to-back firewalls

A setup in which the DMZ network is located between two firewalls; the two firewalls are between the Internet and the DMZ; and the DMZ and the intranet each have two network cards, as does the server within the DMZ.

Bastion host

A computer that stands outside the protected network and defends it by using two network cards: one for the DMZ and one for the intranet. Network communication isn't allowed between the two network cards in the bastion host server.

Biometrics

A method of authentication that uses a person's physical trait—such as a fingerprint, retinal scan, or voice print—to secure an account or resource.

Birthday attack

A brute-force attack that exploits the mathematics of the birthday paradox probability theory to guess an unknown password.

Blowfish

A public-domain symmetric block cipher that uses 64-bit blocks and variable-length keys with zero- to 448-bit keys.

Bluebugging

An attack in which hacker takes control of a victim's phone to make calls and perform other functions as if the hacker had physical possession of the device.

Bluejacking

The act of sending unsolicited messages over Bluetooth wireless links to other devices.

Bluesnarfing

Any form of unauthorized access of a device over a Bluetooth connection.

Brute-force attack

An attack that creates and tries all possible combinations of characters that a password might be composed of.

Buffer overflow attack

An attack that manipulates the maximum field input size variable and then enters data much larger than the database is prepared to accept, thereby causing memory reserved for other data to be overwritten.

CA (certificate authority)

The person or entity responsible for issuing certificates.

Centralized key-management system

A system that places all authority for key administration with a top-level entity.

Certificate policy

A set of rules indicating the "applicability of a certificate to a particular community and/or class of application with common security requirements" (IETF RFC 2527).

CGI (Common Gateway Interface)

An extension of the HTTP protocol that allows Web servers to manipulate data and interact with users.

CHAP (Challenge Handshake Authentication Protocol)

An authentication method used by Point-to-Point Protocol (PPP) servers. CHAP validates the remote client's identity at the beginning of the communication session or at any time during the session.

Checksum

A value that's calculated by applying a mathematical formula to data.

CIDR (Classless Inter-Domain Routing)

An IP addressing scheme that allows you to use variable-length subnet masking (VLSM) to create additional addresses beyond those allowed by the IPv4 classes.

Cipher

The pair of algorithms that encrypt and decrypt data.

Cipher lock

An electronic, programmable lock that uses either a keypad or a card reader.

Ciphertext

Encrypted plaintext.

Cookie

A small file that is stored on a user's hard drive and is used by websites to store information.

CPS (certificate practice statement)

A published document that explains how the CA is structured, which standards and protocols are used, and how the certificates are managed.

CRL (certificate revocation list)

A data structure containing revoked certificates.

Cryptographic token

See *physical token*.

Cryptography

The science of encrypting and decrypting data; or a set of standards and protocols for encoding data and messages so that they can be stored and transmitted more securely.

CS (certificate server)

A server that maintains a database, or repository, of certificates.

DAC (discretionary access control)

An access control model in which a file owner uses an ACL to define who can access a file and what the users can do with the file.

DCS (Data Collector Set)

A Performance Monitor feature that gathers information for a period you specify so that you can review a computer's performance over time.

DDoS (distributed denial-of-service) attack

A network attack in which the attacker manipulates several hosts to perform a DoS attack.

Dead zone

A network that resides between two routers and uses a network protocol other than TCP/IP.

Decentralized key-management system

A system that places responsibility for key management with the individual. The key and certificate are stored locally on the user's system or on some other device, and the user controls all key management functions.

Decryption

The technique of converting an encrypted message back into its original form.

DES (Data Encryption Standard)

A symmetric block cipher operating on 64-bit blocks of data, using a 56-bit key and 16 rounds of processing to compute the ciphertext.

Diameter

A successor to RADIUS; a new protocol that defines a minimum set of AAA services and functionality.

Dictionary attack

A brute-force attack that compares the hash for each word in a standard English dictionary against an unknown password.

Diffie-Hellman

An asymmetric cipher in which, through a series of mathematical steps, the sender and receiver calculate the same shared secret key by using undisclosed private keys.

Digest

See *hash*.

Digital signature

An electronic proof of origin calculated through components of public key cryptography.

Distribution group

A collection of users, and sometimes other groups, used for sending e-mail.

DMZ (demilitarized zone)

An area between the private network (intranet) and a public network (extranet), such as the Internet.

DNA scan

A biometric authentication method that compares a sample of a user's DNA with information stored in a database.

DNS (Domain Name System)

A protocol supporting a hierarchical naming system that provides common naming conventions across the Internet.

DOS (denial-of-service) attack

An attack that consumes or disables resources so that services to users are interrupted.

DSA (Digital Signature Algorithm)

An asymmetric encryption system designed for digitally signing communications.

Dual-homed firewall

See *bastion host*.

Dual-homed host

See *bastion host*.

Dumpster diving

The act of digging useful information out of an organization's trash bin.

Dynamic knowledge-based authentication

A process by which a public database is queried and the individual is asked to verify the information.

EAP (Extensible Authentication Protocol)

A protocol that includes multiple authentication methods—such as token cards, one-time passwords, certificates, and biometrics—and runs over the Data Link layer without requiring the use of IP.

E-C (elliptic curve)

An asymmetric cipher that generates a pair of keys based on the algebra of elliptic curves of large finite fields.

Elevation prompts

The UAC dialog boxes that prompt users to approve elevated privileges for an application.

ElGamal

An asymmetric cipher in which keys are generated using the mathematical principle of the cyclic group.

Encryption

A technique through which source information is converted into a form that cannot be read by anyone other than the intended recipient.

Encryption key management

The systems used to manage encryption keys throughout their life cycle.

Event Viewer

A Windows logging utility.

Eye scanner

A biometric hardware security device that scans the surface of a user's retina to obtain the blood vessel patterns found there and then compares it to information in a database.

Fingerprint scanner

A biometric hardware security device that scans a user's finger and compares the print to information in a database.

Firewall

A device or software that selectively permits or denies network traffic based on rules.

Forensics

The science of investigating an event in the context of a legal action. Computer forensics is typically taken to mean an investigation of a security incident, typically for the purpose of taking legal or procedural actions following an attack.

GPMC (Group Policy Management Console)

The Windows tool used to define group policy settings in a domain environment.

Group policy

A Windows feature that allows administrators to control the actions users can perform on their computers and to automatically configure software.

Group Policy Object Editor

The Windows tool used to define the settings you want to use in a local GPO.

Hand geometry scanner

A biometric security device that scans the entire hand of the user, measuring the length and width of the fingers and hand, and then compares the result to information in a database.

Hardening

The process of modifying an operating system's default configuration to make it more secure from outside threats.

Hardware token

See *physical token*.

Hash

A unique fixed-length mathematical derivation of a plaintext message.

HIDS (host-based intrusion detection system)

Typically, a software-based system for monitoring the health and security of a particular host. A HIDS monitors operating system files for unauthorized changes and watches for unusual usage patterns or failed logon requests.

Hierarchical trust

A trust model in which a top-level CA, known as the root CA, issues certificates to intermediate (or subordinate) CAs.

Honeynet

A network designed to deceive or trap attackers.

Honeypot

A system specifically designed to deceive or trap attackers.

Hotfix

A set of code that fixes errors in the operating system code.

ICMP (Internet Control Message Protocol)

A protocol that controls and manages information sent using TCP/IP.

IDEA (International Data Encryption Algorithm)

A symmetric block cipher that operates on 64-bit blocks using a 128-bit key, performing a series of eight identical rounds and finishing with a half-round output transformation.

Implicit deny

A security tactic in which you block access by default, and then enable specific exemptions on an as-needed basis.

Inoculation

The process of calculating and recording checksums to protect against viruses and worms.

Internet Protocol suite

An internetworking protocol that provides guaranteed delivery, proper sequencing, and data integrity checks. Also called TCP/IP.

Intrusion detection

The process of detecting and possibly reacting to an attack on your network or hosts.

IP (Internet Protocol)

A routable, unreliable, connectionless protocol; its sole function is the addressing and routing of packets.

IPSec (IP Security)

A standardized network protocol that encrypts data at the Network layer (OSI layer 3) of the protocol stack, providing security for both TCP and UDP traffic.

IPv4

Version 4 of the Internet Protocol; supports 32-bit IP addresses, providing up to 2^{32} addresses.

IPv6

Version 6 of the Internet Protocol; uses 128-bit addresses, providing 2^{128} addresses.

IRM (Information Rights Management)

A mechanism that allows individuals to specify access permissions for e-mail messages.

Java applets

Internet applications, written in the Java programming language and downloaded from Web servers to client hard disks, that can operate on most client hardware and software platforms.

JavaScript

A scripting language developed by Netscape to enable Web authors to design interactive sites.

KBA (knowledge-based authentication)

An authentication method that involves asking the potential new user to provide information that only he or she would be likely to know.

Kerberos v5

The primary authentication protocol used in Active Directory Domain Services environments.

Key

A piece of information that determines the result of an encryption algorithm.

Key archiving

The storage of keys and certificates for an extended period of time.

Key escrow

A form of key archive that allows third-party access (such as for law enforcement or other government agencies) without the cooperation of the subject.

Key hardware storage

The practice of storing a private key on a hardware storage medium, such as a smart card, memory stick, USB device, PCMCIA card, or other such device.

Key life cycle

The stages of a key's use: generation, distribution, storage, backup, and destruction.

Key recovery agent

A person within your organization who has the authority to recover a key or certificate on behalf of a user.

Key software storage

The practice of storing a private key in a computer file on the hard drive. The owner encrypts the private key by using a password or passphrase, and stores the encrypted key in a restricted file.

L2F (Layer 2 Forwarding)

An obsolete Cisco VPN protocol.

L2TP (Layer 2 Tunneling Protocol)

A standardized tunneling protocol, described under RFC 3931, that combines the best features of PPTP and L2F to provide tunneling over IP, X.25, Frame Relay, and ATM networks.

LDAP (Lightweight Directory Access Protocol)

The industry-standard protocol for network directory services.

LM

The hash used to store Windows passwords prior to Windows Vista.

MAC (mandatory access control)

A non-discretionary access control method in which all users and resources are classified and a security level is assigned to each classification. If the user's security level does not match or exceed the security level of the resource, access is denied.

Man-in-the-middle attack

An attack that tricks e-mail servers into sending data through a third node.

Man-trap

A set of doors that are interlocked—when one door is open, the other door can't be opened.

Masquerading

See *spoofing*.

MBSA (Microsoft Baseline Security Analyzer)

A tool from Microsoft designed to help security managers determine the current state of security for Windows-based systems.

MD5

A hash algorithm that creates a 128-bit digest from variable-length plaintext.

Mesh trust

See *Web of Trust*.

MPVPN (Multi Path Virtual Private Network)

A proprietary and trademarked data transmission protocol developed by Ragula Systems Development Company.

Mutual authentication

A system that requires both the client and the server to authenticate to each other, instead of having just the client authenticating to the server as in other authentication systems.

NAC (Network Access Control)

A process or architecture through which computers are verified to be in compliance, and are brought into compliance if they fall short, before they are permitted access to the network.

NAP (Network Access Protection)

Microsoft's implementation of NAC; offered as a new feature in Windows Server 2008.

NAT (network address translation)

A protocol that maps multiple private internal IP addresses to a single public external IP address.

Nessus

A free security scanner published by Tenable Network Security (www.nessus.org); used to scan one or more computers on your network to determine their operating system and patch levels, security state, and vulnerability to known exploits.

Network mapper

A tool you can use to scan your network and to build a map (or inventory) of the systems, open ports, running services, operating system versions, and so forth.

NFS (Network File System)

The standard distributed file system for Unix-based environments, which allows users to share files on both similar and dissimilar hardware platforms.

NIDS (network intrusion detection system)

A device or system designed to monitor network traffic on a segment or at a network entry point, such as a firewall. A NIDS monitors network traffic volumes and watches for malicious traffic and suspicious patterns.

NPS (Network Policy Server)

The Windows Server 2008 implementation of a RADIUS server.

NTLM

A challenge-response protocol that's used with operating systems running Windows NT 4.0 or earlier.

One-factor authentication

The use of a single type of authentication, typically something you know.

Online attack

An attack that uses instant-messaging chat and e-mail venues to exploit trust relationships.

OOB (out-of-band) identification

An identity-proofing method that makes use of a channel outside the primary authentication channel.

OpenVPN

An open-source VPN project that uses a variant of the SSL/TLS protocol to provide transmission security by encrypting the entire protocol stack.

OTP (one-time pad) cipher

A cipher combining the plaintext message with a key of equal length. The key is never reused and is kept secret. The plaintext characters are rotated forward some number of characters, and each character is rotated by a different value. The key is a stream of numbers indicating by how much each character should be rotated.

OVAL (Open Vulnerability and Assessment Language)

A project sponsored by the U.S. Department of Homeland Security and managed by Mitre Corp. OVAL standardizes the way systems and applications are tested for vulnerabilities and how those vulnerabilities are described and reported, and provides a central repository of vulnerability information.

PAP (Password Authentication Protocol)

An insecure authentication method used by the Point-to-Point Protocol (PPP) for remote dial-up access.

Password

A secret code associated with a username, used to authenticate a user.

Password crackers

Applications you use (or attackers use) to attempt to determine or decipher the passwords associated with user accounts.

PAT (port address translation) device

A device that performs NAT services, mapping multiple private internal IP addresses to a single public external IP address. The PAT device uses port numbers to differentiate between internal servers sharing this single address

Patch

A temporary or quick fix designed to fix a security vulnerability, compatibility, or operating problem.

Penetration testing

The act of attacking your own systems by using the same tools and techniques an attacker might use to attempt to breach the security of your network or hosts.

Phishing

An attack in which an e-mail message that appears to be from a trusted sender directs the recipient to a website that looks like the impersonated company's site and then records the user's logon information.

Physical token

A material object, such as a smart card, that stores a cryptographic key, which might be a digital signature or biometric data.

PKI (public key infrastructure)

A formalized and feature-rich system for sharing public keys, distributing certificates, and verifying the integrity and authenticity of these components and their issuers.

Plaintext

Original, unencrypted information.

Pop-ups

Web browser windows that open on top of the current window you are viewing.

Port scanner

A tool that examines a host or network to determine which ports are being monitored by applications on the scanned hosts.

PPTP (Peer to Peer Tunneling Protocol)

A VPN protocol developed by Microsoft; once a link has been established, the client is added as a virtual node on the LAN, and packets between the two are encrypted using Microsoft Point-to-Point Encryption (MPPE).

Preset lock

A lock that's opened or closed with a metal key or by turning or pressing a button in the center of the lock.

Proxy server

A server that acts as an intermediary between computers on a network and the Internet.

RA (registration authority)

An entity that collects and stores identifying information—such as contact information, users' public keys, and system capabilities—in order to authenticate a requestor's identity.

RADIUS (Remote Access Dial-in User Service)

A wireless-transmission-encryption system that uses a specialized server for authentication and uses WEP for data encryption.

Rainbow tables

Tables that you can download or create which are used to crack passwords.

RARP (Reverse Address Resolution Protocol)

A protocol that translates between IP addresses and MAC addresses; used when the IP address is unknown and the MAC address is known.

RBAC (role-based access control)

An access control method in which users are placed in groups based on roles within an organization, and then groups (rather than individual users) are assigned permissions to resources.

RC5

A symmetric block cipher that has a variable block size (32, 64, or 128 bits) and that supports variable key sizes (0 to 2040 bits) and a variable number of rounds (0 to 255).

RC6

A derivation of RC5 created to meet the entry requirements of the Advanced Encryption Standard contest.

Realm

A defined namespace in RADIUS that helps determine which server should be used to authenticate a connection request.

Real-time antivirus scanner

Software that runs each time a computer is turned on and is designed to scan every file accessed on a computer so it can catch viruses and worms before they can infect a computer.

Remote-access VPN

A VPN that enables users to securely access corporate network resources via the Internet.

Replay attack

An attack in which an attacker reuses valid transmission data to gain access to a network.

Rijndael

The AES cipher with both key and block sizes of 128–256 bits, in multiples of 32 bits.

Risk analysis

The process of determining the sources of risk that face your network, along with your organization's tolerance for accepting that risk.

ROT13 ("rotate 13")

A symmetric cipher in which characters are replaced with the character whose ASCII value is thirteen higher.

Router

A network management device that sits between different network segments and directs traffic from one network to another.

RSA

The best known asymmetric public key cipher, in which two users each generate a pair of keys: a private pair and public pair. To send a secure message to the second user, the first user obtains the second user's public key and encrypts the message with it. Only the second user's private key can be used to decrypt the message.

Screened host

A router used to filter all traffic to the private intranet while allowing full access to the computer in the DMZ.

Security group

A collection of users, and sometimes other groups, used to assign permissions to computers and resources.

Security policy

A document that defines rules and practices that the organization puts in place to manage and protect information within the organization.

Service pack

A collection of updates packaged as a single installation.

SHA-1

A hash algorithm that creates a 160-bit digest by using principles similar to those used to create an MD5 digest, leading to $2^{64}-1$ possible digest values.

Signature verification

A security method that compares the general characteristics of a user's signature to verify the person's identity.

Single sign-on

A system in which a user logs on once to gain access to multiple systems without being required to log on each time another system is accessed.

Single-authority trust

A trust model in which a third-party central certifying agency signs a given key and authenticates the owner of the key.

Site-to-site VPN

A VPN that links the networks at two locations via the Internet.

SLA (service-level agreement)

A contract documenting the service level expected between a service provider and the end user.

S/MIME (Secure Multi-Purpose Internet Mail Extensions)

A protocol that adds security to MIME formatted e-mail messages.

SMS (Short Message Service)

A method of sending short (up to 256 bytes long) IM messages to cell phones. Provided by most cell phone carriers.

Smurf

An attack in which a host is flooded with ICMP packets.

Social engineering

An attack that exploits trust between people to gain information which attackers can then use to gain access to computer systems.

Spam

The e-mail equivalent of junk mail.

Spoofing

An attack in which a user appears to be a different user who is sending messages. Also, presenting credentials that don't belong to you in order to gain access to a system.

Spyware

Software that gets installed on a system without the user's knowledge and gathers personal or other sensitive information, potentially changing the computer's configuration.

SSH (Secure Shell)

A popular tool for remote command-line system access and management, with current implementations supporting secure file transport (over Secure FTP, or SFTP).

SSL (Secure Sockets Layer)

A protocol that enables an encrypted communication channel between a secure Web server and users' Web browsers.

SSL/TLS (Secure Sockets Layer / Transport Layer Security)

A data transmission protocol that can either encrypt the entire protocol stack or be used to provide a proxy between client and network.

Steganography

A system by which a message is hidden so that only the sender and recipient know that a message is being transmitted.

Switch hijacking

An attack that occurs when an unauthorized person is able to obtain administrator privileges of a switch and modify its configuration.

Symmetric cipher

A cipher that uses the same key to encrypt and decrypt a piece of data.

SYN flood

An attack in which a server is inundated with half-open TCP connections, which prevent valid users from accessing the server.

TACACS+ (Terminal Access Controller Access Control System)

A proprietary authentication protocol developed by Cisco Systems that provides centralized and scalable authentication, along with authorization and accounting functions.

TCP (Transmission Control Protocol)

An OSI Transport-layer protocol used to transmit information across the Internet, providing acknowledged, connection-oriented communications, as well as guaranteed delivery, proper sequencing, and data integrity checks.

TCP/IP hijacking

An attack in which someone takes over an established session between two nodes that are already communicating.

TDES (Triple DES)

The application of the DES cipher three times, with different keys for each round.

Third-party trust

See *single-authority trust*.

Three-factor authentication

Authentication based on three items; typically something you know, something you have, and something you are.

Three-homed firewall

A setup in which the entry point to the DMZ requires three network cards—one connected to the Internet, one to the DMZ network (or perimeter network), and one to the intranet. Traffic is never allowed to flow directly from the Internet to the private intranet without filtering through the DMZ.

Trojan horse

An application that's designed to appear harmless but that delivers malicious code to a computer.

Two-factor authentication

Authentication based on two items; typically something you know plus either something you have or something you are.

UAC (User Account Control)

A feature of Windows Vista and Windows 7 that prevents applications from making unauthorized changes in the operating system.

UDP (User Datagram Protocol)

An OSI Transport-layer protocol used to provide connectionless, unacknowledged communications. It uses IP as the protocol carrier, and adds source and destination socket information to the transmission.

Update

An enhancement to the operating system and some of its features.

Username

A name that uniquely identifies you to a computer or network system when you log in.

Virtualization

A technology through which one or more simulated computers run within a physical computer.

Virtual LAN (VLAN)

A virtual network segment enabled by a Layer 2–compatible switch.

Virus definition

An antivirus software update.

Voice verification

A biometric security method that uses a record of a user's voice—intonation, pitch, and inflection—to identify the person to the system.

VPN (virtual private network)

A private communications network transmitted across a public, typically insecure, network connection.

War chalking

The process of marking buildings, curbs, and other landmarks to indicate the presence of an available access point and its connection details by utilizing a set of symbols and shorthand.

War driving

The practice of scanning for open wireless access points in a region.

Web of Trust

A trust model in which the key holders sign each other's certificates, thereby validating the certificates based on their own knowledge of the other key holder.

Web spoofing

Attacks in which users are tricked into visiting a website that looks and acts like an official, legitimate website. The imposter website is set up to dupe victims into providing information such as user names, passwords, credit card numbers, and other personal information.

WEP (Wired Equivalent Privacy)

A wireless-transmission-encryption technology that uses a 64-bit or 128-bit symmetric encryption cipher, where a key is configured on both the access point and the client.

Wi-Fi hijacking

An attack in which a hacker configures his or her computer to present itself as a wireless router to intercept a user's communication.

Worm

A program that replicates itself over the network without a user's intervention.

WPA (Wi-Fi Protected Access)

A wireless-transmission-encryption technology that uses the RC4 symmetric cipher with a 128-bit key.

WPA Enterprise

A wireless-transmission-encryption technology that works in conjunction with an 802.1X authentication server, which distributes unique keys to each individual.

WPA2

A technology that builds upon WPA by adding more features from the 802.11i standard. Notably, WPA2 uses the AES cipher for stronger encryption.

XSS (cross-site scripting) attack

An attack that takes advantage of the lack of input validation, so that instead of entering valid data, a script can steal data and redirect it to the attacker's server instead.

Index

A

Acceptable-use policies, 13-8
Access control list (ACL), 4-19, 9-4
Account lockout policies, 3-24
Acronym list, A-2
Active Directory
    Certificate Services, 6-10
    Container objects in, 4-11
Addresses
    Loopback, 8-16
    Reserved, 8-14
Advanced Encryption Standard, 2-5
Adware, 1-34
Airsnarfing, 10-27
Antivirus software, 1-36, 1-37
Anycast addresses, 8-18
AP isolation, 10-9
Application layer, 8-3, 9-3
    Protocols, 8-5
Application logging, 12-14
Application-layer firewalls, 9-12, 9-33
Applications
    Hardening, 1-21
    Types of attacks on, 7-7
    Vulnerabilities in, 1-19
ARP, 8-7
ARP poisoning, 8-29, 8-32
Assessments, types of, 12-3
Attack surface, 12-3
Authentication
    Emergency, 3-4
    Mutual, 3-5
    On WLANs, 10-9, 10-16
    One-factor, 3-3
    Protocols for, 3-9
    Three-factor, 3-4
    Two-factor, 3-3
    Vulnerabilities in, 3-23

B

Backdoors, 1-34
Backup media, 14-17
    Rotation of, 14-19
Backups
    Restoring, 14-21
    Storing, 14-17
    Types of, 14-16
    Utilities for, 14-16
Baseline configurations, 1-21

Bastion hosts, 9-23
Biometrics, 1-27
BIOS, updating, 1-14
Birthday attacks, 3-29
BitLocker, 5-5
Black box testing method, 12-6
Blowfish cipher, 2-5
Bluebugging, 10-26
Bluejacking, 10-26
Bluesnarfing, 5-23, 10-26
Bluetooth device paring, 5-21
Botnets, 1-34, 8-26
BPDU handling, 9-5
Bridges, 9-4, 9-27
Brute-force attacks, 3-30
Buffer overflow attacks, 1-20, 7-7
Business continuity teams, 14-3
Business impact analysis, 14-2

C

Cable traps, 1-30
Centralized key-management systems, 6-2
Certificate authorities, 2-25
Certificate policies, 2-26
Certificate servers, 2-25
Certificate services, 6-10
Certificates
    Canceling, 6-6
    Commercial, 6-32
    Dissemination of, 6-4
    Generation of, 6-3
    Renewing, 6-6
    Retrieving, 6-4
    Revoking, 6-6, 6-22
    Suspending, 6-7
Chain of custody, 12-31
Change management procedures, 13-20
Christmas packet attacks, 8-23
CIA triad, 13-3
Cipher locks, 1-29
Ciphers
    Asymmetric, common, 2-18
    Symmetric, common, 2-5
    Types of, 2-3
Classless Inter-Domain Routing (CIDR), 8-15
Cloud computing, 9-47
Code of ethics, 13-14
Cold sites, 14-7
Command injection attacks, 7-8
Common Access Cards, 1-26
Configuration weaknesses, 1-3

Content filters, 9-13
Contingency plans, 14-4
Control types, 13-4
Cookies, uses of, 7-8
Cross-site scripting (XSS) attacks, 7-7
Cryptography
  Asymmetric, 2-16
  Defined, 2-2
Cryptoprocessors, 5-8

D

Data Encryption Standard, 2-5
Data Link layer, 9-3
Data, destroying, 13-11, 13-27
DDoS attacks, 8-26
Dead zones, 9-24
Decentralized key-management systems, 6-2
Demilitarized zones (DMZs), 9-21
Device logging, 12-14
Dictionary attacks, 3-30
Diffie-Hellman cipher, 2-18
Digests, 2-9
Digital certificates, 2-22
  Types of, 2-22
Digital signatures, 2-21
Directory traversal attacks, 7-8
Disaster recovery planning, 14-3, 14-5, 14-9
Discretionary access control (DAC), 4-20
Disk duplexing, 14-10
Disk mirroring, 14-10
Disks, encrypting, 5-5, 5-7
Distance-vector algorithms, 9-7
DLP systems, 5-2
DNS, 8-6
DNS poisoning, 8-29, 8-34
DNS spoofing, 8-34
Domain GPOs, types of, 4-11
DoS attacks, 8-20
Double encapsulation, 9-37
Drive-by downloads, 1-34
DSA cipher, 2-18
Dual-key certificates, 2-30
Due care, defined, 13-8
Dynamic ports, 8-10

E

EAP, 10-11
Effective permissions, 4-19
EFS, 5-3, 6-20, 6-26
ElGamal cipher, 2-18
Elliptic curve cipher, 2-18
E-mail
  Securing, 7-13
  Security risks of, 7-10
  Signing and encrypting, 7-16
EMI, shielding from, 14-26
Encryption, 2-2, 5-2
  For wireless communication, 10-9
  Of files vs. disks, 5-3
  Symmetric vs. asymmetric, 2-4
  Whole disk, 5-5
Encryption key management, 6-2
Event Viewer, 12-10
  Event types in, 12-12
Evil-twin attacks, 1-43, 10-22
E-wallet systems, 5-24

F

Failover systems, 14-9
Failsafe vs. failopen reactions, 12-19
Fault tolerance, 14-9
Fiber taps, 9-16
Files, encrypting, 5-3
Fire extinguishers, types of, 14-23
Fire suppression, 14-22
Firewalls
  Back-to-back, 9-24
  Host-based, 1-16, 1-36
  Proxy servers as, 9-13
  Rules-based, 9-32
  Three-homed, 9-23
  Types of, 9-12
Forensics, 12-28
  Gathering evidence for, 12-30
FTP, 8-5
Fuzzing, 1-22, 7-3

G

Grandfather method, 14-19
Gray box testing method, 12-6
Group policies, configuring, 4-10
Group Policy Management Console, 4-12
Group Policy Object Editor, 4-6
Group policy objects, 4-5
Groups, security vs. distribution, 4-15

H

Hardware
  Disposal of, 5-16, 13-28
  Reusing, 13-29
Hardware security modules, 5-8
Hashes, 2-9
  Algorithms for, 2-10
  Vulnerabilities of, 2-11
Heuristic scanning, 1-37
Hierarchical trust model, 2-28
High-availability systems, 14-9
Honeynets, 12-24
Honeypots, 12-24
Host wrappers, 12-22
Host-based firewalls, 1-16, 1-36
Host-based intrusion detection system (HIDS), 12-21
Hot sites, 14-7
HTTP, 8-5
HTTP header manipulation, 7-9

Hubs, 9-4
Human error, 1-4
Human resources policies, 13-13
HVAC scheduling and monitoring, 14-25
HVAC systems, 14-25

I

ICMP, 8-7
ICMP redirects, 8-29
ID cards, 1-25
IEEE 802.11 standards, 10-2
IEEE 802.1x standard, 11-10
IMAP4, 8-7
Implicit deny, 9-33
Incident response policies, 13-16
Injection attacks, 1-20
Instant messaging, 7-29
Interference attacks, 10-22
International Data Encryption Algorithm, 2-5
Internet layer, 8-3
Intranets, 9-21
Intrusion detection system (IDS), 12-15
Intrusion prevention system (IPS), 12-16
IP address spoofing, 8-30
IP addresses
    IPv4, 8-14
    IPv6, 8-16
    IPv6, scopes for, 8-18
    IPv6, types of, 8-18
IPSec, 9-30, 11-17, 11-19
IV attacks, 10-22

K

Kerberos, 3-10, 3-15
    Process, 3-16
    Weaknesses of, 3-18
Key escrow, 6-5, 6-25
Key recovery agents, 6-26
Keyloggers, 1-34
Keys, 2-3
    Administration of, 6-4
    Archiving, 6-5
    Destruction of, 6-7
    Hardware vs. software storage, 6-4
    Life cycle of, 6-2
    Managing, 2-4
    Public, 2-16
    Recovering, 6-5, 6-25
    Setup phase, 6-3
    Weak, 3-29
Knowledge-based authentication (KBA), 3-6

L

Laptops
    Securing, 5-16
    Vulnerabilities of, 5-13
Layer 2 Tunneling Protocol, 11-17

LDAP, 11-7
LDAP injection attacks, 7-8
LEAP, 10-11
Link-state algorithms, 9-8
Load balancing, 9-13, 14-9
Locks, types of, 1-29
Log files, 12-10
Logic bombs, 1-34
Loopback address, 8-16

M

MAC flooding, 8-32, 9-5
Malware
    Effects of, 1-34
        On mobile devices, 5-21
        Software for blocking, 1-36
        Types of, 1-33
Mandatory access control (MAC), 4-19
Man-in-the-middle attacks, 8-29
Man-traps, 1-30
Masked attacks, 3-31
Material safety data sheets, 14-23
Mathematical attacks, 3-29
MD5 hash, 2-10
Mean time between failures, 14-7
Microsoft Baseline Security Analyzer, 4-3
Mobile devices
    Infrastructure issues with, 10-27
    Mitigating risks of, 5-25
    Securing, 10-25
    Vulnerabilities of, 5-20
Multi Path VPN protocol, 11-18
Multicast addresses, 8-18
Mutual authentication, 3-5

N

Near-Field Communication, 5-24
Need-to-know information, 13-9
Nessus, 12-5
Nested arrays, 14-12
Network Access Control (NAC), 9-29
Network Access Protection (NAP), 9-29
Network address translation (NAT), 8-15, 9-10
Network hijacking, 9-16
Network Interface layer, 8-3
Network intrusion detection system (NIDS), 12-18
Network isolation, 10-9
Network layer, 9-3
Network loops, 9-5
Network mappers, 12-4
Network Policy Server, 11-12
Networking devices, 9-4
    Managing weaknesses with, 9-18
    Physical attacks on, 9-16
    Security issues with, 9-15
Network-layer firewalls, 9-12, 9-33
Networks
    Packet-switched, 9-7

Perimeter, 9-21
　　Route selection on, 9-7
NICs, wireless, 10-5
NTLM, 3-10, 3-12
Null sessions, 3-20
　　Preventing abuse of, 3-21

O

One-time pad cipher, 2-6, 2-31
Open Vulnerability and Assessment Language
　　(OVAL), 12-5
OpenPGP, 5-7, 7-19
OpenVPN, 11-18
Operating systems
　　Hardening, 1-6
　　Updates, removing, 1-10
　　Updates, types of, 1-6
Order of volatility, 12-29
OSI model, 8-2, 9-3
Out-of-band identification, 3-6

P

Packet filters, 9-12, 9-33
Password crackers, 12-4
Passwords
　　Changing default, 9-18
　　Cracking, 3-29
　　Managing, 3-23
　　Methods of guessing, 3-30
　　Policies for, 13-10
Patches, managing, 1-10, 1-21
PEAP, 10-11
Penetration testing, 12-5
Perimeter networks, 9-21
Peripherals, securing, 5-15
PGP, 7-16
　　Signing messages with, 7-24
　　Using, 7-22
Pharming, 1-43, 8-34
Phishing, 1-43, 1-46, 7-10, 8-34
Physical access, controlling, 1-24, 1-29
Physical layer, 9-3
Ping-of-death attacks, 8-23
Pod slurping, 10-27
Policy weaknesses, 1-3
POP Before SMTP, 7-14
POP3, 8-7
Pop-up blockers, 1-36
Port address translation (PAT), 9-10
Port scanners, 12-4
Ports
　　Blocking, 9-35
　　Commonly used, 9-10
　　Types of, 8-10
Prefix hijacking, 9-16
Presentation layer, 9-3
Principle of least privilege, 3-24, 13-9
Printed documents, securing, 5-13, 5-17

Protocol analyzers, 3-26
Protocols
　　802.1x, 11-10
　　FTP, 8-5
　　HTTP, 8-5
　　In the IP suite, 8-7
　　IPSec, 9-30, 11-17, 11-19
　　L2TP, 11-17
　　LDAP, 11-7
　　Path-vector, 9-8
　　PPTP, 11-17
　　Secure HTTP, 8-5
　　SFTP, 8-6
　　SSH, 11-19
　　SSL, 8-5
　　SSL/TLS, 11-18
　　TACACS+, 11-9
　　TCP, 8-8
　　TCP/IP, 8-2
　　Telnet, 8-6
　　TFTP, 8-6
　　UDP, 8-8
　　Weaknesses in, 3-24
　　WiMAX, 10-4
Proximity cards, 1-25
Proxy servers, 9-13
Public key cryptography, 2-16, 2-31
Public key infrastructure (PKI), 2-25, 6-2

Q

Quantum cryptography, 2-31

R

RADIUS, 10-9, 10-10, 10-16, 11-3
RAID
　　Considerations for using, 14-13
　　Levels, 14-10
　　Levels, nested, 14-12
　　Software vs. hardware, 14-14
Rainbow tables, 3-31
RARP, 8-7
RC5 cipher, 2-6
Realms, 11-4
Recovery point objectives, 14-4
Recovery time objectives, 14-4
Registered ports, 8-10
Registration authorities, 2-25
Remote network access, 11-2
Removable media
　　Securing, 5-15
　　Vulnerabilities of, 5-13
Repeaters, 9-4
Replay attacks, 8-36
Reverse authentication, 3-5
RFI, shielding from, 14-26
Rijndael cipher, 2-5
Risk assessment, 12-3, 13-4
Role-based access control (RBAC), 4-20

Rootkits, 1-34, 1-37
Routers, 9-7
   Secure configuration of, 9-39
Routing and Remote Access Service, 11-22
Routing tables, 9-7
RSA cipher, 2-18
RTBH filtering, 9-39
Run As Administrator, 3-24

S

S/MIME, 7-16, 7-17, 7-19
SAM files, 3-31
Sandboxes, 1-37
SCP, 8-7
Screened hosts, 9-22
Secure coding practices, 1-22, 7-3
Secure HTTP, 8-5
Secure Shell (SSH), 11-19
Secure Shell FTP, 8-6
Security baseline document, 4-2
Security policies, 13-7
Security threats, types of, 1-2
Security zones, 9-20
Security, goals of, 1-2
Separation of duties, 13-9
Server clustering, 14-9
Service packs, 1-12
Service-level agreements, 13-10
Session hijacking, 7-8, 8-29
Session layer, 9-3
SHA hashes, 2-10
Signatures, antivirus, 1-37
Single sign-on environments, 1-26, 3-7
Single-authority trust model, 2-26
Single-key certificates, 2-30
Skimming, 1-43
Skimming attackts, 3-5
Slurping, 10-27
Smart cards, 1-25
SMTP, 8-7
Smurf attacks, 8-23
SNMP, 8-7
Social engineering, 1-42
   Countermeasures for, 1-44
Social networking, risks of, 1-50, 7-26
SPA protocol, 7-14
Spam, 1-48
Spear phishing, 1-43
Spim, 1-43, 7-29
Spoofing, 7-11
   Types of, 8-30
Spyware, 1-34
SQL injection attacks, 7-7
SSL, 7-13, 8-5
   Enabling, 6-34
SSL/TLS, 7-13, 11-18
STARTTLS, 7-13
Steganography, 2-13

Striping, 14-10
Subnet masks, 8-14
Switch flooding, 9-37
Switch spoofing, 9-37
Switches, 9-4
   Security problems with, 9-15
SYN flood attacks, 8-21

T

TACACS+, 11-9
TCP, 8-8
TCP/IP, 8-2
TCP/IP hijacking, 8-36
Technology weaknesses, 1-3
Telnet, 8-6
TFTP, 8-6
Threat assessment, 12-3
Three-homed firewalls, 9-23
Time-of-day restrictions, 1-27, 13-9
TMP chip, 5-5
Tokens, 1-26
Tower of Hanoi, 14-19
Traffic filtering, 9-25
Training programs, 13-22
Training, types of, 13-25
Transitive attacks, 8-37
Transparent data encryption, 5-2
Transport encryption, 9-30, 11-19
Transport layer, 8-3, 9-3
   Protocols, 8-8
Trojan horses, 1-33
TrueCrypt, 5-3, 5-7
Trust models, 2-26
Tunnel encryption, 9-30, 11-19
Tunneling, 11-16
Twofish cipher, 2-5

U

UDP, 8-8
Unicast addresses, 8-18
Unified threat management, 9-14
USB flash drives
   Securing, 5-15
   Vulnerabilities of, 5-12
User Account Control, 1-17
User certificates, 6-20
Users, educating, 13-22

V

Vampire taps, 9-16
Virtual applications, 9-42
Virtual desktops, 9-43
Virtual LANs, 9-28
   Securing, 9-37
Virtual machines, 9-41
   Risks of, 9-44
Virtual private networks (VPNs), 9-30

Client connections to, 11-24
Creating, 11-21
Protocols used for, 11-17
Security models for, 11-17
Technologies used in, 11-16
Virtual servers, 9-43
Viruses, 1-33
Vishing, 1-44
VLAN hopping, 9-37
VPN concentrators, 9-30, 11-21
Vulnerability assessment, 12-3

W

War chalking, 10-22
War driving, 10-22
Warm sites, 14-7
Web beacons, 1-49
Web of Trust, 2-28
Web servers, securing, 6-31
Web spoofing, 8-29, 8-34
Well-known ports, 8-10
WEP, 10-10
Whaling, 1-44
White box testing method, 12-6
Wi-Fi hijacking, 9-17
Wi-Fi scanners, 10-22
WiMAX, 10-4
Windows Defender, 1-40

Windows Firewall, 1-16
Windows Update, 1-7
Wireless access points, 10-6
Configuring, 10-12
Wireless Auto Configuration, 10-16
Wireless LANs
Client/AP isolation, 10-9
Encryption methods for, 10-9
Securing, 10-8
Security risks, 10-7
Vulnerabilities of, 10-20
Wireless Zero Configuration, 10-16
Worms, 1-33
WPA Enterprise, 10-10
WPA Personal, 10-10

X

X.509 certificates, 2-22, 7-18
XML injection attacks, 7-8
XSRF attacks, 7-7

Z

Zero-day attacks, 1-34, 7-9
Zeroization, 6-7, 13-11
ZFS file system, 5-3, 5-7
Zombies, 8-26